DIVORCING TRADITIONS

Divorcing Traditions

Islamic Marriage Law and the Making of Indian Secularism

Katherine Lemons

Cornell University Press

Ithaca and London

First published 2019 by Cornell University Press

Library of Congress Cataloging-in-Publication Data

Names: Lemons, Katherine, author.
Title: Divorcing traditions : Islamic marriage law and the making of Indian secularism | Katherine Lemons.
Description: Ithaca [New York] : Cornell University Press, 2019. | Includes bibliographical references and index.
Identifiers: LCCN 2018032569 (print) | LCCN 2018033069 (ebook) | ISBN 9781501734786 (epub/mobi) | ISBN 9781501734793 (pdf) | ISBN 9781501734762 | ISBN 9781501734762 (cloth) | ISBN 9781501734779 (pbk.)
Subjects: LCSH: Divorce (Islamic law)—India. | Divorce—Law and legislation—India. | Islam and state—India. | Secularism—India. | Legal polycentricity—India.
Classification: LCC KNS577 (ebook) | LCC KNS577 .L46 2019 (print) | DDC 346.5401/6—dc23
LC record available at https://lccn.loc.gov/2018032569

CONTENTS

Acknowledgments

Like all books, I imagine, this one has been shaped and sustained by many people, in ways small and large. My debts to friends and interlocutors in Delhi and Lucknow are deep, and I am especially grateful to the *qazis*, *muftis*, *mahila panchayat* leaders, and disputants who took the time to teach me some of what they know.

My interest in the ideas and problems I address here was sparked while I was at Berkeley. Lawrence Cohen has provided guidance, insight, and a model of capacious and creative intellectual life since I first met him. His support has been unwavering. Marianne Constable has been an unfailingly generous and careful reader since the beginning. Her vision for where this project could go exceeds what the book has accomplished; perhaps a work on the rhetoric of anthropology is yet to be written. Saba Mahmood's fierce intellectual determination, commitment to the stakes of anthropological research, and uncompromising standards undergird the efforts of this book. All three have continued to support and nurture this project in the years since I left Berkeley, for which I am tremendously grateful. Barbara Metcalf generously read and commented on parts of the manuscript, and her insights have been influential.

At Berkeley, friends propelled my intellectual life. To the rhetoricians—Diana Anders, Nima Bassiri, Michelle Dizon, Alice Kim, Yannick Thiem, Andrew Weiner, Yves Winter, and Ben Young—thanks for teaching me so much. To the anthropologists (and their allies)—Michael Allan, Dace Dzenovska, Angie Heo, Cindy Huang, Lucinda Ramberg, Tahir Naqvi, and Pete Skafish—thanks for welcoming me into the discipline and helping me learn my way about.

My research in Delhi was made possible and enjoyable by people beyond my immediate circle of interlocutors. I thank Nisha Kirpalani, Harpreet Anand, and Sajida Khan and her family for helping with and sharing housing. Chitra Padhmanabhan and M. K. Venu have made Delhi a home. In their apartment I have been questioned and encouraged by many, among them Hartosh Bal, Nonika Datta, Basharat Peer, Sarim Naved, and Ananya Vajpeyi. Among the academic friends in Delhi who have read and discussed parts of this book with me are Ulka Anjaria, Jon Anjaria, Leo Coleman, Shalini Grover, Deepak Mehta, and Rajni Palriwala each of whom has contributed to my thinking. At Jamia Millia Islamia, I was welcomed by Dr. Kahkashan Danyal, Dr. Akhtarul Wasey, and Qazi Obaid ur Rehman Hashmi. Dr. Hashmi's family—Mehnaz Obaid, Sana, Saba, and Amaan—warmly welcomed me into their home.

A number of friends and colleagues have read chapters over the past few years, helping give shape to my ideas. They include Gretchen Bakke, Rachel Berger, Dace Dzenovska, Saida Hodzic, Sarah Pinto, Lucinda Ramberg, and Theresa Ventura. I have, furthermore, been lucky to have received robust and probing comments in a number of workshops. I thank the following groups and participants for their generous but rigorous engagement: Rupa Viswanath, Nathanial Roberts, and Srirupa Roy, as well as the other members of CeMIS in Göttingen, Germany; Mayanthi Fernando, Joan Scott, Michael Allan, Judith Surkis, and Saba Mahmood; Tamir Moustafa, Jeffrey Sachs, Michael Peletz, and the other participants at the workshop on Islamic Law at Simon Fraser University; Arzoo Osanloo, Nada Moumtaz, Aria Nakissa, and the other participants in the workshop on Islam and Forgiveness at the University of Washington; Leslie Orr and the working group on Religion and Women's Studies at Concordia University; the members of the Montreal working group on religion and media—Hillary Kaell, Setrag

Manoukian, Kristin Norget, Armando Salvatore, and Jeremy Stolow; and those who asked astute questions at the Johns Hopkins University Department of Anthropology. For their interest in and ongoing discussions about this material I thank Srimati Basu, John Bowen, Joyce Burkhalter Flueckiger, Jeff Redding, Mengia Hong Tschalär, Gopika Solanki, and Sylvia Vatuk.

In Montreal, where I wrote most of this book, I am lucky to be surrounded by colleagues and friends who have offered critical guidance and feedback. My colleagues in the anthropology department at McGill University—Diana Allan, Nicole Couture, John Galaty, Sandra Hyde, Eduardo Kohn, Setrag Manoukian, Ron Niezen, Kristin Norget, Tobias Rees, Colin Scott, Lisa Stevenson, and Ismael Vaccaro—have been collegial and supportive, making this a hospitable environment in which to think, write, and collaborate. Beyond the anthropology department, Poulami Roychoudhury and Narendra Subramanian have both been astute interlocutors. I am grateful to the students in my 2017 seminar on secularism for their energetic engagement with much of the material that informs this book. Catherine Larouche has provided invaluable help with the detail work required for publication. My undergraduate research assistants Myra Sivaloganathan and Samar Nisar worked diligently with me on various court records.

I am humbled to have received five insightful anonymous reviews on the manuscript, and I thank these scholars for their seriousness and generosity. I hope the revisions reflect my appreciation for what they have done to make this a better book. I thank Jim Lance for his enthusiasm about the manuscript and his help with the publishing process. Thanks to Matthew Wyman-McCarthy for a careful final edit and to Zahra Sabri for expert transliteration. The research and writing of this book have been supported by the American Institute of Indian Studies, the Fonds de Recherche du Québec Société et Culture (FRQSC), and McGill's internal Social Science and Humanities Research Council Award.

I owe Dace Dzenovska a special debt of gratitude. She has been discussing this project with me for over a decade; her incisive questions reflect her intellectual generosity and her abiding commitment to argument. She has, through it all, been an unwavering friend. Finally, I thank my kin. Yves Winter's scholarly acumen has both inspired and challenged me; his endless energy for discussion and debate, his unflagging belief in the project, and his companionship have been both a source of energy and a ballast. I appreciate the aplomb with which my children, Anouk and Nasim, have taken my absences for research and writing. The indomitable Anouk has brought me laughter and joy and new perspectives on our shared world; Nasim's unfettered love for all of us has made our lives richer. I thank my parents, Daniel and Mary Lemons, for support of every kind, from interest in my research to childcare. Their determination and energy inspire awe, and their unwavering love humility. I rely on my brother, Peter, for his insights and for his ability to make me laugh. My sister, Sarah, has taught me much about determination. My parents-in-law, André and Karin Winter, have always stood behind me; Ada Winter's carefully-timed visits enabled me to do follow-up research in Delhi. Jaron Winter could not be a more dedicated brother-in-law. Without the professional and loving labors of my children's daycare teachers, I would not have been able to complete this project.

Several sections are reproduced from past publications, with permission from the publisher. Parts of chapter 1 have appeared in "The Politics of Livability: Tutoring Kinship in a New Delhi Women's Arbitration Center," *Political and Legal Anthropology Review* 39(2): 244–260. Some of the research presented in chapter 4 has been published in September 2018 as "Sharia Courts and Muslim Personal Law in India: Intersecting Legal Regimes," *Law and Society Review* 52(3). Finally, a different version of the second half of chapter 5 has been published as "Paying for Kinship: Muslim Divorce and the Privatization of Insecurity," *History of the Present: A Journal of Critical History* 7(2): 197–218.

Divorcing Traditions

PART I

The State

Chapter 1

Regulating Kinship under Legal Pluralism

"Salam 'alaikum," the woman quietly uttered, subtly bowing her head and raising her right arm in a deferential greeting. The woman entered the office of the *qazi* (judge) hesitantly, seemingly unsure what to do. I was sitting with Qazi Kamal in his south Delhi office that morning in the late spring of 2006, chatting with him as he read the stack of Urdu-language newspapers that his *peon* (assistant) had delivered. The qazi and I both looked up when the woman entered, and he asked what she needed. The woman, who wore a tired black burqa indicating her membership in a pious but poor family, respectfully asked the qazi to open a divorce case on behalf of her daughter, whose husband was allegedly abusing her. The qazi took out a form with the title, printed in Urdu at the top of the page, "Darkhwast Dene Ka Form" (complaint form). The form noted the name of this *dar ul-qaza* (shari'a court) they were currently in, which it called, parenthetically, a *shari'a panchayat*. The form also provided space for a case number, the name of the *mudda'i* (complainant) and *mudda'a-alaih* (respondent), their parents (*wald-i* or *bint-i*), and their full addresses, including *dak-khana* (post office), *thana* (police station), and *zila'* (district). The last printed line of the header read, "Gu-zarish hai kih . . ." (The plea is . . .), a phrase in Persianate Urdu unused in everyday conversation, followed by an expansive blank page.

The woman looked at the form and told the qazi she was unable to read or write. The qazi replied that she should take it with her, have someone else write down the complaint, and return with the completed form. The woman silently took the form, and, muttering a *khuda hafiz* (God be with you), turned and left the room. She returned a week later with her daughter and handed the qazi the form completed in the devanagari script in which Hindi is writ-ten. The qazi impatiently returned the form to her, insistent that it must be presented to him in the nasta'liq script, in Urdu, the language in which Muslim clergy in India are trained and in which they write. Qazi Kamal, like most of the other clerics I met during my fieldwork in Delhi, could also read Hindi and English, but neither was the language of Muslim scholar-ship and adjudication. Urdu literacy is one of the things that marks experts in Islamic legal practice as distinct from legal experts in the Indian state courts, whether Muslim or non-Muslim. Case files in the dar ul-qaza are written in a neat hand by the qazi himself, who takes down witness testimonies, tran-scribes cross-examinations and statements of fact dictated by the parties to the cases, and, finally, records his *faisalahs* (judgments).

Unlike the other dar ul-qaza in which I conducted fieldwork, this one was not located in a *madrasa* (a school that offers instruction in Islamic religious and legal knowledge). Yet the qazi insisted that the complainant find some-one in the neighborhood to fill out her form. The request reflected the dar ul-qaza's geographical and demographic location. It was located in a neigh-borhood dense with Muslim institutions. On the paved road not far from the office, the renowned Jamia Milla Islamia University was always full of stu-dents, some of whom read and write Urdu; down the pitted unpaved alleys of the office's immediate neighborhood, the Islamic Fiqh Academy buzzed with students and with clerics writing *fatwas*; a bit further down the road, in what was technically another neighborhood, the Jamaat-e-Islami's head cam-pus housed students and teachers of Islamiyat, or Islamic sciences. Though the neighborhood was crowded, with its infrastructure—from roads to elec-trical service—in poor repair, it was home to professors from Jamia Milla Islamia, Islamic legal scholars, and Muslims from across the class spectrum, including middle-class professionals and working poor, like the woman seeking to help her daughter. The composition of the neighborhood reflects the pattern of Muslim segregation from non-Muslims in Delhi: as in other predominantly Muslim neighbors, Muslims of all social classes mix together in this one. Sometimes such class mixing is an effect of family histories, with well-off Muslims living in ancestral homes. But it also reflects the difficulty Muslims have finding homes in non-Muslim neighborhoods because of anti-Muslim prejudice.

The morning the woman left the dar ul-qaza for the second time, she appeared disheartened and frustrated that the qazi would neither read her form completed in Hindi nor examine her daughter's bruises, the latter of which was material evidence of ongoing spousal abuse. For this woman, providing written material in Urdu appeared to have been too steep a condition for entry to the dar ul-qaza. Or, perhaps, she found that the qazi's gruff manner did not bode well for her daughter's case. Either way, she and her daughter did not return to have a divorce adjudicated. However, even though this woman did not end up initiating a case in this dar ul-qaza, her decision to approach the qazi is revealing. It indicates that family disputes among Indian Muslims can be dealt with by consulting a religious legal scholar rather than by bringing a case in the state courts or registering a complaint with the police. The woman's apparent hesitation to approach even the qazi also reflects the difficulty people have taking marital disputes to an outside party, as most family matters are dealt with within and among family units. Her decision to come to the dar ul-qaza, prior to seeking recourse elsewhere, suggests that, for some, a local religious legal expert is easier to approach than a state institution. This is in part because the qazi's office is accessible—it is local, the consultation is free (while filing a case costs very little), and it lacks both the chaos and the layers of intermediaries between disputants and judges characteristic of the district courts (see Mody 2008). In contrast to these forums, the dar ul-qaza appears to be informal. Yet the qazi's insistence that the complaint form be filled out properly tells a different story. It indicates that this is in fact not an informal setting, but rather a deeply procedure-oriented legal forum whose protocols, although different from those of the state courts, are nonetheless formal. The qazi is qualified to adjudicate cases because of his Islamic legal knowledge and the dar ul-qaza constitutes a domain of expertise.

Dar ul-qazas operate according to Islamic traditions of adjudication and appear in this anecdote to occupy a space beyond and untouched by the state courts. Yet it is my contention throughout this book that dar ul-qazas, like other nonstate forums I analyze, are both separate from and entangled with state legal adjudication forums and jurisprudential traditions. In the case of the qazi, this means that although he did adjudicate according to Islamic legal norms and traditions, and these are distinct from the state courts' norms, procedures, and laws, his work of adjudication was part of, not separate from, a broader legal system that includes state courts. While I do not know where the woman who approached the dar ul-qaza went next, my research and that of other scholars indicates that she is likely to have approached any number of other forums: the local Women's Cell—a police station where women file domestic violence complaints; a *mahila panchayat* (women's council) where local women adjudicate family disputes; a *mahalla* (neighborhood) committee; any number of Muslim women's organizations; or even the family courts. The dar ul-qaza is set apart from these other forums by its religious legal character while simultaneously operating in dynamic relation to them.

Divorcing Traditions is an ethnography of Islamic legal expertise and practices in the secular state of India, where Muslims are a significant minority—numerically, legally, and politically—and where Islamic judgments are not legally binding. I conducted the research for this book between 2006 and 2013 in four different types of nonstate dispute adjudication forums: two dar ul-qazas, a *dar ul-ifta* (fatwa-giving office), a Sufi healing practice, and a mahila panchayat (women's council). None of these institutions are part of the state's formal legal system, which means that the decisions, judgments, and advice they offer are not legally binding from the perspective of the state. Nor are they upheld by its enforcement mechanisms.

The forums I study are best understood, more specifically, as practices of shari'a rather than as practices of state law. Shari'a here should be understood as being broader than "law": it is a guide for how one ought to live as a Muslim, which involves abiding by Islamic legal precepts. As such, it is a form of moral, ethical, and legal guidance that all Muslims seek to follow. Each institution has a different aim and procedure that cannot, therefore, be conflated. Dar ul-qazas are adversarial settings that gather testimonial evidence, mediate between parties, and culminate in a faisalah, considered binding on the parties and not by the state but in the eyes of God. Dar ul-iftas are forums where lay Muslims seek authoritative advice from a learned *mufti* (jurist). Fatwas are not binding, according to Islamic legal traditions and the state; it is up to the parties involved to decide whether to follow the advice they receive. The spiritual healing practice is controversial among Muslims, but as a popular modality of adjudicating disputes and guiding Muslims into better relationships, it too, can be understood as a practice of shari'a. The mahila panchayat is, on the other hand, led by lay Muslim women who make their own efforts at teaching women to deal with marital conflict. It is most tenuously connected to the variety of practices easily recognizable as shari'at and is, yet, part of the Islamic tradition in that the adjudicators, who are Muslim, draw on the sources of the Islamic tradition (the Quran and the Hadith) to help disputants comport themselves better in their marriages as Muslims.[1]

Divorcing Traditions argues that together these institutions animate a legal landscape that is plural, and that together they make up the system of secularism in India. Although the outcomes of the processes in these forums are not considered binding by state courts, the forums themselves have been recognized, variously, by the Supreme Court of India, district court judges, the Delhi Commission for Women (a local government agency), and an array of judgments at every level of the Indian judiciary. One effort of this book is to examine where, how, and with what effects the state recognizes these forums. The book's overarching argument is that marital dispute adjudication in these Islamic legal forums is central rather than peripheral both to Indian legal pluralism and to Indian secularism.

By secularism, I do not refer to the "separation of church and state," or the promotion of religious freedom in private coupled with the curtailment of religious practices in public. Instead, I understand secularism to be an ongoing project that aims to establish and maintain an appropriate relationship between religion and politics. Secularism is what Hussein Agrama (2012) has called a "questioning power": a demand to assert where a line ought to be drawn between religion and politics. A secular state is, therefore, always secularizing: it is engaged in a process that is never complete, but instead always fails in its efforts to separate religion from politics. The more the state attempts to separate religion from politics, the more intensely it intervenes in and regulates religion, thereby undermining the separation it sets out to secure. The question raised by the study of secularism, then, is where this process of perpetual intervention takes place. My argument is that, in India, one of its principle locations is the adjudication of Muslim divorce.

Muslim divorce proceedings reveal the labor required to separate an ostensibly private sphere of family, home, and religion from an ostensibly public sphere of politics and exchange. During divorce proceedings, disputants demonstrate that marriage is as much a space of exchange and of jockeying for resources as it is the domain of care, intimacy, and affection. The separation of family, home, and religion from politics and exchange does not, therefore, precede adjudication, but rather is one of its key outcomes. This is largely because Islamic legal forums limit their jurisdiction to matters that fall within the purview of religious authority granted by the state legal system. This compartmentalization has two consequences, both of which I demonstrate throughout the book. First, kinship is central to secular governance. Second, it is not only or even primarily the secular state that carries out the labors of separating these spheres, but religious legal institutions that operate beyond its purview.

Personal Law and the Religious Family

That divorce is central to secular governance and to debates about secularism in contemporary India is in part a result of the country's colonial and postcolonial legal histories, which linked religious regulation to the regulation of kinship. The religious legal adjudication of kinship has the unexpected effect of generating the ostensibly separate domains of religion and law. The character of this separation is not analytical or conceptual; my research shows that it is a distinction instantiated both in state and nonstate religious legal practices and in the relations between them. The separation between "religion" and "law" is, in other words, an effect of Indian legal pluralism. A brief analysis of the eighteenth-century Hastings Declaration and judicial plan helps to clarify the present-day workings of legal pluralism in India, as this declaration established the separate but overlapping jurisdictions that continue to regulate matters pertaining to the family.

In India, as in other former British colonies and protectorates, marriage, divorce, adoption, succession, and inheritance disputes are adjudicated according to religious personal laws (Agnes 1999; Williams 2006).[2] Personal law, referred to in most such systems as personal *status* law, is law that applies to a person rather than to a territory and that regulates relationships accordingly (Sturman 2014, 7). Yüksel Sezgin has called postcolonial Indian personal law a "unified semi-confessional" system because state judges apply the religious personal laws of certain designated minorities—Muslims, Christians, Jews, and Parsis—to these groups and apply Hindu law to everyone else, including not only Hindus but also Sikhs, Jains, and Buddhists (2013, 7).

In the colonial period, preexisting power relations both influenced the legal system and persisted in it. The rulers of Mughal India governed a religiously plural subject population with a legal system that adjudicated disputes based on the religious law of the parties involved (Eaton 1993; Metcalf 2002, 7; Yusuf 1965, 4, 8). As Eaton shows, under Mughal law, Muslim judges even enforced sanctions against Muslim coreligionists who had offended local Hindu norms (1993, 179–183). *'Ulama* (Islamic scholars) held prominent judicial positions during this period (Guenther 2003).

Religious legal adjudication of kinship by means of personal law was revised in the colonial period as part of an effort—riven with well-documented ironies—to govern Indians according to indigenous norms.[3] The legal framework that would become personal law in independent India was formulated by Warren Hastings, then Governor-General of Bengal, as part of his judicial plan of 1772. Hastings presented the judicial plan as a clarification of the "ancient constitution" of India rather than as a new legal system, and he argued that it made only two interventions into existing jurisprudence: it clarified the distinction between criminal and civil law, and it moved the central courts to Calcutta (Travers 2007, 117). Robert Travers describes the plan as a "rhetorical assertion of the exclusive rights of sovereignty" intended to address the decentralized Mughal legal system, which seemed to British East India Company officials to be too unregulated (2007, 118). Coupled with the effort to centralize legal practice and thereby to assert Company sovereignty, the judicial plan aimed to enforce indigenous laws. Thus, the plan famously stated that with regard to "inheritance, marriage, cast [*sic*] and other religious usages, or institutions, the laws of the Koran with respect to the Mussalmans, and those of the Shasters with respect to the Hindoos, shall be invariably adhered to" (quoted in Travers 2007, 118–119). This brief sentence defines inheritance, marriage, and social status (caste) as religious institutions, as well as names the texts relevant to addressing and regulating religious matters for Hindus and Muslims.

The Hastings plan narrowed the scope of personal law relative to its Mughal precursor, specifying that it applied only to Hindus and Muslims.

Sharafi suggests that Hastings did this for two reasons. The first is that British administrators assumed that other religious minorities—Jains, Jews, Armenian Christians, Buddhists, and Parsis—had no developed body of religious law and therefore did not elaborate separate personal laws for them (2014, 131–138).[4] The second reason is that in Calcutta, the capital of Bengal, the British and the local landowners (*zamindars*) had previously debated which matters fell under whose jurisdiction. As a result of these debates, Hindus and Muslims were often exempt from appearing in British courts (Travers 2007, 119), and instead approached Hindu or Muslim religious leaders, respectively. Furthermore, at the time the Hastings Declaration was drafted, British administrators were involved in two distinct but simultaneous conversations with Hindu and Muslim leaders about how to govern their communities. They were not having similar conversations with leaders of other religious communities.

Conversations about the Hastings Declaration also lend insight into the specific shape of the domain that it designated as subject to religious authority. The Calcutta council that authored Hastings's judicial plan of 1772 seems to have been influenced by Muhammad Reza Khan's account of Mughal law administration, which the judicial plan explicitly sought to preserve (Travers 2007, 119–120). Khan, the *na'ib diwan* (deputy revenue officer) of Calcutta, argued that under Mughal law, civil matters—in particular inheritance, marriage, and "other disputes, which can be determined by the express dictates of Mohammedan Religion"—should be adjudicated by religious legal authorities (quoted in Travers 2007, 120). Hastings's delineation of religious authority may, as Duncan Derrett argued, also have resulted from contemporary British legal distinction between ecclesiastical and temporal courts (1968, 233). Cohn attributes this decision to Hastings's general view of India as a theocratic place; but while this point is well taken, it does not help to explain why he drew the boundaries of religious authority where he did (see Cohn 1996, 65). The judicial code Hastings introduced consolidated the sphere of religion by specifying that other areas, notably commercial disputes, fell within the jurisdiction of British arbitrators. The plan thereby simultaneously delineated areas to which religious legal authority would apply and pointed to certain domains to which it would not.

The Hastings Declaration appears to enunciate a primary link between religious texts and inheritance and marriage, thereby removing these relations from the purview of the state. However, from these first formulations, the claim to noninterference and the enactment of a private sphere of the religious family (Parashar and Dhanda 2008) activated new ways for the secular state to regulate religion by means of regulating kinship, now explicitly religiously marked. Even as religious authority was formally mapped onto the domain of kinship, religious legal experts were removed from state courts and religious legal precepts translated into English so that British judges could adjudicate personal law disputes (Kugle 2001). The effect of this was that British judges were given religious authority—the authority to adjudicate matters understood to be essentially religious. The Hastings Declaration had designated that the family would be regulated by religious laws and that its disputes would be adjudicated by religious legal experts whose decisions would be upheld by the British.[5] As British judges took over for religious jurists, the religious content of disputes and/or the religious identities of parties was disarticulated from the religious identities and training of the adjudicator. By reconfiguring the relationship between religious legal matters and religious authorities—who were no longer recognized as *legal* authorities—religious personal law became official law while the scope of religion was reduced to include rituals and practices considered irrelevant to the British. It is for this reason that Rachel Sturman argues that the religious personal law system created not *religious* Hindu law, as the name indicates, but instead *secular* Hindu law (2012). Along with eliminating religious legal experts, new personal law practices emphasized property rights and were oriented around the question of equality, leaving aside questions of ritual status (2012). Another way of putting this is that gradually the British folded the religious legal sphere into British jurisdiction, thereby muddling the distinction between religious and nonreligious law that Hastings had set out to differentiate. This happened in spite of Queen Victoria's 1858 Proclamation that authorities "abstain from all interference with the religious belief or worship of any of our subjects." One peculiarity of this legal organization of religion was that it implicitly differentiated between legally relevant religious interpretations and practices and aspects of religion toward which British law was indifferent. Religious personal law thus regulated religion by splitting it in two—into religious personal law matters and legally indifferent religious matters. This legal bifurcation simultaneously split "law," as it determined which claims were subject to (secular, uniform) criminal or civil law and which to (religious, differential) personal law.

The personal law system established by the Hastings Declaration has been carried into Independent India.[6] However, in practice postcolonial India is marked by the distinctions Hastings put into place that were in some measure undone when British judges began to adjudicate personal law disputes. In the forums I discuss in this book religious legal experts rather than state court judges adjudicate matters that fall within the parameters of personal law—primarily marriage, divorce, and inheritance. Unlike religious adjudication forums under the Hastings Plan, these adjudication forums do not receive recognition by the state and are therefore not formally part of the personal law system. They do, however, adjudicate personal law matters, thereby igniting conflicts between jurisdictions. Analytically, then, they comprise one facet of the Indian legal system's pluralism. Legal pluralism is "the idea that law . . . emanates from a multiplicity of normative orders" (Sharafi 2014, 6).[7] Legal pluralism is evident across the Indian legal system, enabling litigants to navigate between different forums while presenting them with a complex and daunting array of ways to pursue their cases (Galanter 1981; Moore 1993; Randeria 2006; Redding 2013; Sharafi 2014; Solanki 2011). Because of the personal law system and the nonstate forums of marriage and divorce adjudication that complement it, marriage and divorce are sites of regular jurisdictional contest, which are simultaneously tests of the jurisdiction of religious authorities.

Indian Family Law Exceptionalism

The Hastings Declaration of 1772 delineated the family as religious, helping to institute a legal ideology that I call, following the work of Janet Halley and Kerry Rittich, Family Law Exceptionalism (FLE). FLE is the descriptive and normative idea that the family occupies a "unique and autonomous domain" (2010, 754). Halley and Rittich observe that in British and U.S. legal practice the family and family law are treated as domains of intimate, private relationships, as traditional and indigenous, and as sacred. As a descriptive project, FLE merely treats the family as a self-evidently distinct domain regulated by laws particular to it. Normatively, FLE claims that the family "*should* be different because of the unique, special, crucial, affective, altruistic, social-ordering and/or sacred nature of the relationships that it houses" (754, emphasis added). FLE is an ideology: where the family and family law are understood to occupy a distinct sphere, this separateness both describes reality and makes it. The personal law system in India fits this description by treating the family as separate from other legal spheres and entrenching its separateness by placing it within the jurisdiction of religious legal authority.[8] One effect of the way that FLE renders the family a private, affective institution is that it obscures the family's distributive, economic aspect. In this section I argue that in India, even as the personal law system consolidated distinctions between Hindus and Muslims, nineteenth-century legal reforms affected both communities and families, making marriage an instrument for securing property holdings. Ironically, then, the ideal of the private religious family was coupled with practices that made marriage a public, economic institution.

The theorist who most clearly outlined the family's legal particularity in the nineteenth century was the German legal scholar Friedrich Carl von Savigny. Savigny's system of legal classification separated the law of family from the law of contracts on the ground that family law regulated a "nuclear and affective unit," whereas contract law dealt with the "individualist ethos of freedom of contract" (Kennedy 2010, 758). Family law, Savigny argued, should regulate the relations in which people engage in their capacity as interdependent and incomplete beings, relations that arise from the morals and spirit of the particular community in question (its *Volksgeist*). Potentialities law (contract law), by contrast, should regulate people in their capacity as transacting individuals. Halley and Rittich put it this way: "In Savigny's family/contract dichotomy, the rules of contract law were universal (they should be the same everywhere), but the rules of family law were necessarily local (because they made manifest the spirit of the people)" (2010, 771). FLE secures the family as separate, thereby also rendering it culturally particular. For this reason, Saba Mahmood has argued that, in Egypt, the contingent link between religion and the family could be made in and by means of personal law: both religion and the family were understood to hold the culture or Volksgeist, of a community. Religious personal laws could therefore safeguard both together (S. Mahmood 2013).

Even though FLE imagines and treats the family as a separate sphere housing culture and affective relations, Halley and Rittich argue that both past and present families—and marriages and divorces in particular—are sites of distribution impacted by public law. To this end, they show that the formal domain of family law is only one among other types of law that govern the family. Laws with family-specific provisions, such as immigration laws, welfare regimes, and tax laws; laws that structure the ways that family life is lived, such as landlord-tenant law; and informal norms all contribute to the totality of laws governing the family. Public law regulates the family because it is not an isolated sphere but an important distributive institution. Halley and Rittich introduce the idea of the "economic family," a term with which they seek to return family members to the *oikos*, or the household as a site of "production, welfare provision, and consumption" (2010, 758). They establish, thereby, that qualities that anthropologists have long associated with kinship—relations of labor, property, exchange, gender, personhood, inequality, affect, and obligation central to social life—also pertain to marriage-centered nuclear families. Although they do not cite Engels, their argument is reminiscent of his observation that the monogamous family acts as the economic unit of societies that have a regime of private property ([1884] 2010). Halley and Rittich suggest that as an economic unit, the family does more than serve as the repository of inheritance; theirs is a fuller account of the political economy of the family as evidenced in the laws that regulate it.

My research, along with other feminist scholarship, suggests that in India, the family has come to be addressed and popularly understood both as a separate (religious) sphere *and* as a site of production, distribution, welfare provision, and consumption. In contemporary India, marriage, which is treated as the central relationship within the family, is critical to regulating both the privacy of the family and its distributive function, with specific consequences for women. Srimati Basu's analysis of contemporary marital disputes (mostly among Hindus) in India puts it this way:

> Marriage is more than one site of structural vulnerability captured in law; it is at the core of gender trouble . . . Intertwined laws . . . reflect the cultural understanding that marriage protects women . . . economically, sexually, and socially. By this logic, when women legitimately deploy their sexuality in the commodity market of heterosexual marriage, they ought to be set for life: their parents need not consider them entitled to any portion of family resources; they need not engage the labor market, since they are to rely on the income of the husband and affines; they need not worry about having matrimonial property, because if they are good wives they can simply share in the benefits of the household . . . The state of staying married, in other words, is regarded as their primary form of property. (2015, 216)

Basu argues here that ultimately marriage *is* the problem for women in contemporary India because it functions as the source of women's well-being and security. A woman's primary labor is to engage in the kinwork that preserves her marriage; through this labor she secures her primary property, which is her marriage. One consequence of this is the marriage imperative—the view that marriage is the only secure status for adult women.[9] Another is that divorce represents a major economic and financial rupture, for women, their natal kin, their community, and the state. This "cultural understanding" of marriage and its consequences is reflected in the rhetoric and outcomes of many of the cases I analyze in this book. More specifically, these disputes demonstrate that marriage makes women vulnerable because of how it links morality to property: staying married is possible because wives and husbands act morally. Married (and divorcing) women's rights to property rest on this moral uprightness.

The following analysis shows how the Indian economic family was remade by nineteenth-century legal reform projects. Together, the reforms I discuss simultaneously treated the family as a distributive private sphere ruled by patriarchal authority (J. Nair 1996; Singha 1998) and linked it to laws of property. The relevant reforms had two broad facets. First, they entailed massive codification projects that resulted in the 1861 Indian Penal Code, the 1862 Code of Criminal Procedure, and the Evidence Act of 1872 (Fisch 1983; Mantena 2010, 91–92; Singha 1998).[10] Together, these documents standardized criminal, evidence, procedure, and contract law, thereby moving away from the common-law practice of relying on case precedent (Mantena 2010). Second, guided by the established principle that Queen Victoria's proclamation reiterated, family matters were ostensibly left alone, to be regulated by religious personal laws and authorities, which represented the Volksgeist of each community. Yet laws of marriage and divorce were subject to significant reform from the nineteenth century into the postcolonial period. Reforms of marriage and divorce dealt consistently with property, thereby regulating marriage as a distributive institution and limiting the types of property to which women had access. The way such reforms linked marriage and property reflected specific class interests. In the case of landowning families, reforms aimed to curb the division of property; in the case of the poor, the threat of female vagrancy haunted legislation and judgments. Both class concerns converged to make maintenance, rather than immovable property or monetary awards, women's primary entitlement. As Bina Agarwal has argued, policymakers have long assumed that ownership of land ought to be unfragmented to maintain agricultural output, and that women have no need for land title because there is "gender-congruence in interests within the family," with women depending on male breadwinners (1994, 9).

Nineteenth-century marriage law reforms consolidated the close relationship between marriage and property in a way that perpetuated women's dependence on male kin already evident in the eighteenth century (D. Ghosh 2006). Radhika Singha has argued that throughout the early nineteenth century, British legal regulations "sought to domesticate patriarchal authority, [and] to reconstitute the boundaries between household, state, and market" (1998, 122). As in the nineteenth-century U.S., in colonial India patriarchal control over the household increased as slavery was abolished and labor relations were separated from affective relations of dependence (see Halley 2011; Singha 1998). Even as the affective domestic sphere was shored up, women's property rights provoked debate. Mytheli Sreenivas has argued that in the late nineteenth and early twentieth centuries, legal reformers fought for the conjugal couple to replace the joint family as owners and inheritors of property in Hindu law (2004, 957). Sreenivas shows that because the colonial political economy did not encourage capitalist relations in the agricultural sector, merchants and other capitalists supported women's property rights, which represented the triumph of individual over joint family property rights. Agriculturalists, on the other hand, opposed them. This tension was addressed by granting some property rights to women, on the premise that they stemmed from women's "status as dependents entitled to maintenance" (957).

In the twentieth century, reforms to property regimes for both Hindus and Muslims were explicitly linked to their respective personal laws. Early twentieth-century legislation affecting Muslims also sought to protect consolidated agricultural land at the expense of women's property rights. In one early intervention, Muhammad Ali Jinnah, the head of the Muslim League, introduced the Waqf Validation Act of 1913 in response to several court decisions invalidating specific *waqfs* (religious endowments) on the ground that they were not essentially religious in nature but were intended to increase the wealth of concerned families (Anderson 1993, 183). The act, as Michael Anderson has argued, "simultaneously affirmed a scripturalist version of Islam [and] protected the economic interests of certain propertied classes" (1993, 184). It therefore upheld the interests of landholding families. The question of women's property was even more central to the Shariat Application Act of 1937. This act sought to create a governable Muslim collectivity by clarifying that "shari'a" law superseded existing customary practices. It specified that all Muslims were subject to shari'a on matters "regarding intestate succession, special property of females, including personal property inherited or obtained under contract or gift or any other provision of Personal Law, marriage, dissolution of marriage . . . maintenance, dower, guardianship, gifts, trusts and trust properties, and waqfs." The act therefore specifies the kinds of property controlled by families and subject to personal law: maintenance, dower, gifts, and inheritance. Under the act, women would be entitled to their Quranic share of one-half of what men inherit (or in the case of multiple daughters, two-thirds of the property, to be divided among the daughters) (T. Mahmood 2002). However, agricultural land was exempt, which meant that customary law would persist. This exemption was the result of efforts by Muslim landlords in the Punjab and Uttar Pradesh who did not want to extend Islamic inheritance rights to agricultural property (Jalal 2000, 384). In the Punjab, this meant that daughters were generally excluded from inheriting land (Agarwal 1994, 228; Gilmartin 1981). This significantly undermined the rights of inheritance that the act might have secured for women, since most of the property held by Muslims at the time was in the form of agricultural land (Agarwal 1994, 230).[11]

The Hindu Code Bills—a series of bills passed in the 1950s to reform Hindu personal law—reformed subjects, citizens, and family members along with property regimes. Echoing the nineteenth-century scene depicted by Sreenivas, Rochana Majumdar argues that one of Code Bills's major aims was to make Indians into rights-bearing individuals rather than subjects mired in kinship—to "develop capitalist property and liberal citizen-subjects" (2009, 208). For this reason, the Code Bills were hailed as progressive, marking improvements for women in particular. Majumdar argues that dedication to development, an "economic vision," proved decisive in passing these reforms to family-related legal codes. She writes, "This dream of India as a robust and developing economy made up of families whose property remained undivided ultimately clinched the debates about women and family" (2009, 212). The reforms reinforced *stridhanam*—"women's wealth"—given at the time of marriage as the appropriate form of property for women, while simultaneously ensuring that land property remained the usual form of male property. Stridhanam is generally jewelry or property given to the bride at the time of the wedding; it is to be and remain her property (see Basu 1999, 88). As I discuss in depth in this book, postcolonial Muslim personal law has been enmeshed in debates about property, with rights to maintenance having been subject to particularly vigorous scrutiny.

This genealogy of marriage and property in colonial India suggests the longevity and relevance across religious communities of two trends apparent in the marital disputes I study in this book. First, the legally enforced view that women are dependent on male kin has long made claims to property ownership difficult to sustain and rendered maintenance the "natural" form of property and financial support for women in marriage and divorce. This is one significant way that women in contemporary India are made vulnerable by marriage. Second, there is nothing new about marriage as the site of distribution. This is, instead, a constitutive feature both of modern marriage and of efforts to separate a public from a private and a secular from a religious sphere.

The issue of landed property fragmentation could not be more distant from the concerns of the disputants who approach the Islamic legal institutions I analyze in this book. These disputants rarely own immovable property, have modest movable property, and only some of the husbands have salaries sufficient to make substantial maintenance payments. Indeed, by contrast, these cases demonstrate the degree to which literature on divorce, in and beyond India, fails to account for the profound effects of class. Yet the views about women's normative relationship to property that become apparent in the historical debates are now assumed, legally and popularly. The idea that women are entitled solely to maintenance becomes a governing ideal of poor as of wealthy marriages. The effect is that religious and secular courts alike focus on determining maintenance payments, any unpaid *mahr* (dower), and limited amounts of movable property to divorcées. It is for this reason that maintenance has been the key object of dispute and judgment in state and nonstate forums alike. Property and marriage continue to be linked in a distributive private space and are, in turn, tied to and adjudicated according to religious norms.

Together, the religious personal law system put in place by the Hastings Declaration and the reforms in the nineteenth century shaped marriage and divorce in ways that continue to be relevant today. Marriage/divorce and religion continue to be collocated in a nominally single private sphere, and marriage continues to be construed as women's primary form of property, as the cases and disputes under study in this book show. Marriage and divorce also continue to be concerns both because of their moral valences and the family's economies—one, an internal economy of resource distribution and the other, the market economy of labor and property. Because of the contingent link between marriage-property and marriage/divorce-religion, divorce in particular is an event that lays bear families' normative property regimes, leads individuals and families to examine their own economy of distribution, and confronts state courts with immediate, small-scale questions about where religious jurisdiction over the family begins and ends. In this way, divorce at once clarifies the stakes of marriage and renders evident FLE's ideological quality.

Divorce as Reckoning

I have suggested that divorce matters because of India's personal law structure, which makes family an intense site in which religious authority and belonging are secured.[12] Furthermore, I have suggested that to understand the specificity of religious law and secularism in India requires an account of the multiple jurisdictions, sites, and authorizing discourses that comprise the Indian legal system as critically concerned with kinship. But the reason divorce matters to secularism has to do with more than this legal structure. It also has to do with *divorce* as an act of undoing marriage.

Scholars have emphasized the importance of the family not only, as Halley and Rittich have done, as a unit of production and distribution, but also as a regulatory mechanism for the state (Foucault 1978; Donzelot 1997). Specifically, feminists have shown that by setting the terms of marriage, the state constitutes a private sphere in which questions of dependency, financial responsibility, and moral obligation are negotiated (Pateman 1988). But the seemingly private sphere can be governed because marriage, its central institution, and divorce, the undoing of marriage, are subject to public law, not to private contract. Rather than being contracts between consenting individuals, marriage contracts are regulated by the state. Halley shows that the United States' double transformation in the nineteenth century—"from law of husband and wife to law of marriage, and of marriage from contract to status"—separated "the law of familial intimacy from the law of productive labor" (2011, 2). Counterintuitively, this entailed the transformation of the law of the private husband-wife relation into the public law of marriage (52). As marriage transformed from a matter of contract, an agreement between two private individuals, to a matter of legal status, regulated by the laws of the state, it came to be the opposite of contract. Yet laws of marriage secure an ostensibly private sphere where social powers, inequality, and dependency reign, and counterpose it to a public sphere of political equality, wherein individuals can contract freely (Scott 1996; Surkis 2006).

While literature on marriage and the family has been invaluable in explaining the gendered basis for liberal states as well as the fiction of privacy on which political equality relies, its failure to address the specificity of divorce means that a critical site of regulation is missing from the analysis. In *Divorcing Traditions* I argue that divorce, in and between state and nonstate institutions, is both critical to the regulation of families and a site of pronounced anxiety for the state. Divorce is a legal, moral, and financial reckoning. It troubles the boundary between family, on the one hand, and contract and labor, on the other, not from beyond the domain of the family and the laws that function outside of it, but from within it. It is the process whereby the sequestering capacities of marriage are challenged and undone, where the contradictions of marriage are exposed, reopening questions about an individual woman's relationship and rights to property, economic independence, and independent legal identity.

Even as divorce exposes the asymmetries of marriage, it is itself asymmetrical. In the divorces I study in this book this imbalance is apparent in the distinct legal, moral, and financial reckonings that divorce demands of men and women. In India, Muslim women can file for divorce in state courts, under the Dissolution of Muslim Marriages Act, or they can file for maintenance under Criminal Procedure Code 125. Men cannot file for divorce in state courts, but can unilaterally divorce their wives in particular and restricted ways that I discuss in detail in the following chapters.

Women also have recourse beyond the state, to dar ul-qazas, where qazis grant divorce for cause or by adding a clause to the marriage contract (*nikah-namah*), granting them the right to unilaterally divorce their husbands. Women and men need to make different kinds of cases in this forum, each of which carries a particular moral valence. Obtaining a divorce in dar ul-qazas demands that women's devalued reproductive and affective labor be evaluated. This does not mean that women retroactively receive wages for housework (Federici 1975). Instead, in order to be granted a divorce and a maintenance settlement, a wife must prove that she has done her job well: that she has been a good daughter-in-law and wife and has contributed her labor to the household. She must also demonstrate that her husband has failed to provide for her financially, emotionally, or physically. Men who are before qazis either to dispute that a divorce should take place or to contest the financial settlement their wives seek must demonstrate that they have not abandoned their dependents but have provided what they need to live a good life. Divorce disputes push husbands and wives to negotiate about what kind of property a divorcée should receive: mahr, wedding gifts, dowry, and every now and then immovable property—a house or a piece of land. Such morally laden financial negotiations about productive labor in and outside the household, about the household as a site of distribution, and about the interests husbands and wives have in marriage and divorce lay bare the relations between household and markets that feminists have long noted. Both as kin relations and as sites of exchange, divorce proceedings in and beyond dar ul-qazas show that marriage is the site of entrenched gender inequality, with men consistently better positioned to make ends meet after a divorce. Thus, much of the data in this book corroborates the findings in a broader literature on divorce over the past forty years that divorce tends to make women and children downwardly mobile (see Basu 2015; Okin 1989; Simpson 1998; Vatuk 2017; Weitzman 1985).

As it draws attention to the economic relations entailed in marriage, divorce also shows the state's interest in families and in the economics of family breakdown.[13] This becomes especially clear by way of a contrastive negative example. In England, Bob Simpson has argued that because men no longer consider themselves to be familial breadwinners, they also no longer assume that they are financially responsible for their ex-wives. This shift is, according to Simpson, "problematic for the State which, in any case, finds itself deeply at odds with the general shift toward the multiplicity of family forms today" (1998, 107–108). When men do not assume financial responsibility for their families after divorce, as in contemporary England, state welfare programs must pick up the slack; given that women generally have significantly lower earnings than men, this is true even in the case of two-income families. In India, state jurisprudence has been effective at helping to maintain the male breadwinner ideal and at sequestering responsibility for women made destitute by divorce within the family or, failing that, within the community (Vatuk 2001; Basu 2015). This is what makes divorce such an illuminating lens through which to study how an ostensibly private family sphere is made and reinforced by public, state intervention, in and beyond India. One symptom of this dynamic in India is that the state is not particularly concerned to enforce marriage registration, but cares deeply about the financial fallout of divorce.

Anthropology of Secularism and the Indian Case

The renowned scholar and activist Indira Jaising, a senior advocate with the Delhi-based Lawyer's Collective, has argued that religious law is an oxymoron. In a recent article responding to a debate about one type of Muslim divorce, she wrote: "What is law cannot be religion and what is religion cannot be law. Religion, as we all acknowledge, is a matter of faith, not a matter of law. What the constitution protects is the freedom of *conscience* and the right freely to practice and propagate religion" (2017). Jaising argues that allowing religious authorities to regulate nonreligious matters, among which she includes divorce, constitutes a category mistake. She tells us that religion is a matter of faith, which she opposes to law. Kinship is, by contrast, a matter of law. The dar ul-qaza with which this chapter began is one site of religious legal practice: in it, a qazi trained in Islamic traditions of jurisprudence, and not at all in Indian law, hears cases and grants divorces. Religious personal law is, from a certain perspective, another site of religious legal practice in which interpretations of religious law, accepted and partially standardized by the state and carried out by judges and lawyers trained in Indian law govern marriage and divorce. In Jaising's view, both nonstate religious law and, perhaps more egregiously, state-based religious personal laws, are oxymorons. One argument of this book is that religious law is not a category mistake: it does not muddle preexisting separate spheres, and it is not inimical to secularism. Instead, religious legal practices, in particular religious adjudication of marital disputes, simultaneously adjudicate the ongoing question, characteristic of secularism, of the boundaries between domains proper to religious as opposed to secular authority. I am not making a normative argument here: I do not suggest that family *should* fall within the jurisdiction of religious authority. But that it does so is not an indication of Indian secularism's failure but instead indicates one of secularism's ironies.

Divorce, as the object of religious legal adjudication, in state and nonstate institutions, shows how.

The claim that religious law is a site of secular practice relies on insights from the emerging field of the anthropology of secularism. Secularism is generally understood to be a policy that requires separating religion from politics and law; it is most commonly captured by the figure of the separation of church from state. However, in recent years, anthropologists, many following Talal Asad's foundational interventions into the anthropology of religion, have challenged this conception of secularism. Asad argues that modernity is a historical epoch characterized by "the attempt to construct categories of the secular and the religious in terms of which modern living is required to take place, and nonmodern peoples are invited to assess their adequacy" (2003, 14). Asad asks how it has become obvious to divide a secular from a religious domain. This modern project, he contends, is not simply a matter of separating religion from "secular institutions in government." Instead, "what is distinctive about 'secularism' is that it presupposes new concepts of 'religion,' 'ethics,' and 'politics,' and new imperatives associated with them." Asad's genealogy of secularism demonstrates that secularism is best understood *not* as the excision of religion from politics, but rather as a process of reconfiguring various domains of life and regulating religion accordingly (1993, 2003). Anthropologists who have taken up this approach argue that secularism is not the opposite of religion, nor its demise, but instead the organization and reconfiguration of religion (Agrama 2012; Fernando 2014; S. Mahmood 2016).

By engaging both with this literature and with long-standing debates about secularism in India, *Divorcing Traditions* intervenes both in the anthropology of secularism and in the study of secularism in India. The book turns away from the dominant question of whether Indian secularism has succeeded or failed, and instead suggests that practices of Indian secularism, like practices of secularism elsewhere, regulate religion on the premise that it is both possible and necessary to draw a line between religion and politics, but also that this line may shift (Agrama 2012). The Indian case has three further implications for the anthropology of secularism. First, though anthropologists of secularism have shown how religious personal laws can be mechanisms of secular governance, they have tended to work within a narrow conception of law and have overemphasized the role of a putatively unified state. By focusing on India, *Divorcing Traditions* must contend with a radically plural legal landscape that shapes secularism as a practice and renders visible the fractured quality of the state. Second, Indian practices of secularism suggest that divorce adjudication makes secular distinctions between law and religion. *Divorcing Traditions* thus shows how kinship is central to the practice of secularism. Third, *Divorcing Traditions* highlights how secularism governs the Muslim minority precisely by together regulating religion and kinship.

The anthropology of secularism primarily understands secularism according to two models: the Egyptian and the French, both of which suggest that secularism is a project designed and carried out by a rigorously centralized state. In the Egyptian context, shari'a law was "transmuted" into personal status law—whose jurisdiction covers marriage, divorce, succession, and inheritance—by means of colonial codification projects (Asad 2003). The effect has been that "shari'a" in Egypt no longer denotes the decentralized practices of a multiplicity of jurists but instead has become a state-administered legal code governing family life. This redefinition of shari'a as personal status law, Asad argues, "is precisely a secular formula for privatizing 'religion' and preparing the ground for the self-governing subject" (2003, 227–228). It is for the same reason that Saba Mahmood (2013, 2016) has argued that personal laws in Egypt are a mechanism of secular governance, solidifying the distinction between private/particular and public/universal domains. Hussein Agrama (2012) specifies that secular rule of law is characterized by a question: Where ought a line between religion and politics be drawn? On this model of secularism, the state and its rule of law are considered central to regulating even those domains, such as the family, deemed to be properly subject to religious authority.

The French model, by contrast, is ostensibly based not on state regulation of religion by means of instruments like personal status law, but on an aspiration to banish religion from the public sphere. Scholarship on French secularism has therefore addressed the contradictions that inhere in such a project. In France, secularism (*laïcité*) has been understood as the basis for citizens' political equality and in particular of gender equality. Scholars have shown that the guarantee of political equality in French secularism paradoxically requires inequality in the regulation of religion: that is, the state regulates some religious practices more than others (Fernando 2014; Scott 2007, 2011). Mayanthi Fernando has made the point vividly: she argues that French secularism's demand for privatized religion has had the vicious effect of obligating Muslim French[14] women to defend their religiosity and sexuality against the values of a nominally tolerant secular state. The secular demand for privacy has paradoxically manifested as an incitement to public discourse about that which secularism itself has circumscribed as private.

Rather than seeing such an incitement as a betrayal of secularism's nominal mandate of tolerance, Fernando writes elsewhere, "I regard the regulation of religion (and, incidentally, of sex), and the competing imperatives of separation and administration, as crucial to secularism's operation" (2014b, 21). Joan Scott (2007) has similarly argued that interpretations of French secularism have differed significantly in their application to Christian and Jewish, as opposed to Muslim, citizens. Here Scott draws our attention to the politics of secularism and its rhetoric, which treat citizens differently depending on their religious commitments. Both Fernando and Scott show how women's sexuality has become a measure of secularism's success. Women are policed in relation not to a "neutral" code but to secularism's own sexual norms (Fernando 2014a; Scott 2011, 91–116). The contradictions of secularism that this scholarship shows are particular to laïcité, or French secularism, in the sense that they arise from a commitment to the "protection of individuals *from* the claims of religion" (Scott 2007, 15, my emphasis), a commitment initially conceived in opposition to the power of the Catholic Church.

The empirical cases of France and Egypt delineate limits of the new anthropology of secularism that the Indian case challenges. My ethnography suggests that the Indian case brings other facets of secularism into view. One reason for this is that India is a self-described secular, democratic republic[15] that guarantees free practice and propagation of religion as well as disestablishment, but without taking a "wall of separation" approach. This means that Indian secularism has, since independence, entailed deliberating about how to equally respect all religions—an aim that requires both respect for the autonomy of religious practice and state interventions intended to give members of all religious groups equal opportunities. Marc Galanter has astutely argued that Indian secularism, as a practice, entails both a commitment to a secular public order alongside reforms of religion, two processes that he suggests are linked. He writes: "the nature of the emerging secular order is dependent upon prevalent conceptions of religion, and the reformulation of religion is powerfully affected by secular institutions and ideas"

(1998, 311). As his insight demonstrates, scholars of India have long recognized that secularism entails regulating religion, not just attempting to separate it from the public sphere.

Beyond vividly showing that secularism both seeks to separate religion from politics and intervenes in religion, Indian secularism brings into question the assumed centrality of the state to secularism. In contrast both to France and Egypt, in India, secularism is not only a state project, but one carried out by state and nonstate authorities alike. Although religious personal law in India is a mechanism for the governance of religion by means of kinship, as it is in Egypt, nonstate institutions equally participate in such regulation, suggesting greater depth and variety of secular practice. Secularism is not primarily a matter of principle but an effect of jurisprudential practices. The legal practices I study demonstrate the reach of secularism and secularity, what Charles Taylor has called the "immanent frame" (2007).

As Asad has argued, secularity—the sensibilities, categories, and orientations that characterize modern life—is conceptually prior to secularism as a policy. My research suggests that anthropologists of secularism must contend with the possibility that among secularism's generative contradictions is the fact that secularity is not only prior to but generative of secularism, and that secularism is therefore practiced by religious figures who adjudicate beyond the purview of the state. The qazis and muftis and other religious actors I study in this book also engage in practices of secularism. They are important adjudicators in the context of Indian legal pluralism, and in their religious legal adjudication of divorce they undertake the labor of separating religion from law. Along with state actors, they instantiate a system of secularism.

The second way in which the study of Indian jurisprudence contributes to the study of the anthropology of secularism is by drawing attention to the centrality of kinship and its regulation to practices of secularism. This research leads me to challenge Hussein Agrama's effort to identify a space of "asecularity." Agrama argues that the fatwa house (dar ul-ifta) at Al-Azhar in Egypt, where men and women approach muftis to receive authoritative opinions about various life predicaments, is asecular. He argues that because the concerns addressed in the dar ul-ifta do not reflect a commitment to the secular question of how religion and politics ought to relate, it is indifferent to the questions that characterize secular discourse. In order to designate the fatwa house as asecular, however, Agrama must accept that the fatwa and its topics are private matters to which the state is indifferent. My research shows, to the contrary, that it is *precisely* in spaces assumed to be private that the secular labors of separating public from private and law from religion are carried out. This is because, as I showed earlier, matters of divorce, marriage, and property have long been concerns of the Indian state, such that the privacy of the family assumed by Indian FLE, or personal law, is a fiction. This is especially clear in India, where feminist debates about religious personal laws have vociferously questioned whether secularism and gender equality require the abolition of religious personal law. These debates, which revolve around how to reconcile the rights of minority communities with the rights of individual women, clearly show that in India, divorce and other personal law matters regulate religion and kinship together. Thus, even as Muslim women are made to be a measure of secularism's success or failure, the debate itself shows that they are sites for deliberating about the proper place of religion in secular democracy. My argument is that this is part of what makes religious law such a key site not for the undoing of secularism but for its practice.

The Indian case, finally, brings into relief the place of minority difference in practices of secularism. Studies of Indian secularism have long asked whether it has succeeded or failed (e.g., P. Chatterjee 1998, 2004). Alternatively, they have proposed that secularism is simply a misplaced concept in this country characterized in part by the visibility and publicity of religion (e.g., Madan 1987; Nandy 1998, 2007). The success of Indian secularism has been measured in India by means of analyzing tolerance (or intolerance) toward minorities alongside assessments of women's status. For this reason, there have been two ongoing sites of debate and hesitation about Indian secularism's success: intercommunity violence (usually referred to as communal violence) and religious personal law. One notable example is the Babri Masjid, a mosque in Ayodhya, Uttar Pradesh, that Hindu mobs destroyed in 1992, claiming that it was the site of the birthplace of the god Ram (Van der Veer 1994). The destruction of the mosque and the riots it provoked disproportionately affected Muslims and raised the question of whether Indian secularism, as a policy of equal treatment of all regardless of religion, had failed. This question was renewed following riots in the state of Gujarat in 2002 sparked by a conflict between Muslims and Hindus on a train carrying Hindus returning from a pilgrimage to Ayodhya. During this unrest, an estimated one thousand Muslims were killed and about one hundred thousand displaced (M. Chatterjee 2017). Scholars have substantiated the government's participation in these riots and shown that the courts systematically failed to convict perpetrators, thereby suggesting that secularism's promise to protect minority communities has largely failed.[16]

A different interpretation of Indian secularism, with which I concur, suggests that communal violence is a symptom not of its failure but of its success. Thus Aamir Mufti, for one, has argued that the Muslim minority must remain "the other within the modern nation," at once part of the national community and marked as separate (1995, 84). Shabnam Tejani further suggests that this structural position of Indian Muslims dates to the nationalist period, during which upper caste Hindu men consolidated their political ascendency in part by incorporating Dalits into the Hindu fold and in part by resignifying Muslims not as a rights-bearing group but as an identitarian community (2008). The oscillation between governing Muslim divorce and leaving Muslims to reform their own family laws that characterize the relationship between state courts and the nonstate institutions I study in this book suggests that the bind Mufti and Tejani describe persists today.

Even as the Indian cases draw out these four facets of secularism, the anthropological analyses of secularism in Egypt and France suggest that Indian secularism is neither a complete anomaly, nor a failure. My aim in this book is, therefore, twofold. First, it seeks to bring into relief the ways in which the anthropology of secularism enables a rereading of Indian secularism as particular but not exceptional. Second, it seeks to show how practices of Indian secularism push these existing paradigms, in particular by focusing on the secularism of nonstate religious forums.

Four Forums: The Ethnographic Landscape and the Architecture of the Book

Divorce in India does not always require sanctioning by the state or even a religious legal authority. In fact, family and district court records show that only a small number of Muslim marital disputes appear before a state court judge. However, when disputes arise that families are unable to resolve on their own, one spouse or the other may approach a court or a jurist. My argument in this book is grounded in fieldwork conducted over a total of two years between 2005 and 2013 in four different types of adjudication forums in Delhi: an NGO-run women's arbitration center, called a mahila panchayat; dar ul-qazas, usually translated as "shari'a courts"; a dar ul-ifta, an office in which authoritative Islamic legal opinions are given; and a spiritual healing practice. These institutions are all nonstate, but they are not informal. Their normative frameworks are multifaceted and bring together divergent histories, but each has a recognizable logic and consistent patterns of adjudication procedures and outcomes. All of these institutions draw on the Hanafi school of Islamic legal interpretation.[17]

An exhaustive survey of dispute adjudication forums in contemporary Indian legal pluralism would have to include others as well—among them mahalla or neighborhood committees, panchayats, and special police offices called Women's Cells that focus on domestic violence allegations. I have chosen these four institutions because they capture a range of religious adjudication forums available to Muslims and thereby are a useful lens to study the Indian legal landscape. Although the adjudication processes and outcomes in each of these institutions are distinct, the institutions all attend to the same objects of analysis: marital strife and divorce. Each institution responds to different types of marital strife—domestic violence; cruelty and abandonment; woman-initiated divorce; refusal of sexual access; and unilateral male divorce—by employing a distinct method of adjudication.

In chapter 2, I analyze Muslim personal law in relation to the particular conditions of marginality that characterize the Muslim minority in India. I do so by examining a recent groundbreaking Supreme Court judgment on Muslim divorce in relation to the treatment of Muslim kinship in an NGO-run women's arbitration center or mahila panchayat. My research in and about the Muslim mahila panchayat shows that with regard to the Muslim minority, religion is treated as integral to kinship. This has the effect of making pious Muslim women appear unassimilable to empowerment initiatives. Yet in mahila panchayats, Muslim women actively adjudicate cases, drawing both on Islamic sources and the norms they learn in legal training sessions. This chapter provides insight into the bind in which Muslim women find themselves, which is part of secularism's reliance on the particularity of Muslims as India's preeminent minority.

Chapters 3 and 4 discuss aspects of the dar ul-qaza, or shari'a court, drawing on observations of hearings and analyses of case files. Chapter 3 examines the rhetoric of disputing in dar ul-qazas to show how disputes in this venue shore up the ideal of the family as a site of protection and care distant from the public sphere of exchange relations. The major rhetorical pattern through which this view is secured is the obedience-divorce-maintenance paradigm, in which women are able to secure divorces and sometimes property if they are able to convince the qazi that they have been dutiful wives. Chapter 4 focuses on the dar ul-qazas' role in Indian legal pluralism, arguing that while not explicitly governed by the state, the ideological views advocated by the qazis align closely with those articulated by the state. In spite of both the state's and the dar ul-qazas' claims to autonomy, their relationship is one of interdependence that undermines both institutions' claims to priority and originality. To make this argument, the chapter examines both the shared source of dar ul-qaza and state law on Muslim divorce as well as a recent case that was shuttled from the state court to the dar ul-qaza in an apparent act of outsourcing. This dialogue between the state and the dar ul-qaza demonstrates that in India secularism is not solely a state project, but is carried out by both state and nonstate, religious and secular, institutions.

Chapters 5 and 6 examine two different adjudication practices carried out by the mufti of a prominent old Delhi mosque: fatwas and spiritual healing. In chapter 5, I analyze the mufti's fatwa-giving practice, focusing on his advice about a type of divorce called *talaq ul-ba'in*. I examine the jurisprudence on talaq ul-ba'in, which is made up of fatwas and state courts judgments on the subject. A fatwa is authoritative legal advice given by a Muslim jurist in response to a specific question. The mufti's fatwas pronounce on the status of divorces that are carried out unilaterally and extrajudicially, a matter also of interest to the state. By reinforcing unilateral male divorce as beyond the reach of the state, fatwas at once demonstrate the privacy of religious law and provide the opportunity for the state courts to regulate it. The asymmetrical and indirect dialogue this sets up between the Muslim jurist and the state via the question of divorce demonstrates that the state regulation of religion does not only involve direct intervention but is also a subtle and strategic nonintervention.

Chapter 6 turns to the mufti's other adjudication practice: spiritual healing. The mufti treats people suffering from marital and other domestic disputes with amulets inscribed with Quran verses and other ritual prescriptions—the mufti with whom I worked refers to this as his spiritual healing practice. The mufti's healing practice intensifies the distinction between religious and secular domains, inviting Allah and the *jinns* (genies) to mediate troubled relationships by remaking the bodies and minds of those involved in conflicts. Yet the conception, shared by the mufti, his supporters, and his critics, that the connections on which healing relies—between bodies, holy words, and divine beings—are *religious* in character is itself a secular conceit. The debate about the practice, which many Muslims argue is not religious but superstitious, captures the secular work of co-constituting religion and secularism.

It is tempting to create an ethnographic space for these forums that separates them from the cacophony of ongoing public and judicial debate about Muslim men and women's divorces. Indeed, these are forums whose atmosphere, personnel, and methods of adjudication distance them from the state's courts. Unlike any of these forums, the district courts in Delhi, Tis Hazari and Patiala House, as well as the new family court at Saket, are sprawling complexes that take time, and guidance, to navigate. I gave up after my first few attempts to find the judges dealing with personal law cases at Tis Hazari. While I was able both to observe case hearings and to read records in the much calmer Saket Family Court and the shiny new Patiala House Family Court, the atmosphere of the courtroom and relationships among litigants, lawyers, and the judge could hardly have been more different from the atmosphere in the nonstate forums. Thus, different as each of the forums I analyze here is from the others, none of them has the institutional feeling imparted by rows of chairs lined up facing a raised podium on which a robed judge sits, accompanied by a stenographer and an intimidating pile of case files. Lawyers were absent in the forums where I did most of my ethnographic research, and while litigants' interactions with qazis, muftis, and mahila panchayat leaders convey respect, they were nonetheless direct.

But as the qazis, muftis, and litigants concerned were the first to note, they were in no way isolated from the state; indeed, they continuously interacted with its legal system. Throughout this book, I bring out these interactions by introducing relevant legislation and High Court and Supreme Court judgments. In the Indian state courts, women can file for divorce, though they do so on the basis of Muslim personal law—state legislation and case law built on interpretations of certain Islamic legal sources. Men cannot sue for divorce in state courts, which is perhaps one way that state law seeks to balance the availability of extrajudicial unilateral divorce to men. The relevant legislation (the Dissolution of Muslim Marriages Act) enables women to divorce husbands who are unwilling or absent, but its framework is premised on the assumption that men already have this right.

The Possibility of Divorce

This book is about legal cases, and its material is therefore drawn from observations of various kinds of mediation and from case documents and files. At the outset, it is important to note that the cases I analyze do not constitute an exhaustive account of Muslim divorce even in Delhi, let alone in India as a whole. During the course of my fieldwork I came to know numerous Muslim women whose divorces involved neither state nor nonstate forums of adjudication. The three women in this situation whom I knew best all lived with their natal kin (two in their brothers' households and one in her parents'), and all engaged in waged labor outside the home.

One of these women was my longtime interlocutor, Nadia. For the first two years that I knew her, Nadia and her friends told me the reason she lived with her parents was that shortly after the birth of her son she had been widowed. We spent time together regularly while I was conducting my research, between 2005 and 2007, alternating between reading Urdu and English books, helping each other improve our language skills. To contribute to the family income, Nadia tutored local children after school, helping them with their homework in exchange for a small amount of tuition from the children's parents. She and her family were not well off, but they had enough to eat and were comfortable in their house—six rooms, including the kitchen and bathroom, for a family of nine.

During these first years of our acquaintance, Nadia and her friends, with whom I attended a Quran study group, knew I was conducting fieldwork on a range of Islamic legal forums, most of which heard divorce disputes. Nadia and her friends were part of the *Ahl-i hadis* community. The Ahl-i hadis, or Ahl-i hadith, which means "people of the Hadith," is a group of Muslims who place greater emphasis on following the Quran and Hadith than on the opinions of Sunni scholars. I attended the study group not to learn about divorce but to read the Quran. However, as we began to spend more time together we frequently talked about my research. In these discussions, Nadia and her friends expressed much more interest in the healing work by means of which one mufti addressed marital spats than in divorce.

This is because of their conviction that the mufti's healing practice was *shaitani* (evil). In spite of our conversations about divorce and how women secured it, it was not until I returned to do some follow-up research in 2013 that one of Nadia's friends told me that Nadia was in fact not widowed but divorced. When I asked why no one had ever mentioned this before, they told me that it was easier to say she was widowed.

As Nadia and I slowly began to talk about her divorce, it became clear that she was disappointed that her marriage had ended, not because she had wanted to remain with her husband but because she, like most people who marry, had hoped it would work out. I still do not know what led to the divorce. What Nadia did say is that it was clear to her, to her husband, and to both of their families that it would be best if the marriage was dissolved. In consultation with the leader of the local mosque, the *imam*, the families worked out the details of the separation: Nadia received her mahr, some maintenance (alimony), and custody of her son. She and her son then moved to her parents' house. It was important that the negotiations remain amicable, in part because, as is common among Muslims in north India, Nadia's husband was a cousin and therefore part of her extended family. Once everything had been agreed upon, Nadia's husband said, "I divorce you" to her three times, irrevocably dissolving the marriage. Although Nadia is not opposed to the idea of remarrying, she does not expect that she will do so.

I conclude this chapter with the account of Nadia's divorce for two reasons. First, I hope through it readers will be reminded that divorce is a process only part of which is available in the court settings under analysis here. While the material I work with cannot therefore do justice to the variety of ways that women and men live divorce, in India or elsewhere, it does behoove us to recall this variety and the pain and possibilities that can come with it. Second, Nadia's experience shows how in addition to being a site of regulation by the state and a source of volumes of pronouncements by state courts, divorce can also be an act that refuses to engage with the state. This is true for many Indians, regardless of confession, who marry and divorce without ever intersecting with the state and its bureaucratic mechanisms. This fact is key to the secular logic that governs marriage and divorce within and beyond the state: for the All India Muslim Personal Law Board, it marks the flourishing of religious authority, or at least the space where such authority appears to be uncontested. For the state, it is a mark of neutrality, that is, of secularism. It is also, however, an incitement to regulation articulated in popular discourse and in court cases alike. Although outside its direct purview, even Nadia's divorce is not in this way radically beyond the state.

Although most of the cases analyzed in this book reek of betrayal, cruelty, abandonment, and pain, for the women seeking divorce, and for the families who usually support them and the clerics who hear the cases, divorce is an undesirable but sometimes necessary outcome of marriage. Unlike the discourses about Muslim divorce in state courts, where Muslim marriage is depicted as simultaneously too frequent—Muslims are assumed to divorce both at higher rates than Hindus and with little thought—and devastating to women, my conversations with divorced women suggest that divorce was much more multifaceted. For them, sometimes divorce was a relief, sometimes a source of frustration, sometimes a mark of injustice. Sometimes it was all of these at once. But in most cases, it was also an opening: although divorcées returned to live with their natal families, nearly every educated divorcée I came to know beyond the confines of the courts had taken up a remunerated job to help her family pay the bills. These jobs varied according to the woman's education level and social status. Rather than viewing divorce only as tragedy, these women also recognized it as a source of possibility. These divorces remind us to attend to the ways in which the legally and politically salient categories of "religion" and "law" so important to the logics of secularism are constituted by means of a practice that demonstrates the entanglements of kinship, family, dependency, class, gender inequality, and poverty, thereby undermining the separation between private and public.

The inherent multivalence of divorce, as emotional, financial, kin-oriented, state-regulated, and religious, as well as its multiple spheres of impact, from the interpersonal to the political, presents analytical and narrative challenges. In the chapters that follow, I seek to show both the specificity and the legal particularity of divorce for Indian Muslims as well as its broad public significance.

Chapter 2

Muslim Divorce, Secularism's Crucible

In August 2016 the Supreme Court of India banned "instant" Muslim divorce in a 400-page decision in *Shayara Bano v. Union of India*. The type of divorce it banned is colloquially referred to as "triple *talaq*" or "instant" and "irrevocable" divorce because it takes place when a Muslim husband tells his wife, in writing or speech, "I divorce you, I divorce you, I divorce you." This statement "instantly" divorces the couple; and if thereafter they wish to resume the marriage, they must undergo an unpleasant process.[1] The Supreme Court found that the practice was arbitrary and therefore violated the guarantee of equality before the law laid out in Article 14 of the Indian Constitution. *Shayara Bano* was initiated in the Supreme Court in response to the *suo motu* public interest litigation (PIL) *Muslim Women's Quest for Equality*. A *suo motu* PIL is a case initiated by the court in the public interest. The *Muslim Women's Quest for Equality* litigation was not initiated by a Muslim woman or by her lawyers but by the judge in a Hindu woman's inheritance case.[2] In response, many individuals and organizations requested to become parties to the PIL and filed responses. Thus, even the origins of this case reflect the politics of Muslim personal law: it is, the PIL suggests, in the public (or majority) interest to deal with Muslim women's status, as their husbands' right to unilaterally divorce them is a blight on the nation as a whole.[3]

I was home in Montreal when the Supreme Court decision was announced and I first learned of the judgment in a flurry of messages from my Muslim women interlocutors in India. They were happy to see this type of divorce banned. But they also worried about what would follow; specifically, they wondered what the legislation replacing this form of divorce would look like and who would draft it. One woman in particular said that since the Hindu Right's political ascent, marked by its unprecedented electoral victory in 2014, it was hard to trust that state actors have Muslims' best interests in mind. Four months later, in December 2017, the Lok Sabha, or lower house of Parliament, passed the Muslim Women's (Protection of Rights in Marriage) Bill (MWMB).[4] This bill not only banned but also criminalized triple talaq. The bill specifies that not only is triple talaq legally void—that is, nonbinding and unrecognized by the state—but also that a husband found to have attempted to divorce his wife in this way will be imprisoned for up to three years and fined (MWMB 2.4). Furthermore, the offense is classified as "cognizable and non-bailable," which means that the police can arrest accused men without obtaining a warrant. These clauses justify my interlocutors' fear about a talaq act, as they make the stakes of accusing a husband of triple talaq so high that women are unlikely to report if and when it occurs.[5] According to my interlocutors, the act fails to protect Muslim women from the vulnerability of separation while making Muslim men into criminals who, at least while they are in jail, will have no ability to earn money and support their families.

Shayara Bano and the act—which is yet to be passed in the Rajya Sabha, or upper house of Parliament—show the significance of Muslim divorce to Indian secularism. Divorce is a political issue for the secular Indian state in general, because of the personal law system and because of the place of divorce in a broader legally plural landscape where marriage and divorce are adjudicated. But religion has taken on different political casts—and for Indian Muslims, minority politics have been inextricably bound up with the parameters of Muslim personal law and with debates about particular forms of divorce. So although, as some have argued, most of India's personal laws contain gender inequities, Muslim personal law has been the object of popular and political dissection to a degree that other personal laws have not (N. Chatterjee 2010a). This attention is symptomatic of Muslims' position as the "Other" in India—the country's most numerically significant and politically salient minority (Gayer and Jaffrelot 2012). I argue that the significance of the Muslim minority to Indian secularism is *unexceptional*. Like minorities in other modern states, Indian Muslims must perform both their difference from the majority and their loyalty to it. Muslim women figure centrally in this dynamic: their inequality is taken as a sign of the pathology of Muslim kinship and consequently of the community's failure to be fully modern and fully Indian. In this chapter, I examine debates about Muslim divorce and local practices of adjudicating Muslim marital disputes under the auspices of a secular, feminist NGO. Together, these large- and small-scale engagements with Muslim personal law illuminate the bind of Muslim women as central to the performance of secularism.

The most insightful scholarship on Indian secularism suggests that it is, at its core, about governing a political and religious minority. Because Indian secularism contains a dual commitment to equal respect for all religions and to disestablishment, the state actively intervenes in certain religious practices to enable religious flourishing. Such intervention, however, is always subject to scrutiny, especially where the minority community is concerned.[6] This tension between disciplining religion and leaving it alone is a feature of Indian secularism that has ignited some of the most heated debates in the postcolonial period. The personal law system means that marriage and divorce are especially associated with religion and are therefore primary loci of debate about how much state intervention is appropriate. In other words, the personal law system makes kinship a central concern of secularism and makes regulating kinship an exercise in regulating religion. Muslim divorce has thus acted as postcolonial secularism's crucible.

The Uniform Civil Code

The significance of Muslim divorce to the politics of secularism became apparent during the controversy surrounding the 1985 Supreme Court judgment in *Mohd. Ahmed Khan v. Shah Bano Begum* (hereafter *Shah Bano*). Shah Bano, a destitute divorcée, sued her wealthy ex-husband, a lawyer by profession, for postdivorce maintenance. When the High Court decided in Shah

Bano's favor, her ex-husband appealed to the Indian Supreme Court, arguing that according to Muslim personal law he did not have to pay his wife any maintenance once the three-month postdivorce waiting period, *'iddat*, had passed. Affirming the lower court ruling in favor of Shah Bano, the Supreme Court's judgment drew from Islamic sources, including the Quran, to argue that if a woman was left destitute by divorce, her husband was required to provide for her beyond the 'iddat period. In its final paragraphs, the judgment proposed that the state should be more proactive about enacting a Uniform Civil Code (UCC) to replace differential religious personal laws.[7]

Article 44 of the Indian Constitution, states that "the State shall endeavor to secure for its citizens a Uniform Civil Code throughout the territory of India." This is one of the Constitution's Directive Principles, which comprise Section Four of the document. Directive Principles are guidelines for making policies that are unenforceable by the courts. The Directive Principle calling for a UCC articulates the aspiration that all citizens be governed by the same laws and leaves it open to debate when an appropriate time might be to put such a uniform code into place. A UCC remains an unrealized aspiration. The idea of a UCC haunts most major debates about personal law in India, with some calling to finally enact a UCC and others arguing that such a code would undermine minority communities' rights to religious freedom. In the 1930s, the All India Women's Conference (AIWC), an NGO founded in 1927 to support women's "uplift," supported the idea of a UCC to gradually replace religious family laws, enabling all women greater access to divorce among other rights (Agnes 1999, 192). Although—by the time of the 1949 Constitutional Assembly debates—the aspiration UCC was included in the Constitution of Indian in order to more effectively govern rather than to secure either secularism or women's rights (Agnes 2008, 294–295), many supporters of women's equality continued to revere it as holding out the promise of gender equality. Agnes argues that by combining personal laws and the UCC, the Constituent Assembly hoped to alleviate minority citizens' concerns about their rights while making a claim to uniformity for all citizens. Including the UCC in the constitution as an aim indicates that Muslim minority rights were already understood to be bound with personal law.

The Supreme Court judgment in *Shah Bano* argued that India should move more quickly to enact a UCC. This reflected the communal climate in which the judgment was written and provoked anger among Muslim leaders. Sunder Rajan and Pathak have argued that the ruling amounted to an accusation that Muslims had failed to adequately modernize. Muslim women's inequality was taken as emblematic of this inadequacy. Implicit in the judgment was an argument about what Indian secularism's commitment to equal respect for all religions meant: letting religious communities reform their own laws as they saw fit or dispensing with differential religious laws altogether. The argument in favor of a UCC was that uniformity would be *secular* and that secularism entailed an effort to secure gender equality or at least to enhance women's rights.

The controversy that followed the *Shah Bano* judgment forced many members of the women's movement—the multifaceted and internally-conflicted movement for women's equality—to reconsider the relation between secularism, uniformity of law, and gender justice. In response to the Court's pronouncements on the UCC and the Quran, and the communal overtones of these pronouncements, some Muslim leaders, including the All India Muslim Personal Law Board, declared that the state was meddling in personal law (Agnes 1999). Shah Bano herself wrote an open letter refusing on religious grounds to accept the maintenance money that she had been awarded. In the wake of these protests, in 1986 Parliament passed the Muslim Women's (Protection of Rights in Divorce) Act (MWA), which specified that a divorced Muslim woman was entitled to "a reasonable and fair provision and maintenance [to] be made and paid to her within the iddat period by her former husband" (MWA 3.1.a), as a means of support for herself and any of her children. She was also entitled to her mahr. The MWA opened up routes for Muslim divorcées to secure large financial settlements: subsequent judgments in lower courts relied on the MWA's "reasonable and fair provision" clause to grant women generous settlements to be paid during the 'iddat period (Agnes 2008).[8] The act further specified that destitute divorcées were to be cared for by their ex-husbands, their natal kin, or, failing that, the Muslim Community. In other words, it rendered a divorcée's husband, her relatives, or her community responsible to keep her from destitution.

Discussions about *Shah Bano* were animated by the question of how and to what extent religious affiliation should determine a litigants' access to criminal statutes such as the right to maintenance, pitting ostensible secularists against ostensible "fundamentalists" (Sunder Rajan and Pathak 1992). The controversy surrounding the judgment and the MWA disrupted this opposition. A significant reason for this shift was the Hindu Right's support of the judgment, which made it an uncomfortable ally of members of the women's movement. It became clear that gender equality was a useful rhetoric for the Hindu Right in its quest to make India a Hindu nation. Ironically, this project was carried out in the name of secularism (Kapur 1996): by speaking on behalf of downtrodden Muslim women, the Hindu Right sought to mark its agenda as secular (that is, religiously neutral) and progressive. Members of the women's movement could, in such circumstances, no longer simply support the UCC as a straightforward measure to secure gender equality (Hasan and Menon 2004; Parashar and Dhanda 2008, ix). In Flavia Agnes's words, "While gender equality continued to be the desired goal [of the women's movement], the demand had to be reformulated within the context of cultural diversity and rights of marginalized sections" (1999, 106). Shah Bano's refusal to accept the settlement offered by the court (Baxi 2007) intensified this shift in perspective: a legal initiative that obligated minority women to choose between their rights and their religious community—or worse, that approached minority women in the idiom of protection—could not receive the support of the women's movement.

If *Shah Bano* once again raised, and intensified, the debate about the UCC by means of a court case about maintenance, *Shayara Bano* brought Muslim divorce into the limelight. There are certain notable similarities between the 1985 and the 2016–2018 debates. To understand the echoes in the earlier debate of the latter, we need to understand the political context in which these discussions took place. Both in 1985 and in 2016–2018, the Supreme Court deliberated in a Hindu nationalist political climate. In *Shayara Bano*, following the 2014 elections, the Bharatiya Janata Party (BJP) enjoyed unprecedented ascendency, and its term thus far had been marked by a documented increase in violence against those deemed to be "Other," among them both Muslims and Dalits.[9] Once again, Muslim and non-Muslim women's organizations, the All India Muslim Personal Law Board, the judiciary, and the executive branch of the federal government (the Centre) deliberated about the rights of minority women as a litmus test of secular Indian democracy. Once again, Muslim women's inequality—in comparison both to non-Muslim women and to Muslim men—was taken as an indication that Indian democracy enables differential treatment of minority women.

Yet these continuities mask certain critical differences between 1985 and 2016–2018. With *Shayara Bano*, the question from the outset was less about the state's right to intervene in Muslim divorce practices (although this has also been part of the debate) than about the politics of such intervention. This difference may in part reflect changes in the domain of personal law since 1985. As scholars have shown, all of India's personal laws have been reformed, piecemeal (Subramanian 2014), producing, according to some, "harmonization" between the personal laws of different communities (Menski 2008). As will become evident in subsequent chapters, juridical interpretations of several forms of Muslim divorce and of postdivorce maintenance entitlements have altered the practice of Muslim personal law. They have also changed the kind of problems divorce represents. If the major concern about divorce in *Shah Bano* was the problem of destitution, divorce now also causes anxiety because it undoes marriage and overturns the ideological barriers separating family from the public sphere. Indeed, the terms of the debate have changed indelibly *because* the *Shah Bano* decision remains such a pivotal moment in any history of India's secular present.

The positions of some interested parties have also shifted since 1985, in part because Muslim women's organizations interested in reforming Muslim personal law have not shied away from initiatives like the *Muslim Women's Quest for Equality* PIL, even though the Hindu Right also supports it. In 2017, secular and religious *Muslim* women's organizations such as the Bharatiya Muslim Mahila Andolan and the All India Muslim Women's Personal Law Board vocally advocated for reform of Muslim personal law alongside the BJP-controlled Centre. Meanwhile, *secular* feminist legal experts such as Flavia Agnes and Indira Jaising of the Bebaak Collective (an autonomous campaign group that supports women's rights) have argued that there is no need for a ban on triple talaq or for enacting a UCC because triple talaq is already effectively regulated and because the uniformity of rights that a UCC would represent is already available in practice if not in one specific law (Agnes 2016). As Agnes has rightly argued, the notable thing about *Shayara Bano* is that media coverage of the case has failed to cite or acknowledge legislation enacted since 2001, which clarified Muslim women's rights to postdivorce maintenance and made triple talaq difficult to prove in court. Instead, media attention, and by extension public debate, focused on the issues facing the plaintiff (domestic violence, insufficient material support) as *Muslim* issues. The Bebaak Collective's public statement on the case noted that the BJP-led government had taken credit for the results of a Muslim women's initiative to seek a ban on triple talaq, thereby claiming to save Muslim women while by capitalizing on Muslim women's own reform efforts within Muslim communities.

The *Shayara Bano* controversy once again highlighted the capacity of Muslim divorce to provoke heated debate. The controversy, and the positions that Muslim and non-Muslim, religious and secular, parties took in it, lends further insight into Muslim women's predicaments in secular India. Secularism is, as Irfan Ahmad has argued, a promise of equality for members of the Muslim minority (2009). But for Muslim women this promise is often predicated on reforming their religiosity. Muslim women are asked to be equal in spite of being Muslim, not *as Muslim women*. I draw out this predicament ethnograhically in the remainder of the chapter through an analysis of a Muslim women's arbitration center called a mahila panchayat. This center was part of a network of arbitration centers in Delhi, but at the time of my research it was the only one that was located in a predominantly Muslim neighborhood, and the only one with Muslim adjudicators. The mahila panchayat was a site where minority difference was actively negotiated, explicitly and implicitly, in relation to women's rights. My research in the mahila panchayat shows how respect for difference—one of secularism's promises to religious minorities—can inscribe and reinforce such difference and thereby undermine potential solidarity across religious difference.

The Mahila Panchayat

Every Wednesday while conducting fieldwork for this book, I took the new, shiny, air-conditioned metro to the east bank of the Yamuna River, getting off at the Jaffrabad station. The tracks were above ground as they crossed the Yamuna and entered the "trans-Yamuna" section of Delhi, so I could see as we passed the illegal *bastis*, or slums, on the banks of the river and continued into the cinder-block and cement resettlement colonies that were my destination. From the metro station, I walked or took a cycle rickshaw along the congested four-lane road that runs between Jaffrabad and Welcome, then crossed the concrete bridge over the moat-like open sewer that bounds Welcome to reach the mahila panchayat where I conducted fieldwork.

Welcome was initially settled in the 1960s, and its makeup and that of its neighboring colonies changed significantly during the 1975–1977 state of emergency declared by Prime Minister Indira Gandhi in response to efforts to depose her as Prime Minister on charges of corruption. As part of a plan to improve the conditions of the city and urban-dwellers Gandhi ordered massive slum clearance throughout Delhi, displacing many slum-dwellers from the Turkman Gate area in Old Delhi to Welcome in Northeast Delhi (Tarlo 2001). Although Welcome is no longer as far-flung as it was in the 1970s—Northeast Delhi has been connected to Delhi by metro since 2002 (Bhan 2009)—it remains one of the city's most disadvantaged neighborhoods. A study by the Ministry of Minority Affairs (Government of India 2008) found that the area suffered from major structural disadvantages. It was the most densely populated neighborhood in Delhi and had the city's lowest literacy rate. Nearly 40 percent of the households in the area identified as migrants from outside of Delhi and 30 percent as religious minorities, of which Muslims predominated.

The Northeast District shares certain characteristics with other predominantly Muslim neighborhoods in Delhi, and urban India more generally. Muslims comprise 13.4 percent of the Indian population. In 2006 the Sachar Committee Report estimated the number of Indian Muslims to be 150 million (Government of India [2006] 2013), but this population is disproportionately disadvantaged.[10] Unlike Dalits and Adivasis, Muslims on the whole are becoming more rather than less marginal. One way to capture this marginality is in numbers. In 2006 and 2007, two reports commissioned by Prime Minister Manmohan Singh provide such numbers. The first of these, the 2007 Mishra Report, showed that the Muslim community had the lowest literacy rates of any Indian community (cited in Gayer and Jaffrelot 2012, 4). The same report showed that only 23.7 percent of Muslims lived in *pakka*, or stably constructed houses, as opposed to 35 percent of Indians on average. Muslims were also poor, with 31 percent living below the poverty line in 2004–2005, compared with 35 percent of Dalits and Adivasis, 31 percent of Other Backward Classes (OBCs), and 21 percent of upper caste Hindus (Gayer and Jaffrelot 2012, 3). Perhaps even more sobering, Muslims' average earnings appeared to be dropping relative to Hindus' average earnings. Muslims were also dramatically underrepresented in political, judicial, and administrative sectors. For example, only 6 percent of India's 479 High Court judges and 4 percent of India's 3,236 Police Service officers were Muslim.

Indian Muslims are a diverse group in terms of caste and class affiliation. Currently, they are the most urban of India's religious communities; nearly 36 percent of them live in cities, and 16.9 percent of the urban population is Muslim, as opposed to 12 percent of the rural population. Unlike other religious communities, urban Muslims are poorer than rural Muslims.

In Delhi, which was a Muslim or Indo-Islamic city and center of power under the Mughals, Muslims now make up about 12 percent of the population (Gayer 2012, 217). The three districts in which I did research fieldwork have substantial Muslim populations: the Northeast District (27 percent), South District (14 percent), and Central District (30 percent). The specific localities within these districts where I conducted my research have much higher concentrations of Muslims; for example, the part of the South District in which the dar ul-qaza described in chapter 1 is located is estimated to be more than 90 percent Muslim.

The one-room office of the mahila panchayat in the Northeast District was located on the second and top floor of a cinder-block building. A steep staircase led up from the street to a concrete balcony from which one entered the office. In the corner of the office there was a desk and chair, although the only time I saw either in use was when a guest—someone from the office of Action India (the NGO that oversaw Delhi's mahila panchayats) or from the Delhi government—visited. Usually, everyone sat on the mat-covered concrete floor. The two mahila panchayat leaders, Farida and Reshma, kept a small gas burner under the desk, which they used to heat their lunches. There was a shelf at shoulder level on three of the four walls of the room. It was full of notebooks holding the mahila panchayat's logs and case files. The remainder of the wall space was covered with posters about domestic violence, the mahila panchayat, and public health campaigns, and with charts tracking the number of cases and the subjects of disputes that had appeared in the mahila panchayat. The ceiling fan squeaks in the background of all my recordings of meetings and discussions.

The East Delhi mahila panchayat was the only one in Delhi located in a Muslim neighborhood that primarily served Muslim women. It was founded in the early 2000s, and its leaders had been working there for one and two years, respectively. The Northeast Delhi mahila panchayat was part of a network of forty-four mahila panchayats throughout Delhi, the oldest of which opened in the 1990s. The older mahila panchayats were well developed and had strong reputations and voluminous caseloads. I conducted some initial fieldwork in a mahila panchayat in a South Delhi basti, which contrasted sharply with the East Delhi mahila panchayat: it had been hearing cases for fifteen years, and its two leaders had twelve and fifteen years experience, respectively.

The network was founded and overseen by the NGO Action India. Individual mahila panchayats, like the one in East Delhi, are led by local women, such as Farida, who are literate and have received training in gender awareness and law by professionals in these fields. These leaders tend to be poor and share basic life circumstances with the panchayats' disputants, whereas the employees of Action India are mostly middle-class women. The mahila panchayat leaders are paid, as are the NGO employees. The mahila panchayat leaders are expected to meet people (usually though not always women) who come to the office with cases, to keep the case files, issue summons to other parties who need to appear in the course of a hearing, and to adjudicate the case by leading mediations that include parties of the case and members of the mahila panchayat. The members of the mahila panchayat are local women who volunteer their time to help mediate disputes. Mahila panchayat members refer to one another as "sister" (*bahan-ji*) and "auntie," and they address the women who approach them with cases as "sister" (*didi* or *bahan-ji*).

During the course of my primary research, I attended weekly meetings, observed about twenty formal and informal mediations and hearings, read more than one hundred case files, discussed cases with mahila panchayat leaders, studied reports about mahila panchayats produced by Action India, and interviewed staff members. I learned that the mahila panchayat nearly exclusively heard cases about marital disputes. Many of these disputes centered on accusations of ill treatment and physical and verbal abuse, and most involved extended family members. Extended family members' involvement reflected the living arrangements characteristic of the parties. Most women, upon marriage, moved into their husband's family home, which meant that the new wife was expected to contribute to household work under the direction of her mother-in-law. Thus, while most mediations focused on the married couple at the center of the argument, in-laws often played important roles either in provoking or mitigating disputes.

As the leaders of the mahila panchayat in East Delhi, Farida and Reshma opened the office daily at ten in the morning and remained there, on call, until four in the afternoon. Most days, there was little traffic through the office, although occasionally women would drop in to follow up on a case or to discuss difficult situations they were confronting at home. But Wednesday afternoons were different: from one o'clock until about four, the room was crowded. Wednesday was the day that parties involved in ongoing cases were called for mediation sessions. Ten to twenty members of the mahila panchayat joined Farida and Reshma on such afternoons, along with disputants and often the disputants' family members—husbands, siblings, children, in-laws—if there were ongoing cases. Most Wednesdays the mahila panchayat heard only one case, though often the mediation session stretched out over the entire afternoon, beginning sometime after one o'clock and not concluding until three-thirty or four. Rarely, there were no cases to hear. On those occasions, mahila panchayat members would talk amongst themselves for an hour or so, asking about one another's families, discussing their health problems, and talking about local politics, before excusing themselves one at a time to attend to the work, at home and outside, that awaited them.

An individual case at the mahila panchayat usually lasted for a period of several months, as the mahila panchayat call the parties and relatives or other witnesses to the Wednesday meetings to help them resolve the dispute. The mediation process was non-adversarial, though often heated and emotional, as the mahila panchayat members pushed parties for accounts of their problems and pushed them to find solutions. The case files that the mahila panchayat leaders put together resemble court case files more than notes from counseling sessions, with detailed descriptions of each Wednesday proceeding, witness statements, signed documents, and, ultimately, a contract (in lieu of a judgment). The contract was signed by both parties, with the mahila panchayat leaders and all mahila panchayat members present. All those present who were illiterate, which was often the strong majority, signed with a thumb print. The contract stipulated the terms of the decision, which was usually a compromise, and often suggested a follow-up visit. The mahila panchayat has no enforcement power, but is effective at following up with parties, with members often visiting homes, talking to families, and exerting social pressure in other ways. The procedures for adjudicating cases I witnessed at this mahila panchayat were shared by all of the mahila panchayats in the network, as leaders were trained in central sessions.

One Wednesday, a young woman whom I will call Mumtaz entered the mahila panchayat office. Mumtaz stood out immediately, as she wore her hair cropped just above her shoulders and loose rather than long and pulled back, and had applied visible makeup. Farida had already met Mumtaz, and told the assembled members that Mumtaz was having trouble with her father. As Mumtaz began to tell her story, the mahila panchayat members seemed to grow skeptical. Mumtaz said that her father beat her and that he was also mean to her mother, who was disabled. She articulated a number of wishes that fell flat in the room: rather than focus on marriage, she wanted an apartment of her own where she and her mother could live; she also wanted a government job, which would provide her with her own spending money and independence from her father. She told the mahila panchayat members that she liked fashion and that her father unjustly disapproved of her sartorial choices. The mahila panchayat minutes from that day state that she cried as she told her tale. The notes indicate that the young woman had snuck away from home to attend the mahila panchayat meeting and did not want word to get back to her father that she had come. When Mumtaz had finished her account, the mahila panchayat members quickly jumped in to try to persuade her that she should not refuse her father's wishes for her future so quickly. Although Mumtaz did not say that her father had found a fiancé for her, she anticipated that her father expected she would marry—she was about twenty years old, an age at which many women in the neighborhood wed. Mumtaz had hoped to foreclose this possibility by telling her father she did not wish to marry. The members of the mahila panchayat sought to convince her that marriage would provide her with a route out of her father's home as well as a secure future. They did not discourage her from pursuing a job, but they did not encourage her either. Mumtaz never returned to the mahila panchayat during my time in Delhi, discouraged, I imagine, by the coolness of her reception.

Mumtaz's encounter with the mahila panchayat highlights one tension characteristic of this kind of adjudication forum and symptomatic of the broader political and legal context in which it operates. This is the tension between a marriage imperative and an empowerment initiative in a context of significant material constraint and political and legal marginalization. Mumtaz embodied, in her self-presentation and in the aims she articulated, one model of empowerment. She was single and had no desire to marry, and she aspired to be a wage earner and thereby to be able to leave her father's home. Mumtaz's wishes appear to be congruent with the aim of securing economic independence for women—the aim that the mahila panchayat was initially founded to pursue. But her desires were not taken up in the mahila panchayat. Instead, economic empowerment and aspirations to independence from marriage were treated as unrealistic. The tensions evident in Mumtaz's case are not particular to the Muslim mahila panchayat; they are shared across mahila panchayats. These tensions are due both to the aims of the mahila panchayats and to the kinds of disputes that mahila panchayat leaders and members adjudicate.

The name "mahila panchayat" alludes to a forum of local governance and dispute adjudication that has a long and controversial history in India that continues to this day. Broadly speaking, a panchayat refers to a local council that currently exists in various forms, including caste,[11] village *khap*,[12] and *biradari*[13] (Chowdhry 2007). These various panchayats typically enforce their decisions by using social pressure rather than the coercive apparatuses of the state. *Nyaya* (judicial) and *gram* (administrative) panchayats, by contrast, were established by the Indian Constitution and act as local governing bodies (Holden 2003). The vast literature on panchayats demonstrates both the many forms they have taken and the transformations they have undergone throughout the colonial and postcolonial periods, a history to which the name "panchayat" alludes, but of which the mahila panchayat is not a part.[14] Mahila panchayats are among those councils best understood within the Gandhian tradition of supporting local self-governance and adjudication. Just as Gandhi understood the panchayat to be a local justice forum available to be remade from a caste-based organization to a village-level body (Galanter and Baxi 1979), the mahila panchayats aspire to undo the male-centered character of existing panchayats (Action India 2001; Sekhon 1999). Farida, one of the two leaders of the East Delhi mahila panchayat, describes this aspiration as follows: "In villages, and all over India, there are panchayats where five men sit, and call women before them when the women are accused of doing something wrong. In these panchayats women are not allowed to speak, or else they are too afraid to do so. The idea of the mahila panchayat—literally a woman's panchayat—is that it gives women a place where they can speak from their hearts, where they can explain what is wrong, where they do not just have to suffer silently."[15] This account dramatizes women's marginality in caste panchayats and points to the remedy offered by mahila panchayats. As part of an empowerment initiative, mahila panchayats identify kin relations as a site of struggle for poor women, and seek to teach women how to ameliorate their situations by voicing their desires and negotiating with their spouses.

The mahila panchayat network expanded significantly in 2001, when the Delhi Commission for Women (DCW) recognized mahila panchayats as effective mechanisms for promoting women's safety. As part of its "Make Delhi Safe for Women" initiative, the DCW hired Action India to reproduce its mahila panchayat model by working with thirteen NGOs and sixteen Community Based Organizations (CBOs) (Action India 2001, 31). Action India worked with other local NGOs, which in turn found and "motivated" community leaders to begin running their own mahila panchayats. In 2011 the DCW assumed management of the network, which changed the mechanisms and loci of oversight and recordkeeping. One indicative change was that the DCW hired a small NGO to manage its records, to write reports, and to conduct site visits at individual mahila panchayats. In interviews, the NGO's two employees seemed earnest and diligent, though Action India employees were not happy to lose the capacity to oversee the mahila panchayats in their network. In spite of their ever-closer relationship to the Delhi government, mahila panchayats are not technically part of the state's legal apparatus, and their judgments are not legally binding. However, as will become clear in the cases below, they do work alongside state institutions—drawing, in particular, on domestic violence legislation, as they adjudicate cases and draw up contracts. In this way, they are among many institutions active in India's plural legal landscape (Solanki 2011; Vatuk 2013).

The history of Action India lends insight into views about the family and its relationship to women's poverty that inform feminist activism and the positions of conservative clerics alike. The origins of the organization's work in economic justice are reflected in the clarity with which mahila panchayat leaders are trained to identify marital problems as impediments to livability, not only in the emotional but also the material sense. Action India was founded in 1974 when "a group of middle class citizens concerned about the deteriorating democratic and civil rights in India came together to seek the root causes for the growing poverty and to articulate the inequality and injustice in the system" (Action India 2001, 3). The organization was galvanized during the Emergency, declared in 1975 by then Prime Minister Indira Gandhi, that led to the settlement of Welcome Colony (where the mahila panchayat I studied is located). At the time, Action India became involved primarily in providing basic services and food to the roughly 700,000 people—15 percent of Delhi's population—displaced by Gandhi's slum demolitions (Action India 2001, 3). The Action India network still works out of four resettlement colonies in which it was active in the 1970s. Ironically, Action India only began to work in Welcome when the mahila panchayat opened there in the early 2000s.

Action India's six kinds of programs reflect the intertwined issues the organization encounters in its efforts to eradicate poverty. Collectively, they represent a simultaneous movement from economic empowerment initiatives to marital dispute resolution. From the very beginning, its aim was to provide basic services to impoverished and displaced Delhi residents. Action India's founding members recognized the links between economics and kinship. Action India began with labor issues, organizing home-based workers to stand up for their rights. Organizing women workers in domestic spaces led Action India workers to notice several other conditions—notably health problems and domestic violence—that stunted women's efforts as wage earners. In 1984 it therefore founded the Community Health Worker Project and in 1992 the Women, Law, and Social Change Project (Sekhon 1999). The overarching aim of Action India remains "to organize women at the community level where their lives were enmeshed within a patriarchal family and community and were characterized by economic marginality" (Sekhon 1999, 28). Led by the organization's practical efforts to address gendered poverty, Action India's programs began with the view that gender equality requires women's integration into the labor force. Over time, the organization arrived at the position that marriage and the fiction of the private household were central engines of gender inequality—a position that resembled arguments by socialist feminists (Harris 1984; Stolcke 1984). Unlike these socialist feminists of the 1980s, however, Action India advocated not the end of marriage but its reform. Action India thus sought to enable women to enter the labor force by helping them become healthier, more confident in standing up to their male kin, and more knowledgeable about their rights to do so.

From the 1970s onward mahila panchayat mandates reflected Action India's broader aims: to provide women with new ways to resolve their conflicts through legal training and discussion, and thereby challenge prevailing "attitudes and values systems that oppress women" (Sekhon 1999, 30). Mahila panchayats shared this aspiration with other nonstate women's courts in contemporary India, many of which have been founded in response to the state courts' systematic failure to address women's struggles with domestic disputes and violence (Vatuk 2013).

Precarity and Desire

As was evident in Mumtaz's case, mahila panchayat debates about how to improve the lives of individual women did not entail explicit discussions of religion. They instead focused on conditions of economic precarity, domestic violence, and desire and love, issues shared by women who attended all of Delhi's mahila panchayats, regardless of religious affiliation. The predicaments of love and of poverty produced ambivalence in the mahila panchayat leaders and NGO employees alike. Deepa, a founding member of Action India, clearly articulated this ambivalence through the accounts she gave of several memorable cases. As we discussed the problems that arose when reconciliation was privileged over other possible outcomes, in a conversation we had in 2013, she recalled a case where she remains conflicted. Some years earlier, a Muslim woman approached a mahila panchayat because she wanted to leave her husband and their four children to live with her lover. Deepa described the husband as a gentle man. The woman she described as young and beautiful. According to Deepa, the mahila panchayat members told the woman that just because she was young and beautiful now did not mean she would be so forever; they advised her to stay with her husband, who agreed to take her back. However, Deepa intervened, suggesting that the mahila panchayat members not insist that this woman leave her lover and return to her husband—even if they thought it was the safest route. Instead, Deepa urged the members to help the woman do what she wanted.

Implicit in this account of one woman's interaction with the mahila panchayat is a difference of opinion regarding the mahila panchayat's principal aim and proper role. The members, who are also the disputants' neighbors, represent themselves as protectors; in this particular case, they primarily tasked themselves with shielding the woman from the financial precarity that would likely result if she left her family and also lost her lover. Deepa, by contrast, represented the mahila panchayat as an institution charged with helping the woman actualize her desire—even if doing so placed her material security at risk. At stake is a distinction between a pragmatic and an idealistic view of improvement.

Yet Deepa also thought women's claims should not be frivolous. She told me about another woman who, in an attempt for more spending money to buy clothing and go out with her friends, brought a case against her husband.

A young Action India staff member (and mahila panchayat members, who brought up the same case in a later conversation with me) took this to be a sign of progress: women were not only going to the mahila panchayat to secure material subsistence, but also when they felt entitled to confront their husbands in the pursuit of other kinds of desires. In other words, the staffer and the mahila panchayat members viewed this as evidence that women's conceptions of their entitlements were expanding, and that they were increasingly asserting their entitlement to more than just basic subsistence. Deepa voiced two misgivings about this reading of the case as evidence of the mahila panchayat's success. First, she invoked "the feminists" who would regard this as a further entrenchment of the male breadwinner convention by validating the notion that husbands should set "allowances" for their wives, which runs directly counter to the goals of imagining and living lives that do not rely on male benevolence. Second, speaking "as a mother-in-law," she suggested that demanding more money for the purposes of nicer clothes and more outings with friends indicated a frivolous disregard for the family's well-being. In this case, Deepa's question arose from a tension between the pragmatic response to conditions of poverty on the one hand, and on the other the importance of living out one's desires.

Domestic Violence in the Mahila Panchayat

In cases involving domestic violence, which were common, the mahila panchayat members dealt with a different aspect of the tension between pragmatism and the desire to break free. In these cases, in which religion was not part of the discussion, the question was whether and under what conditions couples should be encouraged to reconcile, even in the face of domestic violence. Rehana's case provides insight into such conflicts. Rehana filed her case in the mahila panchayat in late July 2006. The contract in which the case culminated was written and signed in December of the same year. Rehana stated in her complaint that abuse by her husband and mother-in-law prompted her to leave her marital home in Saharanpur, a village about ninety miles from Delhi. During the hearing, Rehana, her infant son, and her four siblings all stayed at her parents' apartment on the ground floor of the two-story building in which the mahila panchayat office was located. Rehana came from a poor family. At the time of the hearing, she was eighteen years old and had a third-grade education. Her thirty-year-old husband had received no formal education.

When Rehana first approached the mahila panchayat, she told its members that she was seeking a divorce. However, the written application did not mention this, suggesting that she only wanted *kharcha* (financial maintenance) and relief from domestic violence. The discussion during the first Wednesday hearing captured the case's trajectory. Rehana introduced her case as follows: "There is a lot of beating and he [her husband] . . . also doesn't earn anything, and my sister-in-law is no good . . . The men [her husband, father-in-law and brothers] give me a terrible time . . . There was so little to eat, and there weren't enough clothes, not enough money, he didn't give me any." The problems described by Rehana, a combination of domestic violence and poverty, were familiar to the mahila panchayat: Rehana's basic needs were not being met. The problem of inadequate clothing stood metonymically for Rehana's deprivation, and she implied that her request for more clothing was met with a threat, motivating her decision to leave. Sufiya, an employee of the Community Based Organization (CBO) that helps run the Welcome mahila panchayat, asked, "Does he have clothing made?"

> *Rehana*:   No. At the time of my wedding I was given things, but since then, he hasn't given me anything. And he threatened to send for my mother [implying that her mother would discipline her for misbehaving in her marital home], so I left to come here.
> *Sufiya*:   How long have you been here [e.g., in Delhi]?
> *Rehana*:   I came five months ago.

Her husband had accused her of infidelity, so she responded to related questioning before changing the conversation's direction.

> *Rehana*:   OK, so what if he leaves me? I'll just stay at my parents' house.
> *Sufiya*:   Where?

Other mahila panchayat members commented:

Your baby needs food and clothing.
Why don't you show your husband what you can do?
Don't stay in Delhi. Be quiet.

Rehana: Here, there isn't much, but there isn't pressure . . . I'm not going there [to her in-laws' home].

Member: Does he have a lover?

Rehana: Yes.

Sufiya: When you need to put pressure on him [to stop acting violently], we can go to the police.

Rehana: No, no, I am not going there [to the police].

The discussion in this case hinged on the question of provision: Rehana accused her husband of failing to provide for her and their son. The mahila panchayat members expressed the view that Rehana should and could make certain demands on her husband and that her position was stronger as a married woman than as a divorcée. The members appealed to the male breadwinner ideal—the idea that the male head of household ought to earn enough to support his wife and children—and to the possibility of kinwork—striving to fulfill one's duties as a family member—as a means of resolution, despite Rehana's skepticism. As the conversation wound down, Sufiya gently said to Rehana: "Char andheri rat phir chandni," which literally means "Four dark nights then moonlight." Her message was clear: you are suffering now, but there is light at the end of the tunnel.

Abandonment or lack of care is a common feature of mahila panchayat cases. Another disputant brought a case to the mahila panchayat after five years of marriage. She had lived separately from her husband for four of these five years. She complained that although her family had provided 1.25 lakh rupees (USD 1,960) worth of *jahez* (dowry), her husband and her in-laws continuously harassed her for more money. After allegedly driving her to her natal home to make her demand additional lakh rupees (USD 1,500) from her parents, which they were unable to give, her husband began to beat her. At this point she left her marital home to live with her parents, and her husband remarried without her permission. By the time she arrived at the mahila panchayat, the disputant had already requested help from the Crimes Against Women's Cell (see Grover 2016). These appeals had not proven useful. Furthermore, her case at the mahila panchayat petered out when her husband did not appear, leaving her where she had begun.

Whereas this disputant had already been to the police, Rehana needed convincing. With Rehana insistent that she would not return to her husband's family, Sufiya suggested "putting pressure on" her husband by involving the police. The mahila panchayat usually disdained the police and courts, but in this particular instance it proposed their involvement, which reflected a recent initiative by feminist organizations to begin bargaining with state apparatuses (Sharma 2008).[16]

In Rehana's case, the mahila panchayat's suggestion that she appeal to the police was impacted by a recent change in Indian law. In 2005, the year before Rehana discussed her case with the mahila panchayat, the Indian government enacted the Protection of Women from Domestic Violence Act (PWDVA) to make Indian law more responsive to domestic violence and stress. Crafted and supported by numerous women's rights organizations (Basu 2008), the PWDVA marked a significant shift in domestic violence legislation: previously only the state could prosecute such cases, but civil legislation could now be "invoked by the victim herself" (Lodhia 2009, 122). The PWDVA offered a civil remedy, including damages, within a clearly laid-out and quick time frame.[17] While Section 498A (the criminal legislation aimed at preventing cruelty) "requires an immediate arrest of the husband and other family members participating in acts of cruelty," marking it as a step so drastic that many women are reticent to take it, the PWDVA does not require immediate arrest (Lodhia 2009, 112–113). According to Jaising, one of the lawyers who worked on writing the act, an underlying conviction was that women facing domestic abuse required protection, medical, legal, and financial support, and the ability to build a life away from her abuser (Jaising 2009, 52). Leaders of Action India hoped that the new legislation would be useful for many of the women who sought the mahila panchayats' services. Sufiya shared Action India's enthusiasm about the act and gave lectures to the membership about its parameters and possibilities. It is not surprising, then, that when Rehana presented her problem, Sufiya urged her to approach the police and thereafter to file a domestic violence case with the help of Action India's lawyer.

Two months later, however, the court still had not heard Rehana's case. She therefore returned to the mahila panchayat on December 9, this time with her husband. I observed the proceedings, and Farida took notes on what transpired. Rehana's husband stated that he was ready to have her come back with him to Saharanpur, and Rehana replied that she was willing and ready to return. Though her mother protested, the panchayat members agreed that Rehana should return to her husband's family—but first the couple was prompted to sign the following contract:

> I, Ahmed, of Saharanpur, on this day, declare before the mahila panchayat that I will go with my wife to Saharanpur, and that when she is there, I will not cause her any more sadness, and we will not fight. And I will do everything that the mahila panchayat has ordered: I will give my wife and my child good and happy lives. And if anyone comes for her wedding gifts, I will not do the wrong thing.[18] If any word gets to the panchayat that I am not doing what they say, they have the right to call me in again. If there is anything wrong, then it will be my responsibility. I make this decision with *hosh o hawas* [full consciousness]. For this reason, I have had this decision written so that it will last.
>
> I, Rehana, wife of Ahmed, today, before the mahila panchayat and others, declare that without any pressure or force but rather by my own free will, I am going with my husband Ahmed to my in-laws. And, in the future, I will never argue with my husband or my in-laws. In my husband's and my in-laws' house, I will accept all things that are *jaiz* [correct]. I will follow the agreement from the mahila panchayat. I will happily lead my life with my husband and child. If I fight with my in-laws or my husband or my mother, the mahila panchayat will have the right to call me in. I am making this decision with full consciousness. I am having this decision written so that it will last.

The agreement interpellated the couple as subjects assenting to explicitly established terms for their relationship.

At the outset of the case, Rehana had made numerous allegations, including that her husband had cheated on her, that he accused her of cheating on him, that her mother-in-law and sister-in-law physically abused her, that her male in-laws tormented her, and that her husband failed to protect her from his family. These accusations were addressed by the contract with clear, if general, prescriptions for action: the couple would not argue, they would accept all things as correct, and they would be happy. As in domestic violence cases before the courts, the couple was encouraged to reconcile (see Jaising 2009, 57). The disputants were, ironically, made into assenting legal subjects even as the case failed to receive attention from the state's formal legal system. In place of a formal legal investigation into domestic violence, Rehana instead agreed to a set of binding terms circumscribed by the kin relations from which her problems first emerged.

Minority Difference

In the cases explored above, the mahila panchayat appears to be a perfectly secular institution, in the sense that it responds not to religiously specific problems, but rather to a condition of economic precarity shared by women across confessional lines. Yet in spite of Action India's commitment to this sort of secularism—indifference to religion—the optics through which the Muslim mahila panchayat I observed became visible emanated from and also reproduced Muslim marginality.

When I was conducting my fieldwork, the Northeast Delhi mahila panchayat was barely five years old, and it was the only one I knew of at the time that was run by Muslim women. This surprised me because of the well-established marginality of Muslims in India. Given that the Indian women's movement has been committed to anticommunalism for decades and that it was common knowledge that Muslims were economically, politically, and legally marginal, I expected a robust representation of mahila panchayats working with Muslim women. That I did not find many such mahila panchayats reflects in part how Muslim marginality is a matter of more than economic vulnerability. It is entrenched by views about who can be empowered and about the exceptional religiosity of Muslim families. Two different encounters made this clear to me.

The first came on March 8, 2006. International Women's Day was much anticipated and greeted with excitement by the members of the Northeast Delhi mahila panchayat. I had been doing research there for over a year by then, and I was invited to join the celebrations, a large extravaganza attended by hundreds of mahila panchayat members from all over Delhi. The festivities were held at Dilli Haat, a market in Central Delhi that sells handcrafted items from all over India and features an outdoor food court with stalls representing the cuisines of each of India's twenty-nine states. Because of its location and because it usually charges admission, Dilli Haat was not a regular destination for the mostly poor members of the mahila panchayats. These women were bused in from their neighborhoods, and once they arrived, they strolled around the market under the sweltering sun waiting for the programming to begin. The program that day included speakers such as Shiela Dikshit, then chief minister of Delhi, and Preity Zinta, Bollywood star, both of whom addressed the importance of women's education and the value of the audience members' contributions as dispute adjudicators in the mahila panchayats.

I met the members of the Northeast Delhi mahila panchayat when their bus arrived. The women wore matching baseball caps along with their nice shalwar qamiz, mostly in bright synthetics. Everyone was in a festive mood, and I was pleasantly surprised to run into a number of relatives of my host family. As we ambled through the market, admiring the handicrafts and talking, it came up that neither Farida, one of the leaders of the Muslim mahila panchyat where I was doing research, nor the other members of her panchayat were wearing burqas, which they usually did when they were in public. Farida explained to me that if she wanted to be taken seriously as a mahila panchayat leader and as a supporter of equality for women, she could not be marked as a burqa-wearing Muslim.

Action India did not in any way explicitly endorse the idea that Muslim women were unsuited to participate in the struggle for gender equality. So the scene at Dilli Haat reflects the far-reaching effects of the view that women from the minority community are particularly unfree. In India, as elsewhere, the veil is read as a sign of such lack of freedom, a sign of inability or unwillingness to leave patriarchy behind (Abu-Lughod 2002; Deeb 2006). When Farida told me that she could not wear a burqa in this context and be taken seriously, she implied that Muslim women's religiosity had to be performed in particular ways. Wearing a burqa made her illegible as an advocate of women's empowerment, following an established logic of secularism that links proper religion to proper gender comportment (Fernando 2014a). According to this logic, a series of associations inexorably tie women who veil to gender oppression: the veil represents dedication to a patriarchal (or "fundamentalist") interpretation of Islam, which renders its wearer either willfully or naively subject to patriarchal control. While the women I spoke to at the mahila panchayat, leaders and clients alike, showed no interest in feminism, they were all there because, like the Hindus and Christians in other mahila panchayats I visited, they sought to escape domestic violence and to be treated with dignity in their families. The aim of these institutions was not equality but empowerment.

A second encounter, this one a conversation I had soon after this event, led me to see that Farida's actions and her interpretations were not idiosyncratic but reflected and responded to views prevalent among organizers of the mahila panchyat network. This conversation took place in Action India's basement office. Located in a middle-class neighborhood of Central-South Delhi several miles from Welcome, the office is simple but contains two columns of desks with computers, a small library, filing cabinets, and a kitchen, lunchroom, and meeting room upstairs. English is one of the languages spoken by all members of the multilingual staff, who range from college-age volunteers, both Indian and foreign, to founding members of the organization, now in their sixties. On one of my visits to this office, I spoke with a senior employee of the organization, Naseema, who also happened to be one of the few Muslims on the staff. She was curious about what I had observed in the Northeast Delhi mahila panchayat, and I, in turn, was eager to learn from her why there were so few mahila panchayats in Muslim areas of Delhi when we all knew that Indian Muslims were disproportionately impoverished. She responded as follows: "We see the Muslim aspect is hard; we see that usually when a Muslim case comes, most of our staff is non-Muslim, so when a Muslim case comes, they are not in a position to handle that case. Because knowing personal law is necessary, knowing Shari'a is also necessary. In our regular trainings, they are about law, but they are not about Muslim law" (interview, March 26, 2007). This analysis was especially interesting given that it followed Naseema's comment that the mahila panchayats were founded without "thinking about caste, class, or anything like that," thereby pointedly refusing the categories around which what she called the "traditional justice system" is organized. Yet while ignoring caste and class appeared at least theoretically possible, Naseema implied that "the *Muslim* aspect" was obdurate. She did not mean "the religious aspect," for she made it clear that the trainings in "law" sufficiently prepared the staff to deal with Hindu and Christian cases— although Hindus and Christians also have personal laws. But Muslim kinship appeared to be different, inseparable from Muslim law, which Naseema alternately called Muslim personal law and shari'a. Her comment was not made with any animus toward Muslim law, but with an air of pragmatism and perhaps respect for the complexity of the Islamic legal tradition. Her comment implied, though, that resolving Muslim women's marital conflicts require religious legal knowledge whereas the same conflicts involving Hindu women do not. Muslim women's kin relations must be addressed through the rhetorical and normative resources of the Islamic tradition.

The claim that Muslim women's disputes must be adjudicated according to Muslim personal laws whereas Hindu women's disputes require no reference to Hindu personal law is jarring coming from a member of a self-described secular organization aimed at women's economic uplift. But it captures the kind of secularism at work in the mahila panchayat as well as the tension between secular and religious discourses and practices that animate it. In a way, it is a merely descriptive comment—for many Indian Muslims, family is indeed understood to be governed by shari'a. But this description has notable consequences: the confluence of the Indian personal law system and Muslims' minority status has both popularized and politicized the idea that the Muslim family is religious and that as such it must always and only be governed by religious authority.[19]

The two examples I have given of the Welcome mahila panchayat being marked as distinctly Muslim capture a predicament that is shared by Indian Muslims and minorities in other national contexts. Saba Mahmood describes this predicament as an irresolvable tension: "On the one hand, a minority is supposed to be an equal partner with the majority in the building of the nation; on the other hand, its difference (religious, racial, ethnic) poses an incipient threat to the identity of the nation that is grounded in the religious, linguistic and cultural norms of the majority" (2016, 25). As an equal partner in building a modern India, one in which women's equality is respected and upheld, Muslims, as much as Christians, must be and are understood as integral. Indeed, from the perspective of Action India there are no meaningful differences between Muslim, Hindu, Buddhist, or Christian women's struggles. Yet Muslim difference *is* marked and *does* affect the way Muslim marital problems are understood. Not only is such difference marked, but it is upheld by a legal system that makes such difference unresolvable. This unassimilable and threatening difference echoes not only through comments about the mahila panchayat but also through debates that surround Supreme Court decisions about Muslim divorce, from *Shah Bano* to *Shayara Bano*. Muslims constitute a limit to the reach and effectiveness of Action India's mahila panchayat program.

Islamic Tradition in the Mahila Panchayat

The foregoing discussion has argued that the mahila panchayat reiterates Muslim difference in a way that brings to light the tension between respectful lack of interference and refusal to work for solidarity through difference.

Farida understood that to fit in with her fellow mahila panchayat leaders she had to remove the garb that marked her as Muslim. Yet the mahila panchayat leadership is in a difficult position, as Naseema's comments show: just because kinship is not naturally or necessarily a religious matter does not change the fact that many Muslims consider it to be so. I conclude this chapter with one example of how mahila panchayat leaders draw on the Islamic tradition to help women navigate family disputes as Muslims.

Here, I follow Talal Asad's conception of an Islamic discursive tradition: "a tradition of Muslim discourse that addresses itself to conceptions of the Islamic past and future, with reference to a particular Islamic practice in the present" (1986, 14). A tradition in this sense is not static, but changes as practitioners—both experts and lay Muslims—learn about and interpret what constitutes correct practice drawing on Islamic legal sources from the past to make sense of how to act in the present. In this sense, dispute adjudication by Muslim clerics ought to be not only a matter of expedience but part of a broader project that aims to teach Muslims how to live well as Muslims. In the Northeast Delhi mahila panchayat, lay Muslim women do sometimes refer to the sources of Islamic law, in particular the Quran, as they adjudicate cases. In so-doing, they help women to think through their predicaments as Muslims. As will become increasingly clear in subsequent chapters, the mahila panchayat leaders' approach to the sources of Islamic law is idiosyncratic, from the perspective of the Muslim clerics with whom I conducted much of my research. Yet in the mahila panchayat, as in the other institutions I analyze in this book, Islamic legal interpretations are harnessed as instruments for regulating marital disputes. In the mahila panchayat, such Islamic resources stand out, as they seem to represent the piety that is unassimilable to Action India's aims. The mahila panchayat leaders intermittently and strategically take up resources from the Islamic tradition, drawing on them within the framework of Action India's goals.

One representative case demonstrates the kind of resource Islamic texts provide in the Northeast Delhi mahila panchayat. Saida approached the mahila panchayat complaining that she was dissatisfied with her seven-month-old polygynous marriage and wished to separate from her husband. Polygyny is legal for Muslims in India (Fyzee 1974), but it is considered socially and ethically acceptable only under specific conditions. Saida said that her in-laws had supported the marriage because her husband's first wife had been unable to have children. Her complaint states: "I was cheated into my marriage.

My husband did not tell me that he was already married; still, I did not complain. But now my husband has stopped giving me *kharcha* [maintenance] and does not have a sexual relationship with me. And he says, 'If you don't have children, I will leave you.' My husband only married me to have children because his first wife also had no children. What am I to do in this situation? My appeal is that you find a solution to my problem [*samasya*]. Thank you." Saida's complaint was not that she was in a polygynous marriage per se, but rather that she was deceived into becoming a second wife and that her husband had not fulfilled her expectations. He failed to give her an adequate allowance, had not kept her company, and established no sexual relationship with her in spite of his ostensible desire for children. Her marriage neither met her expectations nor enabled the life she desired, which, she told the mahila panchayat, would include some financial solvency, freedom of movement, and emotional and sexual companionship. Her implicit understanding of ideal kinship, and the one figured in the mahila panchayat's engagement with her, was as a space of emotional and financial security.

The process of adjudication, in Saida's case as in the others I observed, had two facets, each of which entailed a specific conception of kinship. The first facet of the process entailed adjudication: it was an effort to identify problems, and to create the will and the desire in disputants to rectify these problems by doing kinship differently. To this end the mahila panchayat and disputants came up with strategies and practical actions whose effect would be to alter the quality of kin relations. The process rested on a view of kinship as *kinwork*—as created, not given, and productive as well as constraining.[20] The second facet of the process entailed recording the strategies for improving kin relations in a contract. The contract, designed to fix certain kinds of practices, presumed that even if malleable, kinship can be made stable, restrained if not immobilized.

The kinwork approach undergirded the discussions of Saida's case. The mahila panchayat members suggested that Saida effectively take up and work within her kin position, thereby making reconciliation possible and sustainable, rather than seeking divorce, as she had initially wished. The mahila panchayat sisters parsed Saida's situation through a series of questions. They asked, for example, "Do you think you would have more mobility as an unmarried woman?" In response to Saida's nod, the mahila panchayat members presented several rebuttals. As a married woman, they told her, she would not be suspected of immodest or immoral behavior when she went out or when she entertained visitors, as would a divorcée. Second, if she divorced, it was unlikely that she would be able to get as much money from her husband as if she bargained with him as his wife: divorce would eliminate her kin-based leverage.

Drawing on the Quran, the mahila panchayat members argued that she ought to seek equity in her marriage. To do so, they elaborated the entitlements of marriage based on the Quranic injunction that a polygynous man must treat multiple wives equitably. The Quran says: "Marry such women / as seem good to you, two, three, four / but if you fear you will not be equitable, / then only one, or what your right hands own; / so it is likelier you will not be partial" (Quran 4:3). Sufiya interpreted this demand for equity to mean that men must provide equally for all of the women in a polygynous marriage. She argued that "provision" includes financial, material, and emotional support and *barabar* (equal) treatment. Sufiya did not contest the legitimacy of polygyny when a first wife has proven incapable of having children, but she was skeptical that multiple wives could ever be treated equally.

The Quran is one source among others used to bolster the mahila panchayat's advice that Saida reconcile with her husband. As I have argued elsewhere, the advice also draws on other considerations—the idea that husbands should financially support their families; the legal view that it is easier for Muslim women to win financial support as wives than as divorcées; and the view prominent in this and other Alternative Dispute Resolution (ADR) settings that healing relationships ought to be the aim of marital dispute adjudication (Lemons 2016). The ADR imperative, which Laura Nader has argued focuses on "relationships, not root causes, and interpersonal conflict resolution skills[,] not power inequalities[,] and the search for justice," undergirds the 1986 Family Court Act in India, which prioritizes reconciliation in all marital disputes (see Nader 2002, 141). This imperative is central to the mahila panchayat's approach.

Saida and her husband did ultimately reconcile, signing a contract that stipulated how they would each behave going forward. Their contract closed the process of negotiation and resituated the couple in the domain of kinship; it provided a document and a set of guidelines for moving forward; and it thereby inscribed the possibility of dispute, and resolution, into the kin relations it addressed. References to the Quran or the Hadith, which fleetingly entered the discussion weeks prior to the resolution, were not part of the contract, and other than the disputants' names, religious affiliation was unmarked. Religion, then, on the one hand provided resources to guide disputants toward reconciliation, but on the other hand remained invisible in formal documentation. The Muslim mahila panchayat appears "difficult" from the perspective of Action India, yet the work of religious texts and knowledge was curtailed by training in domestic violence legislation, conflict management, and other strategies and knowledges in which there is seemingly no place for Islamic legal interpretation. This vexed position helps to clarify what is at stake in the *Shah Bano* debates and the *Shayara Bano* case: religion is an instrument for regulating the family. In the case of the Muslim minority, religion is at once the mark of inassimilable difference and an instrument for securing the ostensibly private family as the source of financial support and care.

Conclusion: Minority Difference, Secularism's Crucible

Muslim women's predicament as it appears both in the mahila panchayat and in *Shayara Bano* highlights a "constitutive bind" that religious minorities face in many secular states (Fernando 2014b, 65). In her study of the secular French Republic, Mayanthi Fernando perspicaciously writes: "The insistent repetition of Frenchness reveals the constitutive bind Muslim French find themselves in. The very act of claiming French citizenship only undermines their claim; if they were accepted as French, as full citizens, they would not have to keep asserting their citizenship. The more they assert their Frenchness, the more they reveal the precariousness of their belonging" (2014b, 65). Muslim French, always under suspicion of not being citizens, must assert their political belonging; yet asserting this belonging is evidence that they do not, or are not taken to, fully belong. Belonging would require jettisoning those practices, including religious and sartorial practices that mark them as different. It would require dropping the demand to be *Muslim French*—to claim both citizenship rights and belonging as Muslim.

Fernando's analysis demonstrates the continued relevance of Marx's essay "On the Jewish Question" in understanding the bind of minorities in the modern secular state (1992, 211–243). In "On the Jewish Question," Marx asks what Jewish emancipation in nineteenth-century Europe requires; his starting point is a critique of the left Hegelian Bruno Bauer's argument that Jews must free themselves from religion, recognizing that it is "nothing more than . . . snake-skins cast off by *history*, and *man* as the snake which wore them" (1992, 213). In this way, religion would become irrelevant to the political claims of Jews. Marx argues, against this view, that shedding religion in this way would only emancipate Jews politically by offering formal equality. Such political emancipation would not eliminate religion. Political emancipation from religion, for Marx, would be accompanied by religion's increased significance in civil society, as a divisive force. It would move religion into the realm of the private, against the divisiveness of which the state could fallaciously assert itself as the source of emancipation (1992, 218). Wendy Brown argues that ". . . the state is premised upon that which it pretends to transcend and requires that which it claims to abolish; it reinforces by politically suppressing . . . that which grounds its *raison d'être*. But in addition to its legitimacy, the state achieves a good deal of its power through its devious claims to resolve the very inequalities that it actually entrenches by depoliticizing" (1995, 109). The bind of the Muslim French comes from their refusal to accept political emancipation on the terms of the secular liberal state. The bind in which they are caught comes from the state's reliance on their difference as private particularity—insisting on Muslim French citizenship makes Muslim French rather than the French Republic itself appear contradictory.

Aamir Mufti has brought the Jewish Question into conversation with the Indian Muslim Question, articulating Fernando's bind for Indian secularism. Mufti argues that "secular nationalism offers a particularly Muslim modernism with the following choice: it can either dissolve itself within the nationalist mainstream . . . or be by definition (perversely) communalist, regrograde, and in collusion with the feudalizing policies of imperialism" (1995, 84). During the nationalist period, Mufti suggests, Muslim leadership was not given the option of forging an Indian Muslim political community. It instead had to choose between shedding its Muslim difference and maintaining this difference, as perversion. With this decision comes what Mufti calls the "representational burden" of Muslims, a burden that remains with them in the postcolonial state. This burden of "the figure of the Muslim is precisely that of being the *other* within the modern nation, the continually repeated, *negative* reminder of the nation(alist) self's modernity" (1995, 84). It is precisely this representational burden that Muslim women, in particular, have come to play in debates about secularism. *Shayara Bano* and the predicament of the Muslim mahila panchayat are both performances of this burden.

This chapter has sought to demonstrate how two approaches to Muslim difference together reinforce the significance of religion to and the authority of religion over Muslim families, while normatively implying that shedding religiosity and religiously-based kinship is critical to full incorporation in the Indian nation. Here, the bind of religion that Fernando illuminates is compounded by a bind of gender and kinship. In the case of *Shayara Bano* and the Muslim Women's (Protection of Rights in Marriage) Bill, Muslim kinship is identified as especially inequitable. The assumption here is that making divorce more difficult for Muslim men will address inequalities between both men and women and between Muslim and non-Muslim women. However, the ruling in *Shayara Bano* ignores inequality in marriage as well as Muslim marginality, focusing instead on defective kinship. Such defective kinship, the ruling implies, can be corrected by a better interpretation of Islamic law, one that does away with "instant" divorce and thereby makes access to divorce more difficult. While it is certainly time that the Indian state stopped recognizing triple talaq, which I discuss at length later in the book, it is unclear that doing so will bring about Muslim women's equality. This is especially doubtful given that the act hobbles Muslim women by making triple talaq a criminal offense.

One effect of this mode of regulating religion and kinship in the name of gender equality is to reinforce the family as religious. Another is to augment state control over divorce and thereby consolidate the publicity of marriage and divorce. The mahila panchayat makes visible the effects of these discourses in local efforts to challenge gender inequality as one facet of a struggle for economic empowerment. In the mahila panchayat, as in Muslim personal law, religion and religious sources are instruments for regulating kinship. At the same time, the assumption that religious authority is particularly relevant to Muslim women and their families has the effect of making these women only partially assimilable in the kinds of class and gender solidarity that characterize the basis of the mahila panchayat network more broadly. That is, Muslim families are made out to be governed thoroughly by religious law characterized as foreign to non-Muslims; this view is upheld even by cases, like *Shayara Bano*, that in another way seek to undermine Muslim difference. In this way, Muslim personal law and the mahila panchayat network together demonstrate how the antimajoritarian promise of Indian secularism entrenches minority difference and thereby undermines avenues of interreligious solidarity.

PART II

The Qazi

Chapter 3

Shari'a Courts' Family Values

In the fall of 2006, I joined Qazi Kamal at the All India Muslim Personal
Law Board (AIMPLB) offices, in a simple room serving as his dar ul-qaza,
or "shari'a court." I had been visiting him for months already and had read
many of the case records kept in the dar ul-qaza archives, a large cabinet in
the qazi's room. This was, however, the first time I would be able to observe
the proceedings in his courtroom firsthand; the qazi had offered that if all
of the parties to the dispute agreed, I could attend.

When I arrived at the dar ul-qaza at nine o'clock the morning of the hearing, I sat on the floor in the back corner of the room, as requested, along
with another observer, a PhD student enrolled at a local university who was
conducting research on the AIMPLB. Several minutes later a group of people
arrived: one young man, one young woman, and several older men and
women. They took off their shoes and stepped into the qazi's office: the young
man—the *mudda'i*, or complainant—sat on one side with several middle-aged
men, including his father and uncle; the young woman—the *mudda'a-'alaih*,
or respondent—sat on the other with an older man and woman, her parents.

As the deliberations began I learned that the husband had asked the wife to come to the dar ul-qaza because she had left the marital home following a fight and he wanted her to return—this was, in formal terms, a suit for *rukhsati*. The parties agreed on the basic account of the argument: the husband had given some of the wife's henna (*mehndi*) to his sisters without her permission, and she was enraged. The couple had argued about this, and the husband slapped the wife. The husband and his father told the qazi that he recognized that physical violence is unacceptable, and that he would not hit his wife again. The wife's father argued back that this kind of abuse would not be tolerated and that he required further proof that his daughter was safe in her marital home. As the wife's husband and father spoke, she remained silent.

When after significant prodding the wife would not speak, the qazi sent her father and father-in-law out of the hearing room, leaving only the couple, the qazi, myself, and one other observer. The qazi again asked her to tell her side of the story. She refused, and he continued to push her, saying that it was insufficient to rely on what she had written in her statement. In a voice thick with frustration, she told the qazi that she did not see why she should have to repeat what she had already written for him. As she began to cry, the qazi turned to me and the PhD student and asked us to leave the hearing room so that he could speak with the couple alone.

The qazi called everyone back into the room about twenty minutes later, following these private deliberations and announced that the defendant would return to her husband's home. Her father immediately responded that his daughter could not possibly have agreed freely to this, as she was terrified to return, and that he would not allow her to go somewhere that he was convinced was unsafe. The hearing that day ended in a stalemate; the parties were again sent home, and asked to return in several weeks. Over the next several months, Qazi Kamal sent notices to both parties asking them to return to the dar ul-qaza to continue deliberating about the conflict and to find a resolution. Eventually, after several months of dar ul-qaza dates in which one of the parties was absent, the wife returned to her marital home.

While in certain respects this case is anomalous—in particular because it ended in reconciliation rather than divorce but also because the husband had initiated the proceedings—in many ways it is representative of the content, form, and procedures of hearings in Delhi's dar ul-qazas. Specifically, the case is a marital dispute involving allegations of violence and struggles over property adjudicated according to Islamic law in which the qazi was trained in seminary.

Dar ul-qazas, usually translated into English as "shari'a courts," or into Hindi as "shari'a adalats" or "shari'a panchayats," are indeed courts in the sense that they are adversarial dispute adjudication forums concerned with fact-finding and with supplying verdicts. Cases in dar ul-qazas are heard by a qazi—judge—trained in Islamic jurisprudential traditions and practices. In Delhi, each dar ul-qaza has a single qazi who hears all of the cases in his dar ul-qaza. Describing them as "shari'a" court is not wholly accurate, as shari'a constitutes the totality of guidance as to how a Muslim should live: in other words, shari'a includes abiding by Islamic legal precepts but is not limited to that. It is instead fiqh—the traditions of legal interpretation, the work whereby shari'a is interpreted to arrive at legal guidelines—in which the judge in the dar ul-qaza is trained and that guides his work of adjudication.

This chapter and the next offer analyses of disputes heard in Delhi's dar ul-qazas. In this chapter, I argue that these proceedings rest on and help to consolidate the view that divorce specifically, and marital and kin relations more broadly, are part of a private sphere that overlaps with the religious domain but that is separate from the public sphere of politics and market exchange. I show that disputants in dar ul-qaza cases articulate the financial relations entailed in marriage and divorce as elements of an economy of care, and thereby as consequences of the moral responsibilities kin have to one another. This economy of care is rhetorically separated, sometimes implicitly but sometimes quite explicitly, from the world of remunerated labor and of buying and selling. So although the economics of divorce are recognized, they are recognized as different in character from market economies and isolated from them. The idea that the family's economy is isolated from a broader economy sits somewhat uncomfortably alongside the view espoused by many, Muslims and non-Muslims both, that Muslim marriage is contractual and that divorce is, therefore, a matter of religio-legal rather than moral right, and one that entails certain financial exchanges and settlements. Such a view would seem to make visible how the family is an institution of distribution closely related to waged labor and market exchange and how marriage's home economics extend beyond the home.

To argue that the dar ul-qaza proceedings help to render the family private, the chapter draws out a characteristic feature of dar ul qaza divorce cases evident in the dispute over mehndi described above: property disputes and allegations of violence accompanied by pervasive rhetorics of perseverance, responsibility, and care in marriage. While property disputes and allegations of violence are often central reasons for bringing marital disputes before an outsider for adjudication, complainants articulate divorce claims using a rhetoric of perseverance (claims to have stayed in a relationship despite hardships), responsibility, and care. In making this observation, I do not suggest that complainants are being deceptive. I mean instead to highlight that here, as in other court contexts, there are certain rhetorical tropes that "work." Attending to how violence is rendered legally salient is critical to understanding the way legal speech acts in this court setting. The rhetoric of perseverance morally grounds the legal claim, making it more likely to succeed.

Delhi's Dar ul-Qazas

The mehndi case provides insight into the dar ul-qaza as an institution and into the qazi's approach to adjudicating disputes between kin. This section focuses on the mehndi case to show how the qazi's expertise as a mediator reflects the Islamic legal tradition in which he practices and shapes the character of this legal forum. I conducted my research in two dar ul-qazas located in two predominantly Muslim neighborhoods in Delhi: Jamia Nagar and Kashmiri Gate.[1] The first neighborhood, Jamia Nagar, was founded in the late nineteenth-century by Muslim community leaders as a place for Muslims to live and flourish. Today, Jamia Nagar houses the offices of the AIMPLB and is easily accessible to disputants and other interested parties. The second dar ul-qaza I studied is located at Kashmiri Gate, in the part of Delhi built by the Mughal ruler Shah Jahan. This dar ul-qaza is housed in a small madrasah, whose few students rarely entered the legal offices. The madrasah itself is primarily used for its busy dar ul-ifta (the office in which clerics write authoritative legal opinions called fatwas), but until its qazi became ill in the early 2000s, the dar ul-qaza was also popular. By the time I was conducting my research the qazi had stopped hearing cases altogether, leaving me to work solely with case files. The neighborhoods of Jamia Nagar and Kashmiri Gate are both mixed in terms of socioeconomic class. In 2015, I augmented this Delhi-based research with fieldwork at the Imarat-i Shari'a in Patna, Bihar. This is a Muslim institution that trains large numbers of qazis in addition to hearing a high volume of cases. The AIMPLB qazi trained at the Imarat-i Shari'a, and his adjudication style reflects its approach. While this chapter and the next draw primarily on the Delhi research, I do offer select comparisons with the Imarat-i Shari'a where I find them illuminating.

The kinds of cases that appeared in the two Delhi dar ul-qazas, as well as the protocols that are followed in adjudicating them are strikingly similar. Most were divorce disputes, along with a smattering of inheritance and custody cases. A case in the dar ul-qaza is initiated by a complainant, who comes to the qazi to file a complaint, as in the book's opening anecdote. Once the qazi has received an approved "Darkhwast Dene Ka Form," he mails summons notices to the concerned parties, indicating that there is a case in the dar ul-qaza involving the addressee and giving the date and time the parties should come to the dar ul-qaza. As the case develops, the qazi also sends notices by mail to witnesses, whose testimony is the major source of evidence gathered. The case file that the qazi compiles includes the complaint, usually a counter-complaint written by or on behalf of the respondent, copies of all notices sent, any notices printed in local newspapers, transcribed witness testimonies, accounts of what was discussed and decided at each hearing, additional documents such as marriage or divorce contracts, and, finally the *faisalahs* (decision or judgment). Usually, cases require several meetings— sometimes even ten or fifteen—before the qazi issues his faisalah, although occasionally only one meeting is necessary. According to Qazi Kamal's records, between 2006 and 2010, 70 percent of cases were decided in 6 months or less (*AIMPLB Report*, 31).

Dar ul-qazas judgments are not binding from the perspective of the state, which means its decisions cannot be formally appealed. Because they are not binding, if one party or the other is unsatisfied with the dar ul-qaza procedures, they can decide to approach the state courts. However, the qazi asks parties to state that they wish to have their dispute heard in the dar ul-qaza and that they freely agree to abide by the qazi's decision. The qazi does not have the ability to enforce his decisions; he also does not have the personnel to follow up, as the mahila panchayat members do, to see whether his decision is being followed. My analysis of the dar ul-qazas relies primarily on archival research that I carried out in the Kashmiri Gate dar ul-qaza alongside several observations of cases at the AIMPLB dar ul-qaza and a handful of records from that archive. While I focus on several emblematic cases in detail, an overview of the types of questions facing these dar ul-qazas helps to situate these specific case studies.

Overall, I studied the records of thirty-three cases, the outlines of which I detail below. Eighteen were initiated by wives, twelve by husbands, and two by mutual agreement. One case was brought by the children of a deceased man with a question of inheritance. It is notable that in all but one of the cases initiated by the husband, the immediate reason given for approaching the dar ul-qaza was the wife's departure from her marital home. Men brought cases either in an attempt to bring their wives back (rukhsati) or to verify that they had successfully divorced their wives unilaterally (through *talaq ul-ba'in*, or "triple talaq"). Women more typically brought cases with the intent of being granted divorces. This reflects the legal reality wherein men can secure divorce by talaq—by giving a divorce extrajudicially—whereas women can initiate divorce only judicially, in the dar ul-qaza or the state court. Table 1 outlines the different kinds of divorce available to Indian Muslims. Women are able to seek one of two kinds of divorce in the dar ul-qaza: *faskh nikah* or *khul'*. *Faskh nikah* is "the dissolution or rescission of the contract of marriage by judicial decree" (Fyzee 1974, 168).[2] It is sometimes called judicial separation. Khul' requires the husband to agree to give a talaq in exchange for the wife giving up her mahr—property pledged to her at the time of marriage—and/or other property. Therefore, while both khul' and faskh can be initiated by women, they theoretically effect different property regimes.

In cases of khul' heard in the dar ul-qaza, women often began their claim by stating that they were willing to forfeit some amount of property in exchange for divorce. In one case, marital strife led the wife to leave her husband, and when the qazi's attempts at reconciling them failed, the wife agreed to forgive her mahr if her husband granted her a divorce. Both parties also agreed not to take one another to court in the future. As we will see in the last case analyzed in this chapter, the dramatic relinquishing of significant property claims is a key feature of this form of divorce. In spite of their formal differences, it is notable in comparing cases of faskh and of khul' that their outcomes overlap significantly in terms of the division of property. It seems, then, that in practice the major difference between the two kinds of divorce is that faskh is possible in the absence of the husband (ex parte), while khul' is not.

Of the marital disputes I studied, eight were requests for faskh, seven were requests for khul', and nine were either requests for talaq ul-ba'in or requests that the qazi validate a talaq ul-ba'in that had already been pronounced (see table 2). The four remaining divorce cases were more nebulous—the

Table 1. Types of Muslim divorce and reunion

Type of Claim	Definition	Initiated by	Relevant institution	Entailments
Faskh	Dissolution of marriage	Wife	Dar ul-qaza: by judicial decree	Wife not required to return mahr; entitled to keep any wedding gifts or other gifts acquired during marriage.
Khul'	Divorce	Wife	Dar ul-qaza: qazi issues a document called a khul'-namah	Wife expected to compensate husband for divorce by returning/ forgiving mahr, return wedding gifts and gifts acquired during marriage, not requesting mainte- nance. Reconciliation is possible within the 'iddat period.
Talaq	Divorce	Husband	Extrajudicial: husband declares that he divorces the wife, either thrice in one conversation, or one time per month over three months	Wife entitled to 'iddat maintenance, mahr, wedding gifts, or other gifts acquired during marriage.
			Can be validated by qazi or mufti	If talaq given thrice at once, no reconciliation possible; if given once a month, reconciliation possible until third declaration of divorce given (provided couple have not had sex during those three months).
Rukhsati	Return of wife/ restitution of conjugal rights	Husband	Dar ul-qaza	Wife expected to return to marital home; sometimes results in khul' if qazi deems reconciliation impossible.

Table 2. Divorce cases in Delhi's dar ul-qazas

Type of case	Granted	Denied	Undecided/ Withdrawn	Total
Faskh	3	1	4	8
Khul'	4	0	3	7
Talaq ul-ba'in	4 validations 2 carried out at dar ul-qaza	n/a	3	9
Rukhsati	1	0	3	4
Inheritance	1	0	0	1
Advice/Unclear complaint	n/a	n/a	4	4

complaint was in each case a request for advice about how to proceed in a difficult marital situation. Two were questions brought by husbands whose wives had moved out, and two were brought by wives who wanted to know how to end their marriages. These cases were investigated but never reached any judgment, a common occurance in the Delhi dar ul-qazas (though much less usual at the Imarat-i Shari'a). Of these thirty-two divorce cases,[3] seventeen were either unresolved or their resolutions were unclear from the records.

In 2013 Qazi Kamal, of the AIMPLB dar ul-qaza, gave me a report he had published in 2011, *Dar ul-qaza Janubi Delhi: Ek Ja'iz Riport*, in which he discusses the procedures and overall objectives of the dar ul-qaza, gives examples of different types of cases, and concludes with tables outlining the number of cases heard between 1994 and 2011 (hijrah 1414 and 1432), as well as their duration, and statistics about outcomes. I summarize his findings here because they help to contextualize the cases I analyze. This report states that during this time period, the dar ul-qaza heard 372 cases, 301 initiated by women and 74 initiated by men. There is a minor discrepancy in the qazi's table—he has enumerated 362 decisions in this table and 375 in the previous. I think the table nonetheless offers a useful overview of trends in the dar ul-qaza. Of these cases, 34 resulted in reconciliation by the parties, 85 in withdrawal, and 249 in decisions (faisla); only 7 were undecided. There is a different table that indicates that 351 cases were resolved by means of hall ba-zar'ah in the dar ul-qaza and 17 in counseling sessions. Between 2006 and 2010, the qazi tracked the time it took for cases to receive faisle (decisions) and reports that all but 6 cases (out of 121) were resolved within a year (with most decided in six to nine months). The report offers a table of filed cases by type from 1994 to 2011, which I have. See table 3.

In spite of the discrepancy in the qazi's reported numbers, the table gives a helpful picture of the overall distribution of cases. The qazi's records show that a large portion of the claims concerned maintenance, which differs from what I found in my sample of cases. While some of the cases I have studied include maintenance issues, none were initiated as maintenance cases. In the cases I studied, the outcome of complaints involving missing spouses, cruelty, and maintenance culminated in divorces by faskh, which is how I have categorized them. However, among those cases I have categorized as "advice/unclear complaint," complaints often mentioned missing spouses (both husbands and wives), and one stated that the wife, who was the complainant, did not wish to return to her husband because of his violence.

Delhi has a third dar ul-qaza, located in Jaffrabad, just across the road from the mahila panchayat discussed in the previous chapter. Although I was unable to conduct extensive fieldwork there, on one of the last days I spent

Table 3. Marriage and divorce cases in *Ek Ja'iz Riport* from 1994 to 2011

Type of case	Number
Missing spouse (mafqud ul-khabar zauj)	36
Maintenance ('adam infaq)	121
Battery (zad o kob)	45
Impotence	6
Mutual discord (original translation) shiqaq	27
Khul'	42
Verification of talaq (taqiq-i talaq)	10
Verification of nikah (marriage)	3
Custody/Guardianship (hizanat)	2
Inheritance	1
Claim/title (haqqiyat)	6
Demand to live together well (mutalabah-i husn-i mu'asharah)	11
Rukhsati	43
Miscellaneous	9

in Delhi prior to completing this research, the qazi at the Jaffrabad dar ul-qaza called me in and handed me a pile of eight photocopied complaints (darkhwasts). These complaints stand alone, removed from the greater context that a full file provides and also cut off from their outcomes. Yet they give one more glimpse into the kinds of issues that spur people to approach dar ul-qazas in Delhi. All eight were requests for divorce. In three out of these eight darkhwasts, the wife requested a divorce primarily on the grounds of having been treated cruelly or having been subjected to unreasonable demands from her in-laws relating to dowry. In each of these cases, the wife explicitly stated that she wished to receive a divorce so that she could marry again. In four of the remaining five cases, the wife claimed severe physical cruelty, often also linked to dowry demands, and requested that the qazi either help her to secure a khul' or grant her a faskh. In these cases, each petitioner stated that she had resorted to going to the dar ul-qaza because her husband refused to divorce her, and instead intended to keep her in a state of limbo, neither married nor divorced.

What this overview of cases and decisions in Delhi's three dar ul-qazas cannot show is how, with great regularity, the shift of a dispute to a formal hearing that ended ultimately in divorce—whether in the dar ul-qaza or in the state court—involved a rhetorical shift that hinged not on property demands but rather on questions of proper kin relations. In what follows, I analyze several cases of divorce by faskh, and argue that they together demonstrate that in the dar ul-qaza successful divorce claims were predicated on a marriage's failure to replace relations of exchange and distribution with relations of care and shelter. These cases also imply a conception of divorce that keeps both parts of kinship in the picture: affect and exchange.

Guiding a Case

Adjudication in the dar ul-qaza entails strict adherence to procedures as well as navigating norms of family life and kin relations. In all of the dar ul-qaza cases I studied, the qazi was the guide and driver of this process. A single qazi runs each dar ul-qaza, mediating disputes, keeping records, compiling case files, and issuing notices when people have to appear in court. Each qazi has an assistant whom he tasks with retrieving books, ushering disputants in and out of the hearing room, and bringing *chai* to anyone assembled in the room at teatime. This allocation of labor differs from that described by Brinkley Messick (1993) in Yemen and by Lawrence Rosen (2000) in Morocco. Both Messick and Rosen found that the qazi's assistant was responsible for keeping records in addition to performing menial tasks. In the qazi courts in Kenya that Susan Hirsch (1998) studied, the qazi was assisted by a clerk who talked to disputants to screen the cases the qazi heard. Even in the Imarat-i Shari'a in Bihar, where Qazi Kamal was trained, the two peons and the several clerks with whom disputants initiate cases are indispensable to the workings of the court, enabling the qazi to focus solely on hearing cases. At the Imarat-i Shari'a, qazis in training often serve as scribes. The clerks in these studies of dar ul-qazas closely resemble the local court clerks that Barbara Yngvesson (1988) has studied in the United States. The absence of such a figure in the Delhi dar ul-qaza means that all aspects of the adjudication, including the initial meeting with the qazi, are administered by the qazi himself. Approaching the qazi in Delhi's dar ul-qazas requires as little (or as much) as arriving at the dar ul-qaza office while he is present. Unless they have meetings to attend elsewhere, the qazis in these dar ul-qazas are available in their offices from eight or nine in the morning until early afternoon. It is therefore relatively uncomplicated to get an initial audience with the qazi to explain a case or to request his help. This is apparent in the book's opening anecdote, in which a poor, illiterate woman directly approached Qazi Kamal—the qazi himself *is* the dar ul-qaza's bureaucracy as it is he who writes all aspects of the case up, who sends notices, hears disputes, and issues and offers copies of decisions.

Although the dar ul-qazas are accessible and far less bureaucratic than the state courts, they are not universally available to Muslims experiencing family trouble. Another aspect of the case with which the book began—in which a woman was required to deliver the complaint form in Urdu—highlights the importance of writing and documentation to the proceedings of the dar ul-qaza, a requirement that can be daunting and that favors the educated. It also shows that for the poor and illiterate, dar ul-qazas can be intimidating. The requirement that the records be submitted in writing is therefore not only a defining feature of the form the cases take, but also a condition for entry into the dar ul-qaza more generally. Notably, this condition of entry is the inverse of those found in the state courts, where there is ample help with translation and procedures—albeit at a financial cost—and where talking to the judge outside the context of a formal hearing is nearly impossible.[4]

Delhi's dar ul-qazas appear to be somewhat unusual in terms of their class dynamics. The 300 rupees (USD 4.36) fee for filing a case would seem to encourage poorer parties, but the lack of assistance with writing and filing elements of the case, primarily the complaint as well as letters to the qazi explaining aspects of the claims being made or rebutted, may intimidate poor or illiterate parties. At the Imarat-i Shari'a, not only do peons assist parties as they navigate the office, but there are also young qazis-in-training, called *maulanas*, who are available to write out complaints (darkhwasts). Thus, Sabiha Hussain (2007, 19) writes that the women who brought their cases to the Imarat-i Shari'a were of "lower economic class," although she adds that their fathers "either had petty businesses or were in government service." The woman whom I describe at the beginning of the book appeared to be quite destitute, and while I do not know how her family earns a living, it seems likely that they were of a still lower economic status than the women whose cases Hussain discusses. Most of the disputants whose cases went through Delhi's dar ul-qaza were from families that worked in small business or at universities, or who were overseas.

The fact that the qazi is so accessible to parties is one indication of the dar ul-qaza's remove from the state courts; the qazis' training and approach to judging are another. The qazi at the AIMPLB dar ul-qaza, for example, was in early middle age and was assigned to this particular post because of his dedication to working as a cleric. The qazi began his religious training in the Uttar Pradesh town of Muzaffarnagar, where he attended a seminary for eight years, after which he spent five years at the prestigious seminary Dar ul Uloom Deoband.[5] Finally, after teaching at a madrasah for one year, he was sent to train as a qazi at the Imarat-i Shari'a, widely recognized to be one of the most important centers of Islamic legal practice in northern India, and an institution rooted in the Hanafi legal tradition. As is evident from this brief biography, the qazi traveled to Delhi by way of some of the most influential seminaries in Muslim India and took up his post as a qualified Islamic jurist, not as a lawyer specializing in Muslim personal law, in which he had no formal training. The qazi was selected by other members of the clerical establishment, and the legal norms, rules, and methods of adjudication to which he refers to are shared by others trained in the Hanafi legal tradition. His approach reflects his Imarat-i Shari'a training.

The choreography of the mehndi case reflects the qazi's approach to adjudication more generally. He bases his judgments on "practical information (*hijaj*)" placed within a "framework of doctrine as its point of reference" (Messick 1993, 146). This means that he, like other qazis, need to attend to disputants' accounts of their problems. Qazi Kamal told me that it was important to the process of hearing cases in the dar ul-qaza that the environment be peaceful and quiet. He also needed to be able to configure the proceedings, in part by deciding when different parties to the dispute should or should not share the hearing room. The choreography helped him get a sense of what everyone in the room was thinking, which sometimes required speaking to parties individually. It could be difficult to tell, in these marital disputes, whether the primary problem was between the couple or whether the parents were provoking trouble. The qazi therefore told me that he works to create a space within which vulnerable parties can articulate their grievances, much as was the case with the qazis in coastal Kenya whom Susan Hirsch studied (1998).

In a later conversation, the qazi indicated that such procedural safeguards are necessary but not sufficient to arrive at a correct judgment. After all, he told me, "the one who sits in the qazi's seat is human" (*qazi ki jagah par baithne wala adami hai*). The qazi has the responsibility to recite (*sunana*) God's law (*hukm*) but not to make it. To this end, his responsibility is to gather relevant information in order to interpret and apply God's law. Proper procedure—fairly gathering information and correctly implementing, or reciting, God's hukm—requires not only that the qazi run an appropriately choreographed hearing, but also that he cultivate a certain kind of character and comportment. He must not be greedy (*koi dunyavi lalach na ho*) and should not be biased toward friends, relatives, and acquaintances or against enemies.[6] In adjudicating the mehndi case, the qazi both shifted parties into and out of the room and also stood back to let disputants speak— tactics designed to facilitate information gathering and dispute settlement. These descriptions of the qazi's role hew closely to the requirements for a qazi outlined in the *adab ul-qazi* literature—literature on the habits and comportment of the qazi. A. A. A. Fyzee argues that the adab ul-qazi literature is similar to the "British etiquette of Bar and Profession" (1974, 406). Literature on adab includes notes on procedure, process, and judicial administration, Fyzee shows, but the qazi's etiquette and professional comportment also contribute to the dar ul-qaza's atmosphere and to the qualities of the hearing itself. This principled attention to speech conditions may be one reason why women find the dar ul-qaza approachable.

In the mehndi case, the qazi demonstrated his adab and his knowledge of kinship norms and its lived realities, all of which relate to one another. When the qazi sent both the fathers and us, the researchers, out of the room during the negotiation, it appeared to be his way of simultaneously acknowledging the power of the couple's family to create or perpetuate disputes and communicating to the couple that their relationship was separate from these forces. The other researcher observing that day commented that "in Indian families the in-laws can cause a lot of problems. Sometimes what seems to be a disagreement between the newly married couple is actually the result of the mother-in-law's complaints or of a dispute between the couple's parents." The comment struck me as a truism—one that I heard repeatedly during my fieldwork—and yet also as a cultural construction important to the choreography I had just observed. Other scholarship suggests that this is a pervasive dynamic, and that not only are divorces the culmination of long, drawn-out conflicts rather than the result of a single argument, but that they also very often involve families of the couple (Rafat 2003, 83). Zakiya Rafat and others have established that far more relevant to the outcome of marital disagreement than the disagreement itself, or even than the couple, is the family's reaction to that disagreement and the resources available to the couple and their families to deal with it (Rafat 2003; Bano 2003; Rasheed 2003). Given that permanent separation or divorce never came up during the mehndi case, what the case highlights are the negotiations, which usually remain within the sphere of the family, entailed in marriage.

The qazi's role in a dispute such as the mehndi case is to guide the case to its conclusion by responding to and participating in the labors of doing and undoing kinship. He persuaded the couple and their families to pursue their marriage. These labors are apparent in several other cases as well. For example, in a case at the Kashmiri Gate dar ul-qaza, a disputing couple were instructed, first by the AIMPLB and then by the Kashmiri Gate dar ul-qaza, to try to reconcile. They were, in other words, instructed to continue the labors of kinship, advice the qazi gave when he thought both parties still wished to be together. An unresolved case that I will discuss at greater length later was likewise punctuated by the qazi's requests that the couple find a way to reconcile, even in the context of a heated dispute over dowry (jahez) and land.

However, the defendant's tears in the case sketched above indicate the duress under which disputants present or fail to present their conflicts, even as the qazi attempts to guide them to an amicable solution. While the qazi insisted that talking was the only way through the conflict, the wife's persistent refusal to repeat what she had written suggested that for her this was a needless demand to redouble her pain. Indeed, the outcome of the case appeared to validate the wife's suggestion that in performing her injury for the proceedings it would be transformed into a phase of a process of reconciliation that privileged the defendant's return to her husband's home as the desired outcome. To turn the case for rukhsati into a divorce, she would have needed a different rhetorical strategy, one more insistent on her misery and her unwillingness to remain in her marital home, and consequently different grounds.

Violence and Property in Dar ul-Qaza Divorce Claims

The two precipitating elements of the mehndi case—violence and a property dispute—are emblematic of divorce cases in the dar ul-qazas. In the lead-up to this case's hearing, the complainant had first taken the defendant's henna—perhaps a small possession, but hers nonetheless—and then had hit her. The discussions I observed never made completely clear what this "slap" referred to—whether it represented a single incident or indicated ongoing or severe violence. Scholars have documented women's reticence to admit that their marriages are unhappy or abusive (Hirsch 1998; Jeffery 1979; Oldenburg 2002), while my conversations with litigants corroborates the view that people do not take the decision to approach a legal forum lightly. It therefore seems unlikely that the defendant in the mehndi case would have brought her own family into the disagreement after one incident. It seems just as unlikely that a father would mount such strong resistance to his daughter's return to her marital home if he did not think her situation there was precarious. The qazi, however, did not spend much of the hearing investigating the allegation of violence. He instead focused on assessing the litigants' willingness to reconcile.

The presence of spousal and other forms of domestic violence characterizes marital disputes in every institution I analyze in this book, either as an obstacle to be overcome in the pursuit of reconciliation or as grounds for divorce. In this case, and in disputes adjudicated in the mahila panchayat, domestic violence is approached pedagogically, whereas in the dar ul-qaza cases

I examine below, it constitutes one among other facets of a successful divorce claim. In the mehndi case, the husband and his father clearly articulated remorse for the violence, and the husband stated that he would not hit his wife again, which the qazi took seriously as a reason to work toward reconciling the couple. In the cases that follow, while women acknowledged that they had endured domestic violence, they did not present it as their sole grounds for divorce. Qazis, mahila panchayat leaders, and judges all agree that marriage ought to be preserved if possible, and that a pedagogical approach to domestic violence is an important avenue to reconciliation. The qazi was, however, ready to grant divorces when litigants presented clear and tight cases.

The Neglectful Emigré

In the cases at the dar ul-qaza that I was privy to, allegations of violence always included physical violence and sometimes also entailed other forms of cruelty (*zulm*), such as abusive language, disrespect, and verbal threats. The types of property described in dowry lists[7] and testimonies included mahr, immovable property, monetary gifts or demands, and maintenance. Physical abandonment and financial neglect were frequent precipitating conditions of divorce cases—markers that marital problems had become unresolvable. In this section, I examine the trajectories of property and allegations of violence in dar ul-qaza divorce cases, where both property and violence are usually absent from the final judgment (hukm). While disputants reiterate allegations of theft and violence throughout the cases, they also avoid hinging their cases on these allegations alone, instead emphasizing in virtuosic presentations the ways in which a spouse has failed to live up to his or her marital responsibilities.

I spent months sitting on the floor of the Kashmiri Gate dar ul-qaza reading through case files, drinking tea, and chatting with three muftis as they wrote fatwas. The unwieldy case files—containing documentation from an array of sources, mainly handwritten in Urdu but also sometimes in typewritten English or Hindi—carried me through the simultaneously dry and dramatic genre of divorce proceedings in the dar ul-qaza. Case number 15, which I discuss at length here, hinged on a wife's request for faskh nikah on the grounds that her husband had abandoned her physically and financially. The complainant (mudda'i) had been married for seven years. The first document in the record was a typed request for a fatwa, dated two days before the case opened. The request was addressed to a mufti who worked in the fatwa department of the same madrasah that housed the dar ul-qaza. The fatwa request laid out the complainant's situation: She married her husband in 1995; she did not move in with him (perform rukhsati) until a year later when he returned briefly from the United States, where he worked; she became pregnant at this time, and after he had returned to the United States she gave birth to a daughter. Her husband, known as N in the case records, left her with a USD 25,000 allowance, but when she moved in with her in-laws, as he had instructed, they demanded the money and treated her cruelly, beating her. When she refused to give them the money, they sent her back to her natal kin. The husband and his family kept her dowry, worth 18 lakh[8] rupees (USD 26,000).

Once the complainant moved out of her in-laws' house in 1996, she did not have any contact with her husband. However, in 2000 her brother-in-law informed her that her husband had been in Delhi for a week, during which time he had supplied his parents with U.S. visas and brought them to live with him. The husband had neither brought the visas he had promised for his wife and daughter nor contacted them. When her brother-in-law informed her of this, he also told her that his brother had broken off their relationship (*sare rishte tut ga'e hain*) and that she was not to contact him. Having no contact information for him at the time she requested the fatwa, she was unable to procure his input on the situation. The fatwa request concluded: "All of this suggests that my husband does not want to maintain our relationship. In addition, he has not paid for my expenses for six years. Nor do we have a sexual relationship [*izdawaji ta'alluq*]. I have tried with all my might [*be-hadd*] to keep this relationship going, but they [the husband and his family] are in no way ready to maintain a relationship. Please, in view of this situation, issue a fatwa granting me a faskh nikah to save me and my child from having our lives destroyed. I will be forever grateful for this." While the file includes this request for a fatwa, it does not include a fatwa itself. This is likely because the mufti transferred the request to the dar ul-qaza in the form of a claim petition; a faskh cannot be granted by a mufti but must be granted by a qazi following the correct hearing procedures.

The request and corroborating documents established the terms on which the complainant made her claim. These included three interwoven allegations: property misuse, violence, and betrayed kinship norms. The large dowry, enumerated in detail in the case file, was the first element of property to enter the case. The dowry list included two Qurans; Quran covers; prayer mats; twenty-five bedsheets and pillowcases; thirty-five shalwar suits; eleven *lahngas* (a long, embroidered skirt); seventeen nightgowns for women; and thirteen men's suits. Included also are tea and dinner sets; a makeup box; a sewing box; steel and gold decorations for the house; designer jewelry composed of thirteen *tolas* of gold;[9] garnets; beads; *tika*; a nose ring; fourteen sets of "artificial" jewelry; and silver plates and bowls. Finally, there were two bank accounts; in one there was 1 lakh, 12,000 rupees; and in a second fixed deposit account, 25,000 rupees scheduled for release over five years and 50,000 rupees slated for the period thereafter. This was the considerable dowry to which the complainant referred in the opening fatwa. It served as evidence of the good faith with which the complainant and her family entered the marriage, and simultaneously of the bad faith of her in-laws, who refused to return this property once the complainant's brother-in-law announced that *sare rishte tut ga'e hain* (relations between the spouses had broken off).

Woven throughout the request was evidence that the complainant suffered from violence in her marriage, including being beaten and treated cruelly in her marital home. On several occasions the case file alleged that her brother-in-law beat her. She told the dar ul-qaza that she was finally thrown out of her marital home, suggesting that in spite of the cruelty that defined her life there, she persevered. In other words, the document made the argument that she and her family had met the affective and material terms of the marriage, whereas her husband and in-laws had failed to do so.

Betrayal of kinship expectations was likewise woven through the case. In addition to dowry demands, first of USD 25,000 and then 1 lakh rupees, there were false promises. The most dramatic of these involved false accounts of the husband's professional status and his failure to deliver on his promise to help his wife emigrate. The complainant and her family had been under the impression that the defendant ran a successful business in the United States. Furthermore, at the time of the marriage, the families had agreed that while the husband would return to the United States, he would immediately apply for his wife's visa and arrange for her to join him there. The petition corroborated the fatwa's claim that the husband did indeed return to the United States, taking the marriage contract (nikah-namah) with him, but that he never provided a visa for his wife.

Following a painstaking process of gathering witness accounts, placing advertisements in the newspaper, and issuing notice after notice for the defendant to appear in the dar ul-qaza, the qazi ultimately granted the faskh. The case file included written testimonies from five witnesses who supported some or all of the complainant's claims. The five points that the qazi established were the date of the complainant's marriage, the date she moved in with her husband, the existence of her child, the husband's false promise of a visa, and the husband's neglect. The qazi's ruling (hukm) stated:

> I have terminated the marriage (*faskh de diya*) of the complainant B, daughter of C to the defendant, N, son of the late M, because of the pain he has caused his wife and his neglect of his responsibilities. Now, the complainant is no longer the wife of the defendant. She is now authorized to perform 'iddat. After this, she can remarry.
>   Signed, Qazi Shari'a

With this ruling, the qazi thereby suggested that pain and neglect of mutual responsibilities were the primary reasons for which he granted the faskh. In this way, he took up the complainant's own language: prior to making her final request for a faskh, she had reiterated the ways she and her family persevered in the face of her husband's abandonment. She argued that in spite of years of neglect, they had continued to hope and to strive for reconciliation. She clarified that her husband's abandonment was the central issue in her case and articulated its severity: he had not sent money, he had not called or written, the couple had not had a sexual relationship in six years, and all of her and her family's attempts to renew ties to the marital family had failed. While the qazi's decision mirrored the complainant's own reasoning, it is nevertheless telling in its own right, both for what it said and for its silences. It implied that the husband had responsibilities to financially support his wife and that he was enjoined from causing her pain. Her emotional, physical, and financial well-being were all his responsibility. Just as the wife emphasized her perseverance in the face of abandonment, the qazi emphasized the husband's duties to his wife.

This framework, which relied on the gendered terms of persevering wife and responsible husband, is something that many scholars have found in studies of marital disputes in Islamic courts. The tendency and sometimes the codified requirement to make obedience a precondition for receiving maintenance has been called the "obedience-maintenance" paradigm (Tucker 2008). In her research in coastal Kenya, for example, Susan Hirsch (1998) argues that women tend to win cases in qazi courts when they bring claims based on customary and Islamic gender norms, including perseverance in marriage. Erin Stiles (2009) has found that qazis in the Zanzibari courts emphasize spousal obligations in marriage, failures of which are used as grounds for divorce. Numerous historians (e.g., Agmon 2006; Tucker 1998) have made related arguments, suggesting that women have been successful in such institutions because of their ability to appeal to local interpretations of Muslim women's and men's obligations in marriage. In his study of qazi courts in Malaysia, Michael Peletz (2002) likewise found that women's arguments are usually about men's obligations in marriage rather than about their own rights. Peletz adds to this conversation another dimension: qazi courts are spaces in which men are (also) depicted as untrustworthy, as lying, and as delinquent, qualities that are often attributed to women.

Whereas in the above cases the maintenance-obedience paradigm shapes women's legal narratives and reflects social norms, in other contexts it is a matter of codified personal law. In Egypt, until the 2000 khul' law that granted women the right to initiate and attain no-fault divorce with the agreement of their husbands and for a cost, appealing to this paradigm was essential for women seeking divorce (Kholoussy 2010, 67–74; Sonneveld 2012). Regardless of this new law, an obedience ordinance remains in place, with much the same effect as prior to the khul' law (Al-Sharmani 2013). Likewise, until the 1993 reforms, Moroccan family law defined the husband as family head, required to provide maintenance to his wife as long as she was obedient (El Hajjami 2013). In the new code, husband and wife are defined as joint heads of household. These are but two examples among a range of approaches to the maintenance-obedience relation in recent reforms of personal status laws of Muslim majority countries (see Welchmann 2011). Notably, while the discussion of this paradigm is usually limited to accounts of marriage in Muslim contexts and institutions, studies of no-fault divorce in the United States found that this innovation, meant to improve women's status in divorce, in fact undercut their claims (Weitzman 1985). Unexpectedly, the increase in no-fault divorces has had the effect of decreasing women's bids for property—this is, according to Susan Okin, because of something very similar to the "obedience-maintenance" paradigm: "by depriving women of power they often exerted as the 'innocent' and less willing party to the divorce," no-fault divorce laws "have greatly reduced their capacity to achieve an equitable division of the family's tangible assets" (1989, 162). While the dynamics of no-fault divorce that Okin describes do not pertain to *obedience*, they certainly indicate that arguments that hinge on persevering and remaining blameless in the face of marital distress are equally important in North American divorce courts.

In his decision in the case of the woman abandoned by her émigré husband, the qazi anticipated that the complainant would marry again, which further entrenched the gendered terms in which the case was framed. The formulation of the ruling moved from the husband's neglect to the wife's release, to the wife's responsibility to perform 'iddat, to the wife's availability for remarriage. The transformations in the case from its initiation to the ultimate hukm were profound. First, initial allegations of marital violence were displaced by later claims of neglect. The wife and her family's tremendous losses of property were taken up in the course of the case as evidence of neglect and disappeared altogether in the hukm. Rather than discuss violence as significant in and of itself, or the possibility of recuperating property that could be used to support the complainant, the qazi offered to undo the marriage on the grounds that it had failed to provide the care and shelter it ought.

The qazi's decision to comment on the complainant's ability to remarry and his failure to bring up matters of property provide a depiction of divorce as the end of marriage, rather than as a means to solvency, and as a moral rather than a financial matter. The rhetoric of perseverance, of care, and of responsibility upon which complainant, respondent, and qazi insist delineates divorce as primarily a change in kin relationships. Property transfers appear to be part of marriage but are conspicuously marginalized in divorce.

The Absconding Husband

The disappearance of property was a theme in many of the faskh cases I read. The AIMPLB dar ul-qaza heard a case similar to the one described above in which a woman sued for faskh after seven years of marriage. The defendant, the complainant's husband, was a researcher in Unani medicine[10] at a major Muslim university in north India. After marrying, the complainant moved to Delhi to live with her husband and his family. Two years later, the husband left and never returned. The wife and her in-laws did not know where he had gone. The wife continued to live with her in-laws, but complained in her petition that they had not been treating her well; the entire family was distressed about her husband's disappearance. The complainant's opening petition to the dar ul-qaza stated, "If my husband returned, I would happily go back to him, but if he does not, I would like a faskh nikah. I would like to have a peaceful life." This case file resembled the previous petition for faskh nikah on grounds of abandonment: it contained not only the petitions and letters typical of all dar ul-qaza records, but also testimonies of witnesses who attested to the husband's disappearance, and notices published in the local Urdu newspaper, *Nayi Duniya*, to request the husband's presence at the dar ul-qaza.

The newspaper notice, which was written by the wife as a public summons, stated: "Since you left, I have not heard anything from you. Your brother told me you never arrived in Aligarh. We are all in a bad way, your parents, your brother, and I, and we do not know where you have gone." The notice included a telephone number where the family could be reached and a photograph of the missing husband. The notice was followed in the case file by another letter from the wife, restating her situation. This time she added: "I have waited for him at the house, as have his parents. I have put an announcement in the paper. I have no idea where he is, and I do not receive any *kharcha* [allowance] from him or from his family." Her brother-in-law corroborated her claim in his testimony. He wrote that while he knew the couple was married six years earlier, he could not recall the exact date. He also confirmed that no one had heard from the husband since his disappearance, and that he had not sent any money to his wife as maintenance. No one, he wrote, knew whether his brother was alive or dead, and he affirmed that his sister-in-law needed some kind of financial support. The letters further attested that the complainant's parents-in-law supported her decision to be granted a faskh nikah.

As in the previous petition, here the complainant presented herself on numerous occasions as a persevering and dedicated wife. In spite of having been abandoned, she wrote that were her husband to return, she would remain committed to living with him. She also emphasized that she remained in her in-laws' home even though they had treated her poorly. As the case went on and her newspaper announcement remained unanswered, her rhetoric became stronger: she insisted that she and his parents had been waiting for some time, and that she had begun to lose patience. Her claim was thus predicated on testaments to her patience and her dedication to her husband.

The claim was also predicated on financial insecurity. As in the previous case, the complainant wove indications of her financially precarious position throughout her claim. One of her letters stated that she had been without any allowance because in her husband's absence neither her family nor his provided for her. Yet in formulating her ultimate divorce claim, she made no mention either of mahr or of maintenance. Indeed, her brother-in-law's testimony strategically drove a wedge between the husband's responsibility to maintain his wife and the responsibilities of her husband's family to support her. This was all the more notable given her argument that she had persevered in her in-laws' household—that she had tried to be a good family member, and that she understood that her duties as a wife extended to duties to her affinal kin. Her brother-in-law instead insisted that if the complainant's husband was not available to support her, she should be given a faskh so that she would no longer remain under the in-laws' roof and could find other means of support.

Once the case had run its course and all the relevant documents were assembled, the qazi granted the faskh without mentioning either mahr or maintenance. The subtext was that the issue of financial solvency was distinct from the issue of divorce. Financial neglect was the basis for the claim of abandonment, because it was evident that a husband had shirked his matrimonial duties; but it was not presented as, itself, the grounds for divorce or as an indication that the woman appealing for divorce should be able to live independently. In this way, the qazi's decision reflects a broader, legally instantiated, view that kin relations are separate from economic relations and that women's livelihood rest in the care of the former and not the competition of the latter. The family values on display in this case privilege a view of women as wives to be protected by marriage. Marriage is, at the same time, a relation not only between husband and wife, but with the affinal family. The husband had already practically exited the marriage by the time the case began, and the divorce would therefore more immediately affect the relationship between the wife and her affinal kin than the wife and her husband.

These moralizing views of marriage and divorce resemble those in evidence in Indian state courts, in deliberations involving disputants from a variety of religious communities. Sylvia Vatuk (2001) in particular has studied what she calls the paternalism toward women evident in the Chennai Family Court. This paternalism is evident in judges' assumptions that women are "inherently weak and vulnerable and consequently in need of lifelong material and symbolic support and protection from the men in their lives" (Vatuk 2001, 228). Srimati Basu's (2015) finding that the Kolkata Family Court judges view reconciliation of spouses as their primary aim echoes a similar conception of marriage as a site of protection by male kin. Others have made similar arguments (Mukhopadhyay 1998; Mody 2008). As I show in the next chapter, this view of marriage has roots in colonial Indian jurisprudence and is deeply embedded in contemporary decisions about maintenance.

The Tormenting Husband and Other Unresolved Cases

A final, and unresolved, case from the Kashmiri Gate dar ul-qaza again demonstrates the pattern evinced by the above two cases. In this case, although it was the husband who initially approached the qazi, the last document in the record was a request from the wife for a faskh nikah. The parties agreed only on the barest facts: they were married, the wife no longer lived with her husband in his parents' home, and their marriage was miserable. Beyond this, the allegations were dramatically opposite. While the husband claimed that he married his wife because her father offered him a house, the wife claimed that it was only after the marriage proved difficult that her father offered it to her to live in; prior to the couple's marital problems, the house was not hers. She claimed that if her husband was willing to leave the house in her name, rather than transfer it to his family, she would be happy to continue living with him. Furthermore, while the husband claimed that his wife withheld money from him, she claimed that he repeatedly demanded money from her: first an amount of 10,000 rupees and later an amount of 25,000 rupees, most of which her mother ultimately paid him by selling her own jewelry. In addition, the wife argued that other than a scooter, which she had been able to take back, and her jahez—consisting of about fifteen sets of clothes, four tolas of gold jewelry, and five tolas of silver anklets, in addition to shoes and some other jewelry—remained in her husband's house. Ultimately, the wife alleged that her husband told her he would not divorce her unless she gave him 1 lakh rupees. At the end of this list of allegations, she requested a faskh nikah, stating, "I want you to free me from this cruel man."

Because this case went unresolved, we do not know what happened with the dowry. However, the formulation of the wife's request implied that her husband's monetary demands were strategically motivated to secure a divorce, and that her aim at the dar ul-qaza was simply to divorce without paying him any more money. Her claim does not indicate her intention to push for a financial or property settlement. As in the other cases, her rhetoric in the statement focused on her husband's character: his cruelty, his alcoholism, his greed and rudeness. She also repeatedly stated that if he would treat her as a wife she would return to live with him. Property claims and allegations of violence underpinned her case before the qazi, but appeals to her husband's failure to care for and protect her were the centerpiece of her argument.

What comes through clearly by reading the case of mehndi, the neglectful émigré, the absconding husband, and the tormenting husband is this: Whether or not a woman imagines it as a route to future marriage—some do and some do not—divorce represents the path to a different future, and in that sense a relief. The dar ul-qaza is a last resort aimed at securing a more livable future, even if everyone wishes it did not have to be secured in this way. Some cases that are adjudicated in the dar ul-qazas depict marriages as so unbearable that even a divorce entailing significant financial loss is seen as a desirable outcome. So although one clear effect of the dar ul-qaza, which I discuss below, is to help sequester the family in an ostensibly private sphere, it does at the same time offer a reliable route to divorce, one that is easier and cheaper than in state courts.

Conclusion: The Private Family and the Dar ul-Qaza

The relationship between violence, property disputes, and rhetoric of care in the cases studied in this chapter indicates that one of the effects of the dar ul-qaza process is to evoke the family as private—removed from the public sphere of politics and citizenship—and as a locus of care rather than exchange. In the cases I studied in Delhi, this was evident in the way women won cases by appealing to the maintenance-obedience paradigm, in the process leaving aside or never raising claims to property in the form of dowry, wedding gifts, or even mahr. Marriage, we learn repeatedly, entitles men and women to companionship, to sex, to care. It also entitles women to financial well-being conferred by dependence on a husband rather than by wage labor. *Nafaqah* and *kharcha-pani*—maintenance money and allowance to cover food and expenses—were cited in the cases as materially important but also as symptomatic of care and of a husband's willingness to fulfill his responsibilities. Perseverance in the face of neglect is the perverse underside of this relation. Both the rhetoric of perseverance and that of provision bolster the idea that kinship and the family are private—concerns to be dealt with by appeal to value systems rather than finance or economics. Women reinscribe themselves rhetorically, and with significant legal savvy within a domestic sphere as part of their effort to exit bad marriages.

Feminist theorists have long argued that it has been detrimental to women that the family has been so successfully naturalized as a private institution, a feminized "haven in a heartless world" (Lasch 1995). Socialist feminists argue that this ideology of separation has several insidious effects. The first effect is that it naturalizes unequal gender relations within households in part by accepting that men are the natural heads of households (Harris 1984). This status is not natural, however, but instead is an effect of state recognition: heads of households pay taxes and are counted by the census (Harris 1984). A second effect of the ideology of separation is its assumption that distribution of resources within the household is characterized by generosity, as opposed to the cold logic of economics. In fact, feminists scholars show, distribution within the family is unequitable and follows power dynamics between male heads of households and their wives and children (Whitehead 1984). Meanwhile, women's devalued and unremunerated labor enables capitalist accumulation by reproducing the labor force free of charge (Federici 1975, 2004; Vogel 1995). Overall, this literature suggests that marriage and the assumed privacy of the household, and in particular the assumption that as private the household has its own generous system of distribution, make women vulnerable (Okin 1989). The cases analyzed here were grounded in the broad argument that marriage has not lived up to this ideal and that women are therefore authorized to exit.

It is this last point—that marriage and families are the sites of unequal relations of exchange and distribution—that is particularly salient to my analysis of the dar ul-qazas. Few scholars or observers sustain a belief that divorce is only about affect and untouched by financial concerns, certainly not people in a context where monetary exchanges at the time of marriage—

in the form of mahr and dowry—as well as at the time of divorce are the norm.[11] As these cases bursting with property and financial information suggest, the distinction between moralized family relationships and broader exchange relations is not strictly about finances or economics; rather, it is about the significance attributed to different kinds of property and exchange. Morally upright marriage is marriage that upholds the distinction between appropriate and inappropriate exchange; successful claims for divorce often rest on substantiating that this distinction has been violated.

The historical and ethnographic literature on dowry is particularly illuminating here. Heated nineteenth-century debates over the difference between dowry and bride-price marriages among Hindus reflect anxiety on the part of colonial administrators and reformists alike about the dangerous proximity between the act of giving women (in marriage) and selling women (in prostitution) (Ramberg 2015; Srinivas 1984; Sturman 2012). Dowry marriages, in which the bride was accompanied to her marital home by gifts of movable property and money, represented the ultimate gift. Asura marriages, on the other hand, in which the groom's family gave money or property to the bride's family, represented a sale. Dowry marriage, which was also the Brahmanical form of marriage, achieved a moral quality, while Asura marriage was degraded. In other words, proper marriage was that which clarified the distinction between marriage and prostitution (Ramberg 2015). As Rachel Sturman has argued, part of the process of separating the act of giving a bride in marriage from the act of selling a daughter into slavery or prostitution entailed reconceptualizing marriage as a *moral contract*—the good marriage was good both because it was a marriage based on "mutuality and consent" and because it was a marriage that enabled the contract to transcend its "crass, interested nature" (2012, 168).

In the postcolonial period, as Srimati Basu (2005) has argued, dowry itself has a double character: sometimes it is accepted, and sometimes it is scorned. Basu differentiates between offers of dowry, which most participants in the marriage scene deem acceptable, and demands of dowry, which are considered crass and are disdained. She argues that "it is the demand that is the focus of ire; otherwise women are interested in dowries, especially in items for themselves and the conjugal home, reading it most often as a transfer of resources rather than a marker of hypergamy or gender subordination" (2005, xx). The complaint, then, is about a misuse of the transfer of wealth that dowry is: it should be in the interest both of the bride and of the bride's family, as it will contribute to her ability to live well in her marital home and not to need to return to her natal family for financial help. When it becomes an excuse for excess demands, it is the demands and not the dowry itself that are viewed with disdain.

In the cases studied above, as in Basu's analysis, it is precisely when dowry is excessive, and extends from premarital negotiations into marital relations, that it becomes grounds for divorce—as the crass intrusion of extortion and exchange into the affective sphere of the home. The rhetoric of these cases is exemplary of this, as it shows how allegations of theft, of property misuse, and of violence are transposed into allegations of the husband's failure to act responsibly. The rhetoric indicates a failure to protect, care for, and defend the wife. It also undermines the ostensible separation between exchanges entailed in marriage and those entailed in the market.

The rhetoric and outcomes of disputes in the dar ul-qaza draw attention to the simultaneous importance and dismissal of this political economy of marriage. No marriage, no matter how moralized, is without a property regime, and here we see that the property regime of Muslim marriages disproportionately affects women, who are made vulnerable by it. While divorce threatens to rupture the containment marriage affords, the dar ul-qaza seems to keep this rupture at bay, both to keep divorce in the family and to reiterate it as a matter *of* family. Property, as these cases show, does not disappear. But it is more of a bargaining chip than a bone of contention, much less a source of financial gain. Indeed, the above cases show how even faskh decisions, which technically do not require women to relinquish their mahr and maintenance, can sideline the property disputes that divorce inevitably entails. Women give up claims to property, instead emphasizing their need for separation. The rhetoric of divorce in the dar ul-qaza therefore shores up the idea that family law is exceptional because it sets out to secure specific family values. It does so not as a matter of *mere* rhetoric, but by actually sidestepping property issues in judgments, by actually making divorce in the dar ul-qaza a matter of kinship and not of exchange.

This aspect of the political economy of divorce is perpetuated in part by the legal regime that oversees marital disputes. The Indian legal system is, therefore, exemplary of a particular form of Family Law Exceptionalism (FLE) that binds the family and its exceptionalism to religious authority. As I discussed in chapter 1, FLE describes the historically produced presumption that family law refers to and governs a sphere external to the market, a domain characterized by affect and care rather than by reasoned agonism and exchange. In the context of the U.S. legal system, for example, family law covers matters pertaining to marriage, divorce, and children. It thereby creates the fiction that the family is a set of relations separate from, for example, labor law, tax law, property law, and other matters that clearly pertain to exchange, potential exploitation, and finance. One effect of this nominal difference in legal regulations is that the family is viewed as separate from mechanisms of economic distribution, and legally appears to be untouchable by them: marriage is not broadly thought of as a matter of labor relations and rights or as a relationship shaped by market forces. Instead, those who marry in the United States tend to consider it to be an act of romantic love, a demonstration of the maturity of a particular form of care. This both affects and is affected by family laws that treat marriage, divorce, and custody as neatly separable from public matters.

The process of separating kinship from broader systems of exchange renders fiqh religious and nonlegal. State courts, on the other hand, appear to be the proper site for adjudicating property and financial concerns that exceed the boundaries of the family—they are the place of law. Even as the separation of religion and law appears to be the effect of the Indian legal system, what divorce cases show is that separation is a continuous process. Marital and natal relations are shored up as the primary distributors of economic and emotional well-being, not because a rigid boundary stands between the spheres of law and non-law, secular and religious, but precisely because these supposedly separate spheres are continually being separated. There is, in other words, a dialogical relationship between state and non-state apparatuses of family law adjudication that practically instantiates FLE.

That this is the case is symptomatic of the role of FLE in practices of Indian secularism. It reflects the fact that Indian secularism is carried out in part by forums like the dar ul-qaza that participate in the labor of separating matters of religion from matters of law. For dar ul-qazas introduce a facet to FLE that is not so vividly apparent in Halley and Rittich's (2010) model: religion. Dar ul-qazas are formally distinct from state courts, and their jurisprudence is marked as religious. There is, then, a double move in the privatization of the family in this institution—it is a privatization that also advocates for the idea that the family is best governed by religious norms. The link between FLE and the ostensibly private nature of religion constitutes the foundation for the sexual contract at the heart of Indian secularism: FLE is the primary mechanism by which the family is made and governed. At the same time, FLE is the mechanism through which secular logics of governance are asserted and reproduced.

This is especially clear on closer examination of the relation between the dar ul-qaza and the state courts, to which I turn in the next chapter. Specifically, property claims evaded in the dar ul-qaza appear within the jurisdiction of the courts—that is, as divorce is moralized in the dar ul-qaza, its material aspects emerge as legal claims, and legal claims as relevant to the state courts. Meanwhile, the rules of kinship are reinscribed as falling within the authority of the qazi thus reinforcing the idea that kinship is religious.

Chapter 4

The Converging Jurisprudence of Divorce

In July 2005 a Delhi lawyer filed a suit with the Supreme Court of India seeking to ban "shari'a courts" and Islamic legal opinions in India (*Vishwa Lochan Madan v. Union of India* Petition, 45–47).[1] The suit alleged that so-called shari'a courts (dar ul-qazas) are unconstitutional on the grounds that their decisions are issued by religious authorities and are not overseen by the state's legal apparatus. According to the lawyer who filed the suit, Vishwa Lochan Madan, dar ul-qazas constitute a "parallel legal system" in competition with the state's legal institutions. The *Madan* case concerned what kind of recognition such institutions should be afforded in secular India.

The primary respondent in the suit was the All India Muslim Personal Law Board (AIMPLB), the organization of Muslim clerics that founded and runs several of India's dar ul-qazas. The AIMPLB made three primary arguments in defense of the dar ul-qazas: first, that they are Alternative Dispute Resolution (ADR) forums that complement, rather than compete with, the Indian legal system; second, that they are protected by the Indian

Constitution's religious freedom clause; and third, that they have been a continuous presence in the Indian legal landscape since before independence and should be maintained on grounds of continuity.

Ultimately, the Supreme Court concurred with the AIMPLB that dar ul-qazas are not parallel but alternative to the state courts and should, therefore, continue to practice as before. The ADR forum itself, the Supreme Court agreed, offers a space that is both separate from the state and part of it, stating in its ruling: "According to the Union of India, Dar-ul-Qaza can be perceived as an Alternative Dispute Resolution mechanism, which strives to settle disputes outside the courts expeditiously in an amicable and inexpensive manner and, in fact, have no power or authority to enforce its orders and, hence, it cannot be termed as either in conflict with or parallel to the Indian Judicial System" (*Vishwa Lochan Madan*, paragraph 7). This ruling authorized the dar ul-qaza process while pronouncing it subordinate to the state courts, which, unlike the dar ul-qazas themselves, do have enforcement mechanisms. To the extent that personal law disputes can be settled within the jurisdiction of the qazi and the mufti, the Indian state courts are supportive of such alternatives.

Implicit in the Madan case were three beliefs regarding characteristics of the Indian legal system that my ethnographic research in the dar ul-qazas destabilizes. First, the complainant's premise was that the state courts and dar ul-qazas constituted distinct and competing legal spheres; the AIMPLB agreed that they were distinct, but argued that this made them complementary, rather than competitive. Second, the complainant implied that the distinction between law (state courts) and nonlaw (dar ul-qazas and fatwas) mapped onto a distinction between secular and religious normative orders. Finally, both the complainant and the respondent argued that they and the institutions they supported were centrally concerned with improving the status of women: *Madan* suggested that practitioners of Islamic law infringed upon women's choices, while the AIMPLB insisted that the dar ul-qaza process provided a helpful alternative to the state courts for women involved in family disputes.

My research in Delhi's dar ul-qazas shows, as the Supreme Court has suggested, that they are not part of a parallel legal system. However, I argue here, dar ul-qazas also do not participate in an *alternative* legal system. In the Supreme Court's use, an ADR forum is one that addresses and resolves disputes of no concern to the state and its courts. A parallel legal system, on the other hand, is one that usurps state power by not heeding its ascendency and its legal interventions in matters of concern to it. Dar ul-qazas are neither alternative nor parallel, in this sense. As part of the plural Indian legal system, they intersect with the state's legislative history, and, through individual cases, its adjudication practices in the present. Thus, despite the distinctions between dar ul-qazas and state courts, dar ul-qazas intersect with, rather than run parallel to, the state courts. Together the two legal systems undo the basis for ADR—a neat division between public and private, state and nonstate, secular and religious. Ironically, while the dar ul-qazas appear to be part of a private, alternative, religious legal sphere—which is a key ideological fiction for both the secular state and the dar ul-qazas—their practices reveal this legal sphere to be constructed and porous.

In this chapter, I examine the intersections and points of convergence between dar ul-qazas and state courts, historically and in the present. I begin by asking why the grounds for divorce apparent in faskh cases decided by qazis so closely resemble those laid out in state legislation on Muslim divorce. I show that this intersection reflects the historical interplay between state legislation and clerical opinion, and suggest that this history has helped to produce the dar ul-qaza as a supplement to the state courts: as a site of Muslim personal law adjudication (that is, of the regulation of the family in accordance with state law) as much as a site of fiqh adjudication (that is, the decentralized and uncodified type of legal practice that characterizes nonstate practices of Islamic law). As I will suggest in what follows, this interplay between state legislation and clerical opinion renders moot the question of origins. It is unclear which institution is following which.

The dar ul-qazas illustrate an important facet of legal pluralism: legal pluralism not only provides litigants with alternative forums for legal redress; it sometimes forecloses such alternatives. The intersections between dar ul-qazas and state courts have the effect of consolidating a shared jurisprudence of divorce (faskh and khul') by means of a practical division of labor between the two types of forums. The argument I put forward in this chapter, therefore, is that in spite of the independence and the particularity of the dar ul-qazas, the way they participate in the same legally plural landscape as the state courts makes them key sites of Indian secularism.

Dar ul-qazas participate in the labors of secularism in several ways. First, they accept the secular premise that religious matters, and only religious matters, should be subject to religious authority. They further accept that kinship relations are the only ones (other than the relationship between people and God—relations of worship) that are religious from the perspective of law. In this way they help to uphold a particularly Indian form of Family Law Exceptionalism, which colocates family and religion in an ostensibly private sphere. This colocation makes kinship in general and divorce in particular matters of *secular* governance. As I discussed in chapter 1, by secularism I do not mean the evacuation of religion from the public sphere, but rather the question of where to draw a line between religion and politics. I further argued that the reason divorce matters to Indian secularism is that it is one site where we see religious legal practice producing two distinct spheres: religion and law. The work of separating these categories is, paradoxically, secular. My argument in this chapter is that the dar ul-qazas' role not only indicates the reach of *secularity*—"the set of concepts, norms, sensibilities, and dispositions that characterize secular societies and subjectivities" (S. Mahmood 2016, 3). It also indicates that *secularism* is not solely a state project but instead one carried out by an array of nonstate institutions, a project that thereby decenters and sometimes appears to ignore the state.

The Dar ul-Qaza and the Dissolution of Muslim Marriages Act (1939)

Present-day Muslim legal practices are rooted in a long and dynamic history between legislation, the state, and Islamic legal traditions. Prior to 1938, the only way a Muslim woman in India could successfully divorce on her own initiative was through apostasy, because of the limitations imposed by the conjuncture of the Hanafi school of law (the branch of the Sunni legal tradition that predominates in India) and non-Muslim rule (see Zaman 2008, 57–62). According to Hanafi tradition, a woman could divorce by khul', but this required her husband's consent; she could divorce if her husband did not provide maintenance or if he was impotent; finally, if a minor was married by her father or guardian, she could divorce once she became an adult. The problem, however, was that divorce for any of these reasons had to be carried out by a qazi—a Muslim judge trained in the Hanafi tradition who could adjudicate according to the shari'a. According to Muhammad Qasim Zaman, outside of several princely states with Muslim rulers, qazis had no place in the colonial legal system, as the British had replaced qazis with judges trained in common law. It was these judges, not qazis, who adjudicated Muslim personal law cases during the late colonial period. Zaman implies that the lack of a place for qazis in the legal system also diminished the number of qazis available. According to Muslim personal law in place at the time, a woman whose husband abandoned her was allowed to remarry, but only if a natural life span, ninety-nine years, had elapsed since she was abandoned. This was not much help for a woman without means to support herself. According to the interpretation of Hanafi law accepted by the British, if a woman renounced Islam, she was, de facto, divorced (Zaman 2008, 62). This maneuver worked precisely *because* qazis were not authorized to adjudicate personal law in the British system. If there had been a place for qazis within the personal law system, a woman who apostatized would have been forced to convert back to Islam and remarry her ex-husband.

During the last years of colonial rule, Muslim leaders recognized this limitation on woman-initiated divorce as a political, legal, and theological problem; although it is not clear how many women resorted to apostasy, the Deobandi Maulana Ashraf 'Ali Thanawi and others understood this to be a crisis for the community's coherence and unity.[2] Maulana Thanawi, a jurist, Sufi master, and reformer, addressed the matter with lasting effects: his treatise on divorce serves as the basis both of the Dissolution of Muslim Marriages Act of 1939, which is still in force, and as a basis for divorce given in contemporary dar ul-qazas. Thanawi was a Hanafi jurist, trained at the Deoband Madrasah[3] as well as a prolific writer and a scholar dedicated to addressing current problems by drawing on Islamic sources (Zaman 2008, 2). Thanawi was also a Sufi and became the head of a Sufi lodge in the North Indian city of Kanpur in 1897 (Zaman 2008, 25). Muhammad Qasim Zaman suggests that Thanawi's career can be captured by the overlapping communities in which he participated: the scholars of Deoband; those whom he served as a Sufi master; the community of those who received his reformist writings; the worldwide community of Muslims; and the "evolving Muslim *political* community in India" (Zaman 2008, 31–33).

Thanawi's approach to the problem of apostasy reflected his multifaceted career. He searched for legal bases, within Islamic jurisprudential traditions, to expand women's ability to divorce. To do this, he actively drew on the resources and knowledge of Islamic scholars outside of India. In particular, he requested fatwas outlining the grounds on which women could divorce from

Maliki muftis in Medina (Zaman 2008, 62). On the basis of these fatwas, he published a treatise in 1933, *Al-Hila al-najiza li'l-halilat al-'ajiz*[4] (The consummate stratagem for the powerless wife[5]), which details the grounds on which a woman can receive a faskh, according to Maliki legal principles. In the treatise, Thanawi argued that Indian 'ulama (religious scholars) should change their interpretation of apostasy. They should agree that that it does not affect a woman's marital status, thereby keeping more women in the faith. At the same time, Thanawi argued that 'ulama should work with the resources he had gathered while undertaking research and consultation for *Al-Hila*. 'Ulama could, on the basis of these resources, allow women much broader possible grounds for divorce.

In making the argument that the grounds for divorce should be expanded, Thanawi relied on the legal principle of *takhayyur*, or eclecticism, in which a decision within one school of Islamic law gains authority in reference to a practice or interpretation drawn from another (De 2009; Hallaq 1999). Wael Hallaq (1999) has suggested that takhayyur is of particular importance in the modern period. This established legal practice was central, for example, to the Ottoman Law of Family Rights (Hallaq 1999, 210). But takhayyur was also practiced in earlier historical moments. According to Judith Tucker's (1998, 84) account of seventeenth- and eighteenth-century Ottoman fatwas, Hanafi muftis enabled annulments on the ground of abandonment by asking their Shafi'i or Hanbali assistants to preside over cases. By way of an example, Tucker reproduces a fatwa addressing a situation in which a woman came with three witnesses to testify that her husband married her and then left for four years, leaving her "without *nafaqah* [maintenance], without a legal provider" and without news of his whereabouts (1998, 85). The judge gave the faskh to the woman, although desertion and neglect were not grounds for divorce in the Hanafi tradition.

By bringing together the practice of takhayyur with extensive consultations with Hanafi jurists, Thanawi's *Al-Hila* enabled the 'ulama to "reclaim . . . authority . . . by making *ijtihad* through a collaborative effort at legal reform" (F. Khan 2008, 12). Ijtihad refers to a method of independent legal reasoning contrasted with *taqlid*, which is the invocation of an established legal opinion (Hallaq 1999, 3). As Zaman as argued, Hanafi jurists in India had long been dedicated to taqlid, believing that fidelity to earlier consensus opinions was the best way to maintain Islamic traditions. In response to the perceived crisis of apostasy, however, Thanawi established a new approach of collective fatwa writing, relying as he did on numerous fatwas endorsed by sixty Indian 'ulama (Zaman 2008, 63). Thanawi was therefore able to demonstrate the authority of the 'ulama to offer innovative legal solutions even in colonial India, where they had been stripped of their formal legal duties.

In *Al-Hila*, Thanawi argued that Muslims should work toward legal change: they should seek to re-establish a place for Muslim judges in the state judiciary and reform Muslim personal law so that apostasy would no longer effect divorce. Muslim women would have other grounds to divorce. In 1939, the Dissolution of Muslim Marriages Act (DMMA), legitimated in large part by Thanawi's treatise (see De 2009), was passed, granting women the right to initiate and obtain a divorce under conditions such as desertion, financial neglect, or a husband's imprisonment, impotence, or insanity (Fyzee 1974; Zaman 2008).[6] This legislation, which applied to all Muslims in India and forms part of Muslim personal law, adopted Maliki principles and expanded the grounds for divorce beyond those proposed by Thanawi. Fareeha Khan notes that the DMMA went even further than the reforms called for in *Al-Hila*, given that section 2.7 allows for divorce of a woman married before the age of eighteen, an age never explicitly mentioned in any of the four *mazahib* (schools of law) (2008, 202). *Al-Hila* therefore seems both to be the source of the DMMA and to have impacted the way the 'ulama related to the state, justifying collective ijtihad and reform through engagement with Islamic legal traditions (F. Khan 2008; Zaman 2008).

After the DMMA became law, Thanawi renounced it as insufficiently Islamic because it failed to established local Muslim councils throughout India (De 2009). In *Al-Hila* he had called for local groups of righteous Muslims to form councils, or *jama'at ul-Muslimin*, to which Muslims could take their disputes (F. Khan 2008). Such councils were already approved by Maliki law, and they provided a way for 'ulama to continue guiding Muslims even under a non-Muslim government (Zaman 2008). Zaman cites Thanawi's statement that "just as they [Muslims] establish panchayats [for the settlement of] their worldly affairs, so too should they set up panchayats for their religion and for safeguarding [the interest of] their brethren" (Zaman 2008, 65). Thanawi's call suggests that Muslim survival would require organized guidance by fellow Muslims and, at the same time, clearly limited this guidance to religious matters. In other words, this was a call for true religious adjudication—carried out by and for righteous Muslims—on thoroughly secular terms. These councils would not deal with "worldly affairs," but with religious ones.

Even if the DMMA did not return Muslim judges to the state legal system, Thanawi's call to establish councils of righteous Muslims has been heard. Some councils already existed when Thanawi made his call. Notably, the Imarat-i Shari'a, where Qazi Kamal was trained, was founded in 1921. But more recently, the dar ul-qazas in Delhi and other locations around India have taken up Thanawi's mandate, relying on 'ulama to adjudicate disputes and to grant divorce on Muslim legal grounds. The dar ul-qazas I analyze here carry out this mandate to adjudicate religious (and only religious) matters. Dar ul-qazas's service to Muslims thereby simultaneously conforms to the state's division between religion and law; this is, I argue, precisely why the Supreme Court welcomes their existence.

The dar ul-qaza cases I presented in the last chapter add a contemporary ethnographic dimension to this theological-political history of Muslim divorce. The cases show that the grounds established for divorce articulated in the DMMA have been taken up as consensus in the dar ul-qazas. Furthermore, the qazis in Delhi and beyond trained at the Imarat-i Shari'a evidence their detailed knowledge of the grounds for divorce outlined in *Al-Hila* in their judgments.[7] The AIMPLB's *Majmu'ah-i Qawanin-i Islami*, translated as the *Compendium of Islamic Laws* (All India Muslim Personal Board 2001, 137), records the legacy of *Al-Hila* as it gives the following grounds for faskh: (1) marriage with someone who is not an equal (*ghair-kufu men nikah*); (2) an uncommonly low mahr; (3) marriage before puberty (*khiyar-i bulugh*); (4) husband's failure to fulfill his marital obligations (*huquq-i zaujiyat*); (5) husband's inability to have sex; (6) affliction by an offensive disease; (7) husband's insanity (*majnun hona*); (8) whereabouts of the husband are unknown; (9) desertion by husband; (10) husband's failure to provide maintenance although he could; (11) husband's inability to provide maintenance; (12) husband's physical beating of the wife (*sakht mar-pit karna*); (13) serious discord (*shaqaq*) between the parties; (14) man lied about his state (*halat*) when he married the woman; (15) couple are separated because of lack of affinity; (16) couple are separated because of discord (*fasaad*). Justin Jones (2010) rightly argues that the *Compendium*'s inclusion of a broad array of grounds for divorce is evidence that the AIMPLB has adopted reformist positions. What is even more interesting, though, is that this compendium includes the grounds for divorce from the DMMA, which go beyond those outlined in *Al-Hila*. The *Majmu'ah* does, as

Jones states, give *Al-Hila* as the source for its reasoning in divorce due to husband's insanity and husband's unknown whereabouts. However, the remaining twelve grounds for divorce have other sources. Given that desertion and cruelty are the two primary grounds for faskh claims in dar ul-qazas, the *Majmu'ah*'s debts, and through it those of dar ul-qazas, are both to the *Al-Hila* and to the DMMA.

The significance of this dual and only partly acknowledged debt is that while the AIMPLB sets itself up as a body of righteous Muslims completely separate from the state, its dar ul-qazas in practice implement the same law of woman-initiated Muslim divorce as the state. This does not imply that the dar ul-qaza imitates the state courts, or even exactly takes state legislation as precedential or binding—after all, both traditions have a shared root in *Al-Hila* and an array of other sources, including Maliki sources. Instead, adjudication of faskh demonstrates the complementary relation of the dar ul-qazas to the state courts. In the past dar ul-qazas have been impacted by the state's legal history, while present state courts and dar ul-qazas rely on one another. Given this deep imbrication, it remains to be asked: what grounds and with what effects do both the dar ul-qazas and the state courts insist that they occupy thoroughly distinct domains?

My analyses of faskh cases in the preceding chapter show both dar ul-qazas's independence from the state courts and their overlapping legal interpretations. The point is neither that the state is omnipotent nor that the qazis have been duped, but instead that the governing interests of the postcolonial Indian state are served even without their direct involvement in governing family life—the dar ul-qaza system, while distinct, enforces and produces the very construction of the private sphere of the family, that the state itself is invested in maintaining. Indian law and judicial practice produce and maintain marriage as both within and beyond the state's jurisdiction, while the qazi's adjudication practices simultaneously establish his religious and legal authority over marriage and divorce and dovetail with state legal practices. The postcolonial politics of the AIMPLB have resulted in establishing dar ul-qazas and insisting on their separateness from the state courts, an arrangement they can accomplish because it conforms to the secular demand to separate a sphere of religion from one of law. The following case clarifies that this complementary relation rests on secular presuppositions while also engaging in the labor of separating a sphere of religion from a sphere of law.

Filing for Khul'

A woman filed for a divorce (khul') at the Kashmiri Gate dar ul-qaza in January 1994. In her complaint she described the violence and cruelty (zulm) characteristic of her seven-year marriage. Her in-laws spat on her, hit her, and told her that she was not worthy of her husband. The respondent (her husband), she alleged, threatened that he would "neither keep her nor leave her," implying that he would neither treat her as his wife and a member of his natal household nor grant her the divorce that would enable her to remarry. She recalled the respondent saying to her: "I will make you sick of your life, I will torture you, I will ruin you . . . I will take you for one night and I will destroy your reputation." She further alleged that her in-laws and her husband had launched multiple cases against her: her brother-in-law accused her of taking things that belonged to his daughter, and her husband accused her of cheating on him. She had left her marital home after one year, unwilling to put up with further abuse from her in-laws or her husband. By framing her situation in these moral terms that focus on her in-laws' attempts to prevent her from living well in her marital home, the complainant's rhetoric suggested one type of argument presented in the dar ul-qaza. She sought a divorce. But she introduced her argument for divorce through a description of a marriage that failed, not because she had been an errant wife but because her husband had not lived up to his marital obligations.

The respondent's rebuttle featured a similar approach, but suggested that he, not his wife, had suffered a moral affront. The respondent contested the complainant's claims point by point in the petition, which was written in the form of a letter to the qazi. The respondent's letter was peppered with unsavory characterizations of his wife and her family. Her complaint, he argued, did not suggest anything about *him*, but instead revealed his wife's bad character. "She is ill-mannered and immoral [*bad-chalan*]" he said; "she has lied to the *shari'a adalat* [shari'a court] which shows you what kind of woman she is." The respondent further argued that the complainant's statements to the court showed "the shamelessness [*be-niqabi*]" of the wife and her family, who "lie and give baseless accusations. This is a habit of these people [*in logon ka 'adat hai*]." Like the complainant, the respondent presented his case in moral terms. The complainant and respondent appeared to agree that the pertinent issue was whether the complainant had been a good wife,

or the respondent a good husband. The respondent's rebuttal implied that his wife's immorality and bad behavior were to blame for her misery. He claimed that he never threatened her and never harmed her. Instead, according to his account, he was the party who persevered in the face of adversity. Indeed, he went so far as to argue that he would like to remain married to the complainant, further emphasizing his patience and perseverance.

In her dar ul-qaza petition, the complainant offered to forfeit her mahr and her monthly maintenance to secure a khul'. But this petition, and approaching the dar ul-qaza itself, was only the final chapter in a longer legal battle. This battle began in the state courts six years earlier. Table 4 outlines the trajectory of the case. The case file shows that, in 1988, the complainant left her marital home. On September 16, 1988, the respondent filed a case for Restitution of Conjugal Rights (RCR) demanding that the complainant return to the marital home. The following day, the complainant filed suit under CrPC 125 for maintenance. This suit yielded a small award of maintenance—200 rupees (about USD 3) a month—which both complainant and respondent mentioned in their petitions to the dar ul-qaza. On September 23, 1988, the complainant filed a criminal complaint against the respondent under CrPC 498A/406 of the Indian Penal Code, alleging that her husband had stolen the jewelry and other property that she received at the time of her marriage. Each of these state court cases was framed as a matter of rights in marriage: the requests were, respectively, for a marriage free of violence and theft, for a shared marital home, and for the husband to financially support his wife. None of them yielded a satisfactory result from the wife's perspective, yet as far as the records show, she did not sue for divorce in civil courts under the Dissolution of Muslim Marriages Act. Instead, she turned to the dar ul-qaza.

The case file thus illustrates the relationship between dar ul-qazas and state courts. Here, the state courts (civil and criminal) were the forums in which litigants filed cases that they later withdrew. The dar ul-qaza, meanwhile, was where the litigants argued, brawled, performed acrimony, and labored at compromise. At the same time, disputants sought remedies for marriage in the courts—they sought to strong-arm one another into a livable married life—while in the dar ul-qaza they sought divorce. The specific types of state court cases involved in this particular dispute substantiate the claim that courts were the place to work out marital disputes rather than to secure divorce.

Table 4. Chronology of khulʿ case

Date	Case	Court	Action
September 16, 1988	RCR	Civil Court	Request for wife to return to marital home
September 17, 1988	CrPC 125	Civil Court (criminal claim)	Maintenance request
September 23, 1988	498A/406/34	Civil Court (criminal claim)	Allegation of theft and cruelty
January 9, 1994	Khulʿ	Dar ul-qaza	Suit for khulʿ opened
May 2, 1994	Khulʿ	Dar ul-qaza	Dar ul-qaza agreement to divorce on certain conditions
May 4, 1994	498A	Civil Court	Request for adjournment
September 20, 1994	CrPC 125	Civil Court	Dismissed as Withdrawn
September 21, 1994	498A	Civil Court	Order to dismiss
September 21, 1994	Compromise Deed	Civil Court	Compromise agreement
September 26, 1994	RCR	Civil Court	Order to Dismiss
December 23, 1994	Khulʿ	Dar ul-qaza	Hukm: Khulʿ granted

Source: All India Muslim Personal Law Board, *Ek Jaʾiz Riport* (2013).

The case offers a vivid example of how India's condition of legal pluralism in India impacts divorce adjudication, something we have seen traces of in other dar ul-qaza cases as well. By legal pluralism I mean a legal landscape made up of numerous interrelated forums that draw on different sets of norms and are grounded in distinct authorities. While I am not invested in the terminology of interlegality (Santos 1987, 2002) that Hong Tschalär (2017) takes up, I am sympathetic to her insistence that Indian legal practices take place in a context of intersecting and semiautonomous forums that must be analyzed through their relations to one another. Some of these are official state institutions, others are definitively nonstate forums, and many occupy a position somewhere in between. Such an approach also undergirds Solanki's (2011) study of marriage and divorce disputes among Hindus and Muslims in Mumbai, Holden's (2008) analysis of Hindu divorce in Madhya Pradesh (2008), and Basu's (2006, 2015) accounts of divorce and domestic violence cases in Kolkata. The focus that each of these studies places on the relations between state and nonstate institutions provides a dynamic portrait of Indian law that is especially relevant in the case of marital disputes and divorce.

Part of the reason that legal pluralism in India is composed of intersecting institutions is that litigants forge such intersections by traveling between them. Litigants tend to be savvy about their options, making strategic use of the variety of spaces available to them. Ethnographies of local-level disputes, many of them mentioned above, teem with examples of litigants seeking recourse in multiple forums at once, or sequentially, in order to increase their chances of success. Solanki found that about 40 percent of the litigants she studied in her analysis of marriage and divorce disputes among Indian Hindu and Muslims had approached at least two different venues (2011, 79). These forums are not chosen randomly, but reflect litigants' sense of what is most socially acceptable as well as where they might expect success. This approach to the legal system is often referred to as forum shopping (von Benda-Beckmann 1981; Galanter 1981; Griffiths 1986; Sharafi 2014; Solanki 2011). The literature suggests that forum shopping, made possible by legal pluralism, in and beyond India, both opens up possibilities of maneuver and forecloses the possibility of "escape" from legal regulation. Indeed, even from its outset, this dar ul-qaza case suggests that cases are often comprised of numerous claims, each of which can be taken up as central, guiding decisions about which institution to approach. Holden (2008) has found that state courts are a venue of last resort for marital conflicts and that women and men prefer to handle their disputes in informal or unofficial venues, often finding success in the offices of local notaries. Basu notes that the very last resort is often a criminal complaint, and shows that marital disputes involve "carefully timed movement among civil, criminal, and mediation venues," a process that can provoke "bafflement and anger" (2015, 183). Adding another dimension to this analysis, Hong Tschalär shows that sometimes a litigant's choice of venue is informed by "knowledge-brokers" such as the heads of Muslim women's organizations with the connections necessary to help their clients seek solutions (2017, 169). In spite of the active decisions litigants make in approaching different forums, the metaphor of consumer choice upon which forum shopping relies is, as Basu has written, often off the mark given that as litigants try to make difficult decisions, they are confronted with "overlapping and sometimes contradictory directives," which can lead to detrimental decisions (2015, 183).

Traffic between forums implies more than just filing multiple cases; it entails modulating the tone, argument, and voice to suit the demands of each forum. Women's success and the definition of what constitutes success vary depending on the institutions in which a case is heard as well as on women's ability to translate their claims into terminology that will be effective within a given forum. The rhetorical strategies evident in this case are typical of dar ul-qaza cases discussed in the previous chapter: women and men portray themselves as persevering and as responsible spouses with minimal interest in property settlement.

Convergent Jurisprudence

The khul' case shows how divorce, with its many facets and its messiness, straddles jurisdictions. But if the choices made by litigants are a key reason for this, they are not the only one. The forums themselves, and those who run them, shape these decisions and, as becomes clear in what follows, sometimes appear to determine a case's trajectory. This case furthermore evokes the relationships of power and agency characteristic of Indian legal pluralism, which play out in cases of divorce by means of interactions between religious law in several registers and criminal complaints. To make this clear, I first analyze the details of the three cases filed in civil and criminal courts. These types of cases—498A (for dowry demands and cruelty), CrPC 125 (for maintenance), and RCR (for the wife's return to her marital home)—as well as their outcomes are representative of the Muslim marital disputes filed in state courts. They also lie at the epicenter of feminist concerns with women's legal status and citizenship rights because they articulate the courts' significant ambivalence about whether the state has the right to intervene in the ostensibly private sphere of marriage and family. In particular, the fact that the wives pursue remedies under both 498A and 125 marks a common conundrum for Indian women (not only Muslims). Srimati Basu's excellent analysis of this conundrum concludes that since women rely on their husbands for economic survival, "each remedy works only if the other fails: either violence complaints must be forgone to maintain the cash flow, or economic support must be forgone if symbolic redress of violence is deemed more important" (2015, 191). These three pieces of legislation are part of a legal apparatus that has produced a bifurcation between public and private, and concomitantly has naturalized such concepts as "family" and "household," thus shoring up a gendered division of the world. That a woman can hope for either freedom from domestic violence or maintenance but not both is symptomatic of this effect. Restitution of Conjugal Rights (RCR) contributes to constructing this world, inasmuch as it can be used to demonstrate a husband's good faith interest in maintaining his marriage, undermining his wife's allegations of mistreatment.

This division of the world is affected by, and also effects, "failures of the imagination," as one of my lawyer interlocutors put it, that judicially locate women's material and emotional well-being in a natal or marital household imagined as bounded and private. If the histories of CrPC 125 and 498A demonstrate state regulation of conduct within marriage that seems to defy the posited public/private split, RCR is an excellent example of the state's dedication to upholding the domains of marriage and family as sacred, private, and therefore inaccessible to questions about the universal rights of the citizen. Like the DMMA, these pieces of legislation are tied to the AIMPLB historically, but also through dynamics of adjudication apparent in this case.

On September 16, 1988, some months after his wife left the marital home, the husband in the khul' case discussed above filed suit for RCR. RCR is a suit for the return of one's spouse into "marital society"—this can be interpreted narrowly as being a matter of sex or more broadly as a matter of participating fully in a marriage by living together, treating one another well, and caring for one another. RCR rests on the eighteenth-century British legal view that marriage joins husband and wife, rendering them one legal person: the husband (Agnes 2008, 236). During the colonial period, RCR was introduced into both Hindu and Muslim marriage law by the British. The most commonly told history of RCR indicates the courts' ambivalence about how to treat marriage—as private or as public. In a famous judgment on the matter in 1983, Justice Choudhury opined that RCR constitutes a violation of the wife's right to privacy and human dignity guaranteed to all citizens by Article 21 of the Constitution (*T. Sareetha v. Venkatasubbiah*, AIR 1983 AP 356). This decision was challenged in 1984 by a Delhi High

Court opinion that stated the "introduction of constitutional law in [the] home is most inappropriate. It is like introducing a bull in a china shop" (*Harvinder Kaur v. Harminder Singh*, AIR 1984 Del 66). This view was upheld later that same year in *Saroj Rani v. Sudarshan Kumar Chadha*, which stated that "such a right is inherent in the very institution of marriage itself" (paragraph 1). Furthermore, the justices wrote, restitution "serves a good social purpose, as an aid to the prevention of the break-up of marriage" (paragraph 4). These decisions uphold the privacy of marriage and the exceptionalism of kin relations such that they supersede the rights of individual wives. For Muslims, RCR is only available to men, and it is assessed based on case precedent because there is no legislation on the matter in Muslim personal law. *Mulla Principles of Mahomedan Law*, widely used as the authoritative source of Muslim law in state courts, states that: "where a wife without legal causes refuses to live with her husband, the husband may sue the wife for restitution of conjugal rights" (Hidayatullah and Hidayatullah 2006, Section 281). The legal questions outlined in *Mulla* concern the grounds on which a wife can successfully contest such a suit: cruelty or a husband's decision to marry a second wife while awaiting the outcome of an RCR case against his existing wife. *Mulla* also specifies that the existence of an RCR suit is not necessarily sufficient to contest or refuse a CrPC 125 claim.

The day after her husband filed for RCR, on September 17, 1988, the complainant sued her husband for maintenance under CrPC 125. CrPC 125 allows "destitute and abandoned or deserted wives or children to claim maintenance from their husbands or children, respectively." This version of CrPC 125 dates to 1973, when then Prime Minister Indira Gandhi proposed an amendment to the existing law. She did this because the government had found that Muslim husbands could avoid paying maintenance for destitute wives by divorcing them. Under Muslim personal law, Muslim men were responsible for supporting ex-wives for only three months after a divorce (during the 'iddat period). At that point, if the two had not reunited, the husband was no longer financially responsible to his ex-wife. Gandhi sought to close this loophole by redefining "wife" to "include any woman who had been divorced and not remarried" (Williams 2006, 128). Ultimately, in response to opposition to the change, Gandhi also amended CrPC section 127 so that if a woman had already received some compensation (such as mahr), this amount could be subtracted from what the court ruled she was due (Agnes 1999, 102).

CrPC 125 has played a dramatic role in Muslim divorce jurisprudence in postcolonial India, as it has been implicated in debates about the boundaries of personal law and the ostensible clash between women's rights and minority rights. While the courts decided in favor of Muslim women's maintenance claims under CrPC 125 in several relatively unnoticed decisions (including *Bai Tahira v. Ali Hussein Fidaali Clothia* and *Fuzlunbi v. K. Khader Vali*), it sparked controversy around the issue with its judgment in *Shah Bano*. This case granted the destitute divorcée, Shah Bano, maintenance under CrPC 125 and indirectly resulted in the Muslim Women's (Protection of Rights in Divorce) Act (MWA) of 1986.[8] The complainant in the khul' case filed her CrPC 125 petition only three years after *Shah Bano* and two years after the passage of the MWA, which ostensibly made CrPC 125 moot for Muslim women. The complainant received 200 rupees (about USD 3) a month in maintenance. While 200 rupees a month does not approach the amount of money required to sustain a decent standard of living, it is a fairly typical maintenance award under CrPC 125. There is a ceiling of 500 rupees per month that courts can award under the legislation, but a lower award is typical, perhaps partly due to the well-documented assumption by the courts that a woman is either the ward of her husband or of her father / natal kin (Basu 1999; Mukhopadhyay 1998; Vatuk 2001).

On September 23, 1988, just days later, the complainant registered a complaint with the police, who arrested the respondent under Criminal Procedure Code (CrPC) 498A / 406 Indian Penal Code (IPC), the provision that protects women from dowry harassment and domestic violence.[9] CrPC 498A was written to deal with dowry harassment and suicide, but its language makes it relevant to accusations of cruelty and domestic violence. 498A was therefore doubly relevant here: as an allegation of dowry demands and as response to RCR. Under CrPC 498A, the police are entitled to arrest and detain the respondent for up to twenty-four hours, following which the police file a case in court against the respondent (Mukhopadhyay 1998, 52).[10] Srimati Basu's analysis has shown that 498A is often deployed as a way to secure entitlements in marriage, rather than as a way to exit marriage. It thus "ironically become[s] a conduit cementing the material and symbolic power of marriage" (2015, 178). In this case it appears, instead, to function as a defense against returning to the marital home.

The FIR in this case was filed, more specifically, under Section 406 of the Indian Penal Code, which deals with criminal breach of trust and can be punishable with up to three years' imprisonment and/or a fine. In this case, the police report stated that the husband was arrested for stealing his wife's jewelry after it had been entrusted to him, and for refusing to return it. As it turns out, the respondent's brother, who was jailed along with the respondent, testified to the police that the two had sold some of the jewelry. Since it was not legally theirs to begin with, this constitutes a further breach of trust.

The case file does not indicate why, after the flurry of cases in 1988, the parties stopped litigating—after all, with the exception of the complainant's 200 rupees per month in maintenance, neither party had gotten what they sought. Also undocumented is the reason why the complainant decided to approach the dar ul-qaza on January 9, 1994, six years later, seeking khul'. Whatever the reason, the shift in claim—to divorce (and in venue) to the dar ul-qaza—entailed significant changes in the rhetoric of the case.

Unlike in the two criminal cases, which were based on the complainant's claims of violence in which property played a central role, in the dar ul-qaza the complainant immediately offered to give up her mahr, her maintenance, and the gifts she received from her husband at the time of their marriage. Her dowry (jahez) was not offered up as a concession. It included a gold necklace and earrings that weigh 2.5 tolas [29.25 grams]; one pillow and bedsheet; two tables; a chair; a fan; a cooker; an electric kettle; a sewing machine; a tea set; a bucket; several bowls; twelve plates; a thirty-two-piece steel dinner set; numerous glasses; seventeen sets of clothes for the bride; and nine sets of clothes for men and nine for women. Compared to the 5,000 rupees (USD 75) in mahr, 200 rupees (USD 3) per month in maintenance, and 1,500 rupees (USD 22.50) in wedding gifts that she trades for her divorce, this property list is substantial. Nevertheless, because the woman petitioned for khul', it is routine that she offered to give up her mahr in exchange for the divorce. Many women have never received their mahr, which means that money rarely changes hands.

The complainant's decision to open a dar ul-qaza case had a cascade of effects that illuminate the dar ul-qaza's relationship to state courts. Between January 9 and May 4, dar ul-qaza records indicate that the parties engaged in heated debates about possible divorce. Exceptionally, they each had a mediator, who met with the parties and the qazi (and once, if the records are correct, had a small fist fight outside of court). On May 4, 1994, the dar ul-qaza file contains a note stating that in exchange for specified property exchanges the husband would give a divorce (talaq). The preceding negotiations and this judgment resemble other khul' processes I have observed and khul' case files I have studied.

Under the Hanafi school of Islamic law, a khul' has two basic conditions: "common consent of the husband and wife" and "as a rule, some '*iwad* (return, consideration) passing from the wife to the husband" (Fyzee 1974, 163). There has been debate in Islamic jurisprudence over what kind of compensation a wife is required to give to her husband in exchange for divorce, and also regarding whether such compensation is indeed a requirement at all (Fyzee 1974, 164–165). The AIMPLB's *Compendium of Islamic Laws* (All India Muslim Personal Board 2001, 93–94) states that khul' is a divorce given by the husband and accepted by the wife at either party's request. This divorce is given in exchange for an agreed-upon amount of money or property, which may include mahr or maintenance support during the 'iddat period but may not include maintenance due to dependent children. Although her right to maintenance during marriage had already been recognized, in part, by the Indian court that awarded it to her, the turn to divorce, either through khul' or under Muslim personal law, reversed the entitlement to maintenance. What had begun as four different suits in four different courts had become a single matter before the dar ul-qaza of formally undoing marriage.

The decision to divorce recorded in the dar ul-qaza was followed by new activity in the state courts, this time ending suits. On September 20, the civil court judge requested that the court dismiss the 498A case. The judge argued that justice and the well-being of the disputants demanded that the case be dropped. She argued that since the disputants were Muslim and had "sought the assistance of a qazi and have been able to settle the matter amicably," dropping the property suit would be conducive to the couple's desire to "live peaceful lives." According to Flavia Agnes's study on the impact of 498A on abused women, this is no anomaly and is also applicable to Hindu women. It has repeatedly been the case that when a husband has been willing to grant a mutual consent divorce, the wife would also give up her property rights (1992, 26).

On September 21, the parties signed a compromise deed that stated, among other things, that "the articles given to Respondent by Complainant during the marriage" should be returned after he divorced the Complainant. The deed made the qazi responsible for overseeing the transfer of the goods. It also stipulated that based on a prior written agreement between the parties, the qazi "will have the right to grant divorce" ex-parte (without the presence or cooperation of the Respondent). Finally, on September 26, the court granted an order to dismiss the RCR claim. In December, following another series of discussions, the qazi divorced the couple. The dar ul-qaza file stated that the wife had given over all gifts from her husband, plus 18,500 rupees (about USD 275) that she had accrued in maintenance payments and mahr, and to pay off other debts she had incurred while married to her husband. Upon receiving this divorce, the qazi wrote, she is "free" (*azad*), and neither party can make further claims over the other.

The legal practices evident in this case—which was really four separate cases—lead to several conclusions. First, forum shopping comes with costs, and it is can be more about dividing legal labor than about increasing litigants' options. This is ironic given that the dar ul-qaza network was one of the AIMPLB's responses to the ostensible incursion into Muslim personal law by the state courts following *Shah Bano*. The aim was to offer an alternative to the state courts. Second, the intersection between these forums affects what Muslim divorce looks like. The divorce granted here was both khul'— because it was woman-initiated and required a property exchange—and faskh—because the qazi had the right to grant it ex-parte if necessary. Although the qazi did the mediation work, the judge arrogated to herself the right to grant the qazi the right to divorce (faskh) the couple. Third, the process of proliferating and then collapsing claims secures a division of labor that renders divorce "religious" and proper to the qazi's jurisdiction while it implies that property claims belong in state courts.

In other words, rather than a relation of parallelism or of alternatives, the legal pluralism that is practiced here is best characterized as a convergence of jurisprudence. The convergence institutes and relies on the division of labor I have outlined above, where the qazi's primary domain is the divorce, but it is a division of labor in the service of a shared approach to divorce. When the complainant needed a divorce, she exited the state courts. Yet she brought the state courts with her in the form of a history of cases materially present in photocopies of FIRs and case files. When the qazi had worked out the terms, complainant and respondent returned to the court, both for approval and so that the dar ul-qaza decision could be collaborative. This is reflected in the common practice that before a dar ul-qaza will give a divorce, disputants must formally drop all cases they have pending against one another in the state courts. This case suggests that disputants understand the dar ul-qaza to be a place for divorce—for dealing with the messy matter of undoing marriage. The qazi's expertise and authority inheres in such regulation of kinship. Yet even as the qazi delivers divorces, he does so through a process of converging with the state: the two forums agree with one another's terms. The qazi and the judge implicitly agree that his (religious) authority is over kinship while her (secular legal) authority is both to authorize terms and regulate marriages that are ongoing, with their problems of violence and property disputes. This convergence both rests on and reflects the shared secular view that I have referred to as Indian FLE: in this view, not only is kinship a private matter, subject to religious rather than state legal authority, but it joins religion in its private sphere. Yet this case also exposes the other side of Indian FLE. In the name of leaving the family to religious authority, the judge in this case oversaw its every detail and was instrumental in clearing the way for the khul'. The state is not as absent from the projects of regulating religion and kinship as FLE and secular ideologies would together purport.

Conclusion: Secularism and the Uses of Kinship

The histories and practices of Muslim law in the cases I have analyzed above elaborate the tension I noted at the beginning of the chapter: dar ul-qazas are figured as external to the state but nevertheless both accept the secular premise that religion and law are separate spheres and participate in the secular labor of making and upholding this distinction. There is perhaps no better place to go to capture the dynamics of divorce and personal law as the site of manufacturing law and religion than the Supreme Court case with which this chapter began: *Vishwa Lochan Madan v. Union of India*. The case challenged the Supreme Court to assess the constitutionality of dar ul-qazas, with the plaintiff arguing that they constitute a parallel legal system and therefore undermine the sole authority of the Indian state. The AIMPLB argued in response that dar ul-qazas are neither the same as state courts nor wholly outside their logic. Instead, it argued that dar ul-qazas were ADR forums, which thereby includes them in an increasingly broad category of adjudication forums operating outside of ordinary courtrooms with the aim of amicably settling disputes. This consolidates dar ul-qazas as unthreatening in their capacity as religious institutions whose authority is confined to the domain of kinship. Because, as the Supreme Court pointed out, dar ul-qazas cannot avail themselves of the enforcement mechanisms upon which the state relies, they are all the more nonthreatening and also appear to be subordinate to the state's courts.

The Supreme Court's view reflects the politics of Islamic law in India, both in the present and as they have been shaped since the nationalist movement. For example, Ashraf Ali Thanawi's intervention into the rules of Muslim divorce was part of a larger effort to unify Indian Muslims as a single political community in the face of their impending minority status. In particular, Thanawi argued that Muslims should have their own adjudication forums, which would allow them recourse to religious authorities in matters that concerned them *as Muslims*. While his effort to have such institutions written into legislation failed, it generated arguments for and the reality of a space of adjudication beyond the state in the form of dar ul-qazas. The deeply secular quality of his argument, which posited the need for Muslim authority over Muslim religious matters, closely aligns with the contemporary Supreme Court's defense of the dar ul-qazas.

From the training of its judges to the forms of argument that succeed within it, the dar ul-qaza appears to demonstrate that Islamic law in India constitutes an important exception to the forms of postcolonial fiqh found in other national contexts. Unlike in Egypt (Asad 2003), for example, dar ul-qazas in India practice an Islamic law that is decentralized and largely uncodified. On the one hand, the AIMPLB's *Compendium of Islamic Laws*, published in English and in Urdu in 2001, can be read as a codification of Muslim law for India, designed to "facilitate its implementation within a legal and structural framework set by the state" (Jones 2010, 188). On the other hand, the compendium is not accepted by the state as binding Muslim law. As others have shown, the uncodified character of Muslim personal law has enabled it to change in significant respects over the past decades (Subramanian 2008).

Also unlike in Egypt (S. Mahmood 2013), one of the countries where anthropologists of Islam have begun most intently to study secularism, dar ul-qazas in India seem to comprise an alternative to a civil legal system that is nonetheless open to hearing Muslim family law cases.[11] And yet dar ul-qazas bolster rather than disrupt the state's regulation of marriage and divorce. In the many ways elaborated in this chapter—traffic of cases between dar ul-qazas and courts; shared moral-legal language; shared view of the appropriateness of locating family matters within the purview of religious authority—dar ul-qazas adjudicate as part of the state's legal landscape. Thanawi's effort to secure a separate space of religious law has produced religious legal practices that separate "religion" from "law," each with its own, albeit contested, jurisdiction. The separation of these jurisdictions is, in practice, an ongoing project. It is, and must remain, incomplete, not because of a failing of the institutions, but because as a practice of secularism, it is an effort at separating religion from law, an effort perpetuated by its own incompleteness.

One consequence of this argument is that secularism cannot be satisfactorily understood as solely a state project, or even as a project centered on the state and its practices. In other words, dar ul-qazas constitute secularism as a political and legal practice along with state institutions and along with the other religious forums examined in this book. This unsettles the powerful if implicit assumption in most contemporary studies of secularism that the state is *the* site and motor of secularism as a political project, while nonstate loci of secularism are better understood as sites of secularity.

For Talal Asad (2003), whose work has spurred a recent interest in secularism among anthropologists, secularity is conceptually prior to secularism: secularism as a political project relies on secular ways of being in the world. The leading anthropologists of secularism take up this distinction. For example, Saba Mahmood frames her analysis in *Religious Difference in a Secular Age* as being primarily concerned with political secularism, "particularly the modern state's production and regulation of religious differences . . . and the effects of this intervention on the way religious identity has come to be lived" (2016, 3). Following Asad, Mahmood understands political secularism to be a power of the modern state, specifically the power to define and organize religion and religious life. Mahmood differentiates political secularism from secularity, which entails the proper attitude and sensibilities of a modern secular person. In her insightful analysis of French secularism, Mayanthi Fernando (2014a) looks closely at the state's project of making Islam a religion—an act of secularism—and the presuppositions about who a secular subject is—its presuppositions about secularity—upon which such an intervention relies. In this way, she too is able to draw out the fecundity of secularism's contradictions precisely by analytically separating secularism as an ensemble of state projects from the norms and nonstate forms of the secular.

Although the state's role in pursuing political secularism remains central in Hussein Agrama's analysis of Egypt, he nonetheless works to unsettle the omnipotence of the state. One way he does this is by questioning the conceptual priority of the secular to secularism, instead positing that they "draw one another into existence" (2012, 2). The secular and secularism, for Agrama, are united by their shared concern with questions about how politics and religion ought to relate. Secularism as a political practice has a secular sensibility even as secular subjects are precisely such because they are deeply interpellated by the demands of secularism. For Agrama, what escapes from this mutual imbrication are spaces of asecularity, spaces that do not share a concern with the relationship between politics and religion but which answer to a different set of norms and expectations, in particular with regard to ethical questions.

Dar ul-qazas open up the possibility, which becomes clearer and more pronounced in the context of the fatwas I look at in the next chapter, that secularism—the political project of asking the question of how religion and law/politics should relate—is something that *also* takes place in the kinds of spaces that Agrama calls asecular. The dar ul-qazas are not just guiding Muslims toward correct, ethically upright kin relations. They are actively producing the sphere of kin as ethical, religious, and sheltered. They are at the same time producing the problem of property and finances as problems of law and the state. This *is* the labor of secularism. Secularism, then, is not controlled by the state, and it is not a project exhausted by state initiatives and practices. It is radically multi-sited, and in India it relies heavily on the very legal pluralism the Supreme Court defended in response to Madan's PIL.

This observation has another consequence: it shows that secularism is a practical rather than primarily a conceptual project. Just as secularism is not only carried out at the behest of the Indian state, it is also not carried out in response to a blueprint or a conceptual apparatus that is prior to its practices. Secularism is a matter of legal (and political) practices and of the habits of legal language. In this context, these practices are especially evident in the traditions of divorce adjudication. It is this practicality of secularism—rather than its central question—that gives it its dynamism.

PART III

The Mufti

Chapter 5

"Talaq, Talaq, Talaq . . ."

On one of the many afternoons during which I sat with Mufti Ahmed in his spacious office at the Fatehpuri Mosque in Old Delhi, a young woman entered and handed the mufti a small scrap of paper with something written on it in Hindi. Members of Mufti Ahmed's family have served as the mosque's imam for four generations. As imam, Mufti Ahmed leads prayers, delivers Friday sermons, and gives legal advice (fatwas). Usually, people who want to receive legal advice either mail their questions to him or drop them off at his office in the morning and return in the evening to pick up his response. The exchange between the questioner and the mufti takes place exclusively in writing. At this time in the afternoon, just following the late afternoon 'asr, prayer, there was an unusual lull in the mufti's office, so when the young woman entered and told Mufti Ahmed that she had come for legal advice, he invited her to sit down on the floor mat in front of his low lectern behind him, cross-legged.

When Mufti Ahmed saw that the question was written in devanagari script on a small scrap of paper, he asked the woman to rewrite it in Urdu on a proper piece of paper. She replied that she could neither read nor write Urdu, the language spoken and written by Indian Muslim jurists, which is written in the Perso-Arabic Nasta'liq script. Similar to the dar ul-qaza case in chapter 1, in this instance the mufti instructed the woman to find someone on the premises to transcribe the question for her. There is a madrasah in the mosque, and the woman returned from it ten minutes later with her question written in Urdu on a piece of plain white paper. As he read through her question, the mufti asked for clarification. The woman explained that ten years earlier her husband had said "talaq," or "I divorce you," to her twice. According to the Hanafi school of Islamic law, a man can divorce his wife by saying "I divorce you" to her three times. This form of divorce is legal but disapproved of in Hanafi law, and has been the subject of much debate in the Indian judiciary. As this chapter discusses, its legality is complex and ambivalent.

Knowing that this utterance can effect a divorce, the couple had consulted a mufti who told them that because the words of divorce had been spoken only twice rather than three times, a legal divorce had not occurred and the couple could reunite. A week prior to this visit to Mufti Ahmed, the woman's husband had said "I divorce you" to her again, this time three times. She wanted to know what was required of them now that her husband had said "I divorce you" to her a total of five times. Without speaking to her further, the mufti wrote down his response in the space left at the bottom of the paper that held the question. When the woman asked him to tell her what it said, he referred her to his son, who often helps his father in the mosque, learning the skills that will enable him to eventually take over his father's role. I suspected that I already knew what the mufti had written, and when his son read the mufti's response to her, I could see the woman's face drop. Once the woman had gathered her shoes from outside the office door and left the mosque, the mufti confirmed to me that he had written that the utterance of five "talaqs" during this span of time had indeed effected an irrevocable divorce.

Talaq, Talaq, Talaq

The type of divorce about which the woman consulted the mufti is called talaq ul-ba'in. This way of divorcing is referred to by different names. Talaq ul-ba'in (irrevocable divorce) and *talaq al-bid'at* (innovative divorce) refer to its origins as an innovation in Islamic law. While these two terms refer to the same kind of divorce, they have distinct etymological origins. Collo-quially, this kind of divorce is referred to as "triple talaq" or "instant talaq." Talaq ul-ba'in is a form of divorce "given in violation of the prescribed pro-cedure" (T. Mahmood 2002, 105). It takes place when a husband utters "I divorce you" thrice to his wife. Unlike other types of Muslim divorce, which require systematic statements of the intention to divorce to be produced over a period of several months, talaq ul-ba'in can occur unexpectedly or in a mo-ment of rage. It therefore differs from the other unilateral, extrajudicial forms of divorce available to Sunni husbands who follow the Hanafi mazhab (school of law). The terms for all forms of unilateral divorce—*talaq-i sunnat, talaq-i ahsan, talaq-i hasan*, and *talaq-i ba'in*—"refer to the conduct of the man in pronouncing a talaq" (T. Mahmood 2002, 104). Talaq-i sunnat refers to any talaq that is given in accordance with proper procedure, one that allows for the possibility of reconciliation between spouses. Talaq-i ahsan (better talaq) and talaq-i hasan (less virtuous but acceptable talaq), are ways of giving a talaq-i sunnat. Although technically this speech act, in either its revocable or irrevocable forms, does not require authorization by either courts or religious legal experts in order to achieve legitimacy, Muslims in Delhi, as elsewhere (Masud, Messick, and Powers 1996, 27), have a broad knowledge of major issues in Islamic law and are aware that talaq ul-ba'in is immediate and irre-vocable only if properly carried out. Questions about the success of any given utterance of talaq ul-ba'in therefore often involve requests to have the legiti-macy of the speech acts evaluated by a legal authority.

Talaq ul-ba'in has been the subject of significant debate in the Indian courts and among Islamic legal scholars and practitioners, but most agree that it is a legal but reprehensible act. While not all schools of Islamic law recog-nize the repetition "talaq, talaq, talaq" in one interaction as irrevocable and binding, Hanafi law does (T. Mahmood 2002, 106–107). Indian courts, which apply Hanafi law to Muslims in matters of personal status, until recently widely echoed the conservative Hanafi view that talaq ul-ba'in is "good in law but bad in theology."[1] The question of what particularly makes talaq ul-ba'in "good in law" is, however, a matter of debate, one that is addressed both in fatwas and in courts.

This chapter provides an analysis of the jurisprudence on talaq ul-ba'in. The jurisprudence has been made in two distinct forums and in two legal registers: fatwas and judgments. A fatwa is a piece of authoritative legal advice written by a qualified Muslim jurist (mufti) in response to a specific question (*istifta*) posed, as in this context, by an individual questioner (*mustafti*) (Masud, Messick, and Powers 1996). Although only the advice is the fatwa, the question to which the fatwa is a response is an integral part of it. Fatwas are nonbinding but authoritative: Muslims are not required to follow the fatwas they receive, but because fatwas are the learned opinions of a religious legal expert, they carry significant weight (Agrama 2010). As authoritative opinions given by jurists and unenforceable by the state, fatwas are best understood as practices of shari'a—a guide for how to live as a Muslim—rather than of state law. Fatwas are thus an important source of moral guidance and ethical self-making (Agrama 2012) even as they constitute a register of law. In addition to constituting an element of Islamic legal practice, fatwas are part of the Indian personal law landscape: although they are not considered binding by state courts, Mufti Ahmed has been called to court to explain fatwas he has given for specific matters, and has been chastised by lawyers for failing to include fully elaborated reasoning in them.

Meanwhile, state court judgments have a different process, form, and outcome. Judgments are the culmination of an adversarial process that involves testimony and evidence gathering whose aim is to uncover the facts of the case. In this way, court proceedings are concerned with responding to the question at hand by producing a context for it and by assessing the validity of relevant claims. Finally, judgments are binding in the sense that they are backed, at least theoretically, by the state's enforcement mechanisms. While they are ostensibly only legal, following from case precedent and legal reasoning, such judgments are notably moralizing in tone and in content.

Fatwas and court judgments produce distinct conceptions of the relation between divorce and marriage, yielding insight both into the workings of law and into the role of divorce in postcolonial Indian secularism. In fatwas, divorce appears as a legal instrument for remaking kin relations, one initiated by the parties of a marriage and completed through an uneven collaboration between these legal subjects and the legal authorities to whom they appeal. Likewise, the consequences of divorce, including financial and custody arrangements, are addressed in the fatwa only if they were raised in the istifta. Marriage thus appears as a straightforward and recognized mechanism for economic distribution even as this facet of the marital relation is considered relevant only if the parties of a marriage consider it to be. It is this conception of marriage and divorce, as contractual relationships circumscribed by Islamic legal precepts, that make fatwas well suited to adjudicating talaq ul-ba'in in particular.

In contrast, the state courts frame marriage as the solution to the problem of divorce, rather than the inverse. Divorce is a problem for the state; because it lays bare some of the contradictions of marriage, it raises anxieties. Divorce exposes the way in which marriage constitutes not only an institution of care but also a significant mechanism for financial distribution. This is especially true in India, where people generally avoid bringing marital disputes to the courts—when they do, it is often because the divorcée is destitute, unable to support herself or her children. Such dynamics exacerbate and render visible the economics of divorce: in India and elsewhere, people tend to divorce either because they have a lot to gain or because they have nothing to lose. In this way, divorce calls into question the strict divides between the private and the public, and between care and exchange, that are assumed and inscribed by secular law.

As I have discussed in chapter 1, one of the historical developments of secular modern law in India (as in Britain, the U.S., and other secular states) has been to produce this distinction between public and private, secular and religious, while undermining it in practice. This simultaneous doing and undoing of governing distinctions between family and public takes different forms in different times and places. Thus, in Donzelot's (1997) analysis, the family is a relay, for Foucault (1978) it is a target, and for Halley and Rittich (2010) it is a legally exceptional entity surreptitiously governed by a vast array of laws pertaining its supposed other—the public domain.

Talaq ul-ba'in in particular raises anxieties for the state, as it also appears to mark the limits of sovereign control over divorce and therefore over the family as a site of distribution. As with other forms of unilateral divorce, the state is not needed in these cases. When the courts have the opportunity to rule on them, then, the judgments are in part an effort to address and affect a broader public. In state courts, these anxieties related to sovereign control and maintaining the family as a site of distribution yielded a particular mode of adjudicating divorce: judgments verbosely regulate the conditions governing talaq ul-ba'in, thereby normalizing it as a form of Muslim divorce. Their circumscriptions of the practice simultaneously uphold marriage as the appropriate mechanism for distributing financial resources and security to adult women.

As a seeming indicator of the limits of sovereign control over divorce, fatwas in fact contribute to this regulation, demonstrating its importance by appearing to defy it. This is because fatwas and judgments on talaq ul-ba'in share the same terrain but are in direct conflict with one another. They are different legal interventions: fatwas are nonbinding advice while judgments are the enforceable outcome of an adversarial process. Furthermore, their interventions imply inverse views of marriage and divorce and reveal competing legal philosophies. The *Madan* PIL—which challenged the constitutionality of nonstate Islamic legal forums including dar ul-qazas and fatwas—would imply that this is a matter of distinctions to which both institutions are indifferent. But for reasons of politics and governance both the mufti and the state are aware that their jurisdictions overlap and that they therefore make competing if coexisting claims to authority over divorce.

Fatwas

The first facet of Indian talaq ul-ba'in jurisprudence resides in fatwas. Because talaq ul-ba'in is extrajudicial, it is not carried out in dar ul-qazas, although occasionally litigants do approach these institutions to have their divorces authorized. Scholars of Islamic law in other modern state contexts have argued that one of the notable features of contemporary fatwas is that they tend to respond to questions concerning people's private lives (Messick 1993; Agrama 2005; Skovgaard-Petersen 1997; Masud, Messick, and Powers 1996). In this, Mufti Ahmed's dar ul-ifta [fatwa-giving office] is no exception. Mufti Ahmed addresses a steady stream of istiftas. During the period of my fieldwork, between 2005 and 2007, he collected 107 fatwas for me, of which 60 were related to divorce. Twenty of the fatwas unrelated to divorce responded to questions about property division as part of an inheritance, and thirteen were about marriage. Other istiftas asked about how a deceased man's property should be divided among his multiple heirs; what a non-Muslim woman had to do in order to marry a Muslim man; and what a man's financial responsibilities were to his ex-wife.[2] Unlike in other contemporary Muslim law contexts, in Mufti Ahmed's postcolonial Indian dar ul-ifta, questions were rarely received about religious practice. The questions reported in other studies, ranging from those of colonial India to contemporary Egypt, include a significant number about religious practice ('ibadat). In these studies, family law issues are also prevalent (Agrama 2005; Metcalf 1982).

The selection of fatwas that I analyze here reflects the sum total of the fatwas the mufti copied for me. I assume that this is not a complete set: he probably forgot to copy the fatwas he wrote from time to time, and I know that sometimes when no one was available to make a trip to the photostat booth down the block he simply returned the fatwas without copying them. However, I have no reason to believe that Mufti Ahmed edited his collection to privilege certain questions or topics, and for this reason I understand the collection to be uncurated. This differentiates the collection from, for example, the European fatwas that Caeiro (2011) has studied. Caeiro gives an excellent analysis of the ways in which the European Council for Fatwa and Research addresses the particular situations of Muslims in Europe but notes, referring to Zaman (2002), that this council is an example of how institutionalization has enabled 'ulama to maintain their relevance in the contemporary world. Because the fatwas I study are uncurated in the sense that they have not been culled and edited for the purposes of publication or as guides for other jurists, thematic consistencies demonstrate the narrow focus of Mufti Ahmed's fatwas, as well as the function of fatwa-giving in secular postcolonial India.

Fatwa collections, or *fatawa*, have a well-documented history in India. Indian fatwa collections, which were first compiled in the tenth century, had a distinctive character compared to other Muslim jurisdictions (Masud, Messick, and Powers 1996, 14). Rather than being bound volumes in which questions and responses were listed, the fatwa collections of the Mughal period were compilations of Hanafi doctrine. The most relevant of these collections to this study, because it is referred to by all of the 'ulama with whom I worked in Delhi, is the Fatawa Alimgiri, which was compiled at the behest of the emperor Aurungzeb in the seventeenth century. This compilation of jurisprudence (fiqh) remains a chief reference for muftis in India.

As Barbara Metcalf has shown through her work from the published fatwa collections produced by the dar ul-ifta at the influential Deoband seminary, the form of fatwas collections changed during the colonial period. She describes the aim of the Deobandi 'ulama during the last decade of the nineteenth century and the first decades of twentieth century as a "collection of fatawa as definitive as the famous compilation of the Emperor Aurangzeb" (1982, 146). The published collections were gleaned from the registry of fatwas kept by the 'ulama of the dar ul-ifta beginning in 1911 (Metcalf

1982, 146). Thus, although this was a broad collection, it was made up of actual questions. By contrast, the seventeenth-century Fatawa Alimgiri had been a tome of doctrine in prose. The Imarat-i Shari'a, which I have discussed in the previous chapter, also maintains a dar ul-ifta, and the three-volume fatwa collection it has published is similarly structured around themes, but substantiated through actual questions and fatwas rather than prose commentary. Likewise, the fatwa collection of Mufti Ahmed's father (published in Pakistan by some of his followers) is a compilation of questions and answers that includes only three chapters out of seventeen concerning personal law matters. These fatwa collections are thus both much more exhaustive and more wide-ranging than the fatwa sample I received from the mufti. This variety of topics indicates that while collections reflect editorial decisions and include rarely asked questions in the interest of covering the range of possible topics, the fatwas from which I work here reflect the scope of questions that people bring to the mufti on a regular basis. The focus on matters of personal law suggests both that they are disproportionately vexing to contemporary Delhi Muslims relative to other problems and that they are widely accepted as inherently religious matters. This is especially true of divorce.

I focus my analysis in this chapter on fatwas pertaining to talaq ul-ba'in. Not only is this form of divorce the subject of the preponderance of questions the mufti answers; it is also a suggestive site at which to examine the role of religious divorce in regulating the family, largely because its quasi-extrajudicial character makes it a vexed but productive site of legal intervention.

As with other recent ethnographic accounts of fatwas, mine departs from analyses that consider fatwas as points of doctrine (see Messick 1993). Here I agree with Agrama that fatwas are more personal and specific than accounts that understand them to be points of doctrine suggest (see Agrama 2012, 163). They are, in form and in practice, indeterminate and dialogical. It is, at the same time, clear that Mufti Ahmed's approach to fatwa writing is, as Messick has put it, "recitational," in that it does not require complex analogical reasoning or reflect probing questions into circumstances. Instead, it rests on the mufti's ability to hear a question, quickly categorize it into an existing domain of legal rulings, and recite the relevant response (1993, 149). Recitational fatwa giving, associated with taqlid (the act of following the legal school's established norms) as opposed to ijtihad (independent reasoning), is an interpretive act. Whereas the practice of ijtihad "is the exertion of mental energy in search for a legal opinion to the extent that the faculties of the jurist become incapable of further effort," taqlid is the invocation of an established legal opinion (Hallaq 1984, 3). Scholars have argued over whether ijtihad is a practice that continues in Islamic jurisprudence. Orientalist scholars suggest that the practice of ijtihad no longer existed after the third hijra century (the ninth century CE), and on that basis have claimed that after that date Islamic jurisprudence grew rigid (Schacht 1964; Coulson 1964). Along with rigidity, these scholars argued, came an increasing rift between theory and practice. Another wave of scholarship has questioned the thesis that the "gates of ijtihad" closed in the third/ninth century, and argue instead that the practice continued, even if its forms changed (Hallaq 1984; S. Jackson 2001; Messick 1993). My analysis here draws out the simultaneous consistency and responsiveness of the fatwa form in the present day.

Performative Divorce, Constative Fatwas

Muslim marriage, as many scholars have noted, is considered to be contractual rather than sacramental (Mir-Hosseini 2000).[3] While for some this is emblematic of the weakness of Muslim marriage, because it indicates that husbands and wives relate to each other as parties to a contract rather than as partners bound together by sacred relations of love and care, for others the contract is understood as a mechanism that can be used to inscribe gender equality into a marital relationship. For example, the contract can include clauses granting women broad rights to divorce (Carroll 1982). Because it can be tailored, the marriage contract—nikahnama—has been taken up in recent years as an instrument to improve women's condition in marriage, especially by Muslim women activists (see Hong Tschalär 2017, chap. 4; Lemons 2013; Vatuk 2017, chap. 5).[4] The fatwas I analyze in this section suggest that even where the nikah-namah has not been designed to either grant wives extended rights to initiate divorce or limit the husband's right to it, husbands and wives recognize that their contractual relationship to one another must conform to the precepts of Islamic law. Husbands and wives therefore bring inquiries to the mufti because they seek clarification of the terms according to which their contractual obligations can be dissolved even as they appear to actively make use of these very parameters. The contractual quality of Muslim marriage therefore provides unexpected sites of maneuver.

Fatwas are one mechanism of such maneuvers. The three exemplary fatwas I analyze in this section show how talaq ul-ba'in initiates a dialogue about the entailments of marriage and divorce of which the fatwa constitutes an integral part. They also lay the groundwork for an analysis of how the written medium and temporality of fatwas are well suited to such a dialogue. In Fatwa 79, a man recounts how he told his wife that he would divorce her and then declared, "I have given it [a divorce]," three times. He asked the mufti whether these words had effected a divorce. The fatwa stated that because the man had not said "the words of talaq," "I divorce you," three times, the couple remained married. Fatwa 58 describes a marital dispute during which the wife declared, "I divorce you," three times to her husband. Her husband responded that this declaration was ineffective, but then repeated the phrase four times. "Were they divorced?" the petitioners asked. "Yes," the fatwa stated: the husband had said the words of divorce three times. The predicament in Fatwa 25 is that a husband and wife agreed together to write an oath stating that if the husband drank alcohol again, he would divorce her. The next day, the husband came home drunk and wanted to know whether he and his wife were divorced. The mufti answered that the husband was bound to fulfill the oath.

Each of these questions takes roughly the same form, presenting a marital problem to the mufti in the register of his learned language. Each question begins with a variation of the phrase *kya farmate hain, 'ulama-i din, wa muftiyan-i shari'-i matin, is bat ke bare men?* (What do religious scholars and jurists who interpret shari'a say about the following situation?) The use of the formal verb tense along with a combination of Farsi and Arabic words refigures an intimate problem in reverential language; the choice of the Persian verb "farmana"—"to order"—which the questioner uses to ask the mufti for his opinion emphasizes the weight of the mufti's words and distances the fatwas from everyday banter. The questions culminate in the phrase *Qur'an o Hadis ki raushni men jawab dijiye* (We request that you give us an answer in light of the Quran and the Hadith), emphasizing the mufti's religious authority. These are not empty formulas. They situate the questions, which are written in a layperson's terms, within the learned religious world of the mufti.

In addition to sharing a form, these questions are also substantively similar. In each case the questioner asks, "Are we divorced?" The implication here is that in order to be effective, divorce proceedings must conform to the parameters of a marriage contract that exceeds the individual parties' intentions and that could thereby render their actions effective. In each fatwa, the mufti gives an analysis of the felicity of an utterance of talaq. The mufti gives his answer without elaboration: he does not cite the Quran or relevant Hadith, nor does he otherwise explain his reasoning, following long historical precedent and in spite of having been chided for this omission by state court judges (Masud, Messick, and Powers 1996). Instead, he often gives responses in the conditional, stating the legal consequences if a particular act or event took place. In this way, there is an immediacy to the responses that suggests that they are invocations of rules emerging from the consensus (*ijma'*) of the Hanafi school of law.[5] But these fatwa exchanges are not only sites at which rules are applied. They are also performances—they are produced by individuals acting in particular times and places and predicaments—demonstrating how people adapt to and work through fatwas to negotiate their marital positions.

In order to draw out how talaq ul-ba'in and the fatwas that the mufti writes about them together elucidate this type of divorce as a conventional mechanism for undoing marriage contracts, I turn to speech act theory as developed by J. L. Austin in his lectures *How to Do Things with Words* (1975). I argue that in these fatwas, the husband's declaration is a performative speech act and that what the mufti is asked to do in his fatwa is to authoritatively determine, with another speech act, whether the first performative was successful. Talaq ul-ba'in is rendered performative by the broader rule of marital contracts of which it is a part, but fatwas are appropriate for determining the legitimacy of this performative because they are not instruments wielded by the mufti, but rather speech acts responsive to the quandaries introduced by marital strife. The mufti's fatwa does not determine the outcome but throws the question, along with his elaborations, back to those who initially asked. This is its indeterminacy. Law on this account is itself extended over time and produced by several speech acts, only one and in this case the more belated of which is the mufti's.

Austin's definition of the performative refers to an utterance that performs an act rather than simply describing one. Aptly enough, given the context in which I am taking up Austin's work, one of his central examples of a performative is the statement "'I do (take this woman to be my lawful wedded wife)'—as uttered in the course of a wedding ceremony."[6] In uttering "I do" in this context, the speakers *do* something: they marry. With talaq ul-ba'in, the utterance "I divorce you, I divorce you, I divorce you" divorces the couple in question. Simply uttering the right words is not always sufficient, however. Austin writes, "Besides the uttering of the words of the so-called performative, a good many other things have . . . to go right" in order for the performative to succeed (1975, 14). These "other things" that have to "go right" are what Austin calls *felicity conditions.*

Each of the three fatwas below indicates that the mustaftis had some knowledge of talaq ul-ba'in's felicity conditions and chose to solicit a fatwa to gain clarity and sometimes authorization. In Fatwa 79, which I introduced above, the mufti found that no divorce had taken place on the grounds that the utterance itself was infelicitous. The question and fatwa read:

Fatwa 79

Istifta

What do you command, mufti of the shari'a, about the following issue which concerns a man and his wife? The husband's mother and his wife used to fight. During one of these fights, the husband said to his wife, who has three children: I am going to divorce you [*tumhen talaq dedunga*]. And he said three times: "I have given it, I have given it, I have given it" [*de di, de di, de di*]. Afterward, he felt terrible because he wants to spend his life with his wife and his children. Has his divorce happened or not?

Al-Jawab

The words with which you gave talaq were not the words of talaq, so there has been no divorce. If you have said talaq once, you can take your wife back during the *'iddat* period and you will be reunited.

The husband seems to have *intended* to divorce his wife (he told her, "I am going to divorce you"), but instead of uttering the first person indicative "I divorce you," he switched to the perfect tense "I have given it." The divorce failed because the husband uttered a constative rather than a performative. In other words, to say "I have given it" is to describe what one has done; to say "I divorce you" is to divorce. One way to interpret this particular exchange is to note that in formulating the question as he or she did, the mustafti opened up the possibility for the divorce not to have taken place; and the mufti, recognizing that the felicity conditions were not in place and that the husband wished to reconcile with his wife, took up this possibility in his fatwa. The terms of the dialogue, including a clear indication of the desired outcome, had been set by the istifta to be elaborated in the fatwa.

If Fatwa 79 responds to an infelicitous utterance, Fatwa 58 draws our attention to one of the performative's felicity conditions—the gendered body.

Fatwa 58

Istifta

Bismillah ir-rahman ir-rahim. What do you command, learned mufti, about the issue that follows: Nazimah Khatun is always fighting with her husband Mohammad. One day, Nazimah Khatun said to her husband: "I divorce you, I divorce you, I divorce you." Upon hearing this, Mohammad said, "If a woman says 'I divorce you,' there has been no divorce. I divorce you, I divorce you, I divorce you, I divorce you." Now the question, in this situation, is whether Nazimah has really been divorced. This incident happened on 1 January 2005. The request is that you give us an answer in light of the Quran and Hadis.

Al-Jawab

If a woman gives a talaq, a divorce has not taken place. If a husband says talaq three times, then an irrevocable divorce has taken place. It is necessary for the woman to observe 'iddat. After the waiting period is over, she can marry another man.

This fatwa suggests that the grammar of disembodied words is not sufficient for the performative to succeed. The subject who utters "I divorce you" must be appropriate to the task: he must be a (Hanafi Muslim) man married to the woman whom he addresses. When the wife first uttered "I divorce you" three times to her husband, her husband (and she and later the mufti) recognized that the couple was not then divorced. When her husband uttered the words, the conventional conditions of the performance were restored, and the couple divorced.

There are two notable things about the scene described in this question: it demonstrates that the legal speech act of talaq ul-ba'in needs to be embodied in order to achieve legitimacy, and it demonstrates that as a performance this speech act can be subverted. The question suggests that the wife, in anger, spoke the talaq ul-ba'in to her husband even though both knew that she was not in a position to effect a unilateral divorce. Her unsuccessful performative utterance seems to have provoked her husband into successfully uttering the words of divorce, which coming from him had legal implications. Her success in provoking this reaction also relied on the mufti's understanding of the talaq as a performative: it is unclear whether her husband had initially intended to divorce her, but because the mufti did not consider intention to be relevant to the felicity of the performative, it succeeded. As in Fatwa 79, though, an intention is clear: the wife wished to be divorced from her husband. As I will discuss in greater detail below, the fatwa's use of the conditional indicates that the disputants must decide which of the scenarios took place, and on that basis follow the appropriate consequence.

There is another aspect of the performative speech act that enables this woman to leverage it to her apparent advantage. Austin argued that "a performative utterance will . . . be *in a peculiar way* hollow or void if said by an actor on the stage" (1975, 22, emphasis added). The actor's speech is hollow because on the stage "language is . . . used . . . in ways *parasitic* upon its normal use" (1975, 22). When an actor on a stage utters "I do (take this woman)" the spectators know that this is merely mimicry of a marriage and that it does not *actually* marry the actors on the stage. In *How to Do Things with Words*, Austin excludes such hollow performatives from consideration, focusing instead on speech acts uttered under "normal" conditions. It could thus be concluded that for Austin, the wife's statement "I divorce you" would similarly not warrant consideration: as a purposeful imitation of the unilateral male divorce, the wife's statement is hollow, like the utterance of an actor on the stage.

Famously, Derrida (1982) responded to Austin by arguing that far from being parasitic on "normal use," mimicry was the basis for all speech acts. The reason that the statement "I divorce you," when uttered three times by a Sunni Muslim man to his wife, effects a divorce is that it follows an existing convention—in this case a convention based on a particular interpretation of Islamic legal sources. This means that anytime a Hanafi Muslim man says to his wife, "I divorce you," he is repeating or citing a previous utterance; this is what makes a speech act conventional. This is also how we can recognize when a speech act has not been felicitous: because "I divorce you" conventionally has to be uttered by a man in order to be effective, when a woman utters these words, her husband recognizes that a divorce has not taken place. But as Derrida (1982) pointed out (and as Judith Butler [1991] and others have elaborated), if all speech acts are citations and if citations always run the risk of being incorrectly executed, as we saw in the case of the utterance "I have given it," all speech acts run the risk of failure. The scenario to which Fatwa 58 responds shows that just as all speech acts run the risk of failure, so too a failed speech act may initiate a felicitous one. Through a performance that is *"parasitic* upon" talaq's "usual use," the wife instigates a scenario in which the speech act is uttered under "normal circumstances" (that is, by her husband) and is therefore felicitous. The hollow utterances that are conventionally found in theater here produce effects beyond theater's parameters (see Chambers-Letson 2013).

Another way that women can subvert male control of the performative divorce is by means of a contract that alters its felicity conditions. In Fatwa 25 a couple creates a contractual trigger for the performative utterance "I divorce you."

Fatwa 25

Istifta

What do you say, learned religious scholar, about this issue? In the presence of another person, Zayd wrote this information in a letter to his wife: if I drink alcohol, I will not maintain any relationship with you. This person understood that "no further relationship" means talaq and separation. This was very clear to both parties; this sentence was deeply understood. And it was well understood what the consequences of it would be. This person and Zayd both signed the letter. After this, Zayd left the house and when he returned, he was drunk. My request of you is that you tell me, in light of the Quran and Hadis, whether a talaq has occurred or not. Finis [*Faqat*].

Al-Jawab

About this it is necessary for the husband to keep his oath. God knows best.

The oath here has the effect of enabling the wife to set conditions for a divorce. In other words, the oath is an instrument by means of which the felicity conditions of the utterance can be redefined. Unlike in Fatwa 79, the formulation of the divorce need not be conventional. Instead, a particular act (drinking alcohol) is invested with the performative *effect* of the conventional utterance.

This examination of the performativity of the triple talaq shows how this legal speech act, which is widely recognized as privileging male authority, can in fact be strategically engaged by women.[7] It further suggests that talaq ul-ba'in is recognized as legally binding both by mustaftis and muftis, but that questions about its felicity conditions abound and therefore elicit authoritative interpretation. In other words, the performative utterance of talaq ul-ba'in sometimes becomes the first moment of the fatwa scene, since those who utter and witness this legal performative recognize that it carries with it a risk of failure and turn to the mufti for a diagnosis. In this consultation, we witness how fatwas' legal and ethical entailments meet. The legal question is whether the marriage contract has been severed. The ethical question is whether one is living an upright life. One might ask why a couple who wishes to remain married would admit to a mufti that a triple talaq had taken place. But for some practicing Sunni Muslims in Delhi, one does not only seek a fatwa that will be agreeable; indeed, part of the point of getting a fatwa is to find out if one is living as one should. As Hussein Agrama argues in his work on fatwas in Cairo, when people seek a second fatwa it is "often because they had received one in their favor, which yet somehow made them uncomfortable" (2010, 5). The diagnosis—which both identifies what has happened and simultaneously *calls that which it identifies into being*—takes the form of the fatwa. The fatwa merely continues a dialogue; it does not dictate a resolution. Unlike a judgment, a fatwa's success is not contingent on being obeyed, but on being attended to.

Divorce and the Division of Property

One element of divorce's reconfiguration of kinship, which is implied in some but not all of the fatwas presented thus far, is financial. Divorce not only renders certain otherwise licit sexual relationships illicit and raises questions about children and custody and residence arrangements; it also demands negotiations about financial responsibility. In fatwas concerning talaq ul-ba'in, such financial considerations sometimes remain implicit; however, sometimes they become the direct subject of inquiry. The fatwas on maintenance and property division discussed in this section demonstrate the implicit assumptions that marriage is the primary source of adult women's economic support and that divorce introduces uncertainty because it does not result in an immediate end to this financial and kin relationship, but rather a change in its entailments. Through financial obligations, ex-spouses remain in significant relationships with one another past the date of divorce.

Fatwa 20

Istifta

25.5.2006. What do you say learned 'ulama about the following issue: Mohammad gave his wife Parveen three talaqs but Parveen's parents are not ready to obey the talaq. Parveen is also not ready to accept this talaq. But Mohammad explained that this is much better, and Parveen is ready to live on her own, and she has asked Mohammad for a house in which to live and an allowance for herself and her children. But Mohammad's father says that his son has divorced his wife and that according to the shari'at once this act is done he has no further responsibility for his wife. In this situation, does Mohammad have to give Parveen a house and allowance or does he only have to give allowance for the children? Please give an answer in light of the Quran and Hadis. [As a seeming afterthought in the margin]: The divorce took place about fifteen days ago.

Al-Jawab

A place to live and an allowance during 'iddat is the husband's responsibility. The divorce has been completed. The relationship between the husband and wife is over.

This fatwa directs the questioner to provide a place for the ex-wife to stay and an allowance during the three-month 'iddat period following the divorce. The conversation between the father and the mufti demonstrates the mufti's role in upholding women's rights to property upon divorce. While the father is under the impression that his son no longer owes his wife anything, the mufti refutes this claim. The fatwa therefore provides moral and legal support for the son's instinct that he ought to provide his ex-wife with housing. However, the fatwa places an end date on this responsibility: it is unclear from the fatwa what the wife is expected to do, and where she is expected to live, once the 'iddat period is over.

Fatwa 38 is a question about a divorce and the subsequent division of property. The couple in question has several children, and a house that is in the wife's name. The istifta requests information about who ought to receive the house. The fatwa offers the following advice:

Al-Jawab
If three talaqs have been given, then a foul divorce has taken place. The wife is free of the marriage. It is necessary for her to observe 'iddat. The children are the father's responsibility. The two-year-old child can stay with the mother who will care for her. The father will provide for living expenses. The house is in the wife's name, but the father is now responsible for the children, so the house will be his. The wife is due her mahr and her 'iddat allowance.

Whereas Fatwa 20 backed the woman's right to at least a place to stay and an allowance, this fatwa is more complicated. The wife is entitled to living expenses for the child over whom she has custody, but she is not entitled to the house. The right to the house, even during the 'iddat period, appears to be linked to the other children's needs rather than to the deed of ownership—since the father will retain custody of the older children, he is granted the right to live in the house. According to standard interpretations of Hanafi law in Delhi, the father would also attain custody of the young daughter when she reaches puberty. The only additional entitlement the wife receives is her mahr[8] and an allowance during the 'iddat period. Once again, the fatwa implies that the husband's responsibility to his wife (but not to his children) ends at the close of the 'iddat period.

In addition to being one effect of divorce requiring consultation, property division is a significant factor in deliberations about whether a divorce should be sought at all. The following fatwas consider the consequences of divorce prior to granting it. This is a dramatically different picture of talaq ul-ba'in than in popular discussions of Muslim divorce practices because it appears here that "instant" talaq can be preceded by careful deliberation and information-gathering.

Fatwa 54

Istifta

What do you command, learned religious leader, about the following issue: I, Mohd. Aafaaq Khan was married to Shumaila Sultan on December 20, 2003 according to Muslim rites and rituals. I have one daughter who is two and a half years old. My wife and I have been fighting for a year now, and during that time my wife has been living in her natal home. If I divorce my wife, what do I have to return to her?

1. Mahr
2. The things from her dowry
3. The gold and silver that came from my wife's family and that came from my family.
4. To what is my wife entitled? [*Larki kis chiz ki haqq-da hai?*]
5. What are the rights [*huquq*] of the child after a divorce?
6. In the light of the Quran, what should I do?

Al-Jawab

    The woman (wife) is entitled to her *mahr*, her dowry, the jewelry that came from both sides of the family, and any clothing. After the divorce, it is the wife's responsibility to take care of the child for nine years. You must pay for living expenses. Afterward, you may take the girl.

Fatwa 64

Istifta

Honored mufti sahib. As-salamu 'alaikum. What do you command learned *mufti* about the following issue: Zayd was married four months ago. But the girl has not moved in with him [*rukhsati nahin hui*]. The marriage was arranged by the parents. The girl and boy had not seen one another. Now the girl is saying that she should annul her marriage [*nikah faskh kiya jaye*] because I am now an adult and I was married against my will. The issues are:

1. Should the girl be divorced (talaq) or not?
2. Please also tell me about the *mahr*.
3. The man's [husband's] parents have spent a lot of money: does his money have to be returned or not?

4. Will the girl have to give back the jewelry and other things she received from the groom's family?

Please give an answer according to the Quran.

Al-Jawab

The girl herself wants a divorce so she can get a divorce upon the return of the jewelry and the forgiving of the mahr. It is not her responsibility to return the allowance she has received from the groom's family. If she demands her mahr, you should give her half of the mahr and she will get her jewelry.

Both Fatwa 54 and Fatwa 64 clearly show that the mustafti is a man in a troubled marriage. The marriage in Fatwa 54 had lasted three years, during one of which the wife had lived in her natal home rather than with her husband. The marriage in Fatwa 64 had lasted only four months and had never been consummated, as the sentence "The girl has not moved in with me" suggests. Both fatwa requests indicate that the husbands are considering divorce, but that they are weighing the responsibilities that will devolve upon them if they do pronounce talaq. Far from assuming, like the father invoked in Fatwa 20 did, that a divorced woman can no longer make demands on her husband, these husbands list the assets that the couple received at their wedding. Fatwa 64 is a case of khul': the mufti instructed the man on how to carry this kind of divorce out extrajudicially by settling the matter of compensation before granting the divorce. Yet the fatwa includes a caveat in the case that the wife demands her mahr: if she insists, she can in fact be entitled to half of the mahr as well as all of her jewelry. The mufti appears inclined to keep open the question of property division, and not to insist that her decision to request a divorce requires her to give up her property. One implication of the ambiguity the qazi leaves about property division is that the negotiation of property following a divorce is more flexible than the question of the divorce itself, and it is expected that this negotiation will be resolved through discussions among the parties.

In each of these fatwas, the mufti supports the wife's or the ex-wife's rights to property in divorce. Yet the settlements are never explicitly discussed in monetary terms, and there is no implication that they would be sufficient to sustain the ex-wife for longer than the 'iddat period. Indeed, although property rights are supported by the mufti, they do not appear to be considered a source of substantive and ongoing subsistence. Instead, it appears that a second marriage or support in the natal home are the two expected routes for a woman to take in order to achieve postdivorce subsistence. Like the question of the validity of a particular divorce, questions about the financial repercussions of divorce are part of a dialogue with the mufti, a dialogue constitutive of law.

My suggestion to focus this analysis on the dialogical and indeterminate aspect of fatwa-based talaq jurisprudence reveals that law is constituted through both performatives and constatives.[9] In the context of fatwa scenes, law is made through a series of discrete speech acts. The performative uttered by the husband changes the world (it divorces the couple); the fatwa that subsequently evaluates the performative functions to define it, framing the changed world and its entailments in legal terms (that is, the wife is legally permitted to remarry after observing a waiting period).[10] While the performative force of the fatwa scene lies in the initial speech act uttered by a husband, the mufti's constative authorizes what has happened. As written documents, fatwas can circulate back into the disputes or uncertainties that gave rise to them, declaring and defining newly established divorces and thus the newly organized lives of the couples involved; or they can be ignored, forgotten, or refused. Fatwas remain incomplete until and unless they are taken up by those who have requested them. In this way, fatwas produce law, not in isolation, but through a process of fragmented dialogue with the mufti's interlocutors, close to the messiness of intimate life. It is this indeterminacy that I examine in the next section.

The Temporality of Dialogue

Attending to the fatwa as a diagnostic legal speech act captures how its language enables a particular type of intervention into an ongoing lived conundrum. It also implies that the fatwa has a particular temporality—belatedness—that places the mufti in a position of responsiveness to the mustafti, as his fatwa hews closely to the terms of the mustafti's question. Here, I draw out one important consequence of this belatedness: the fatwa is not a determining but rather an inherently indeterminate[11] dialogue that addresses an ongoing scene or conundrum that it does not, and cannot, complete. As Setrag Manoukian has argued, as dialogues, fatwas appear asymmetrical, given the sometimes full narrative accounts in istiftas coupled with brief fatwas given in reply (2005, 171–172). Such asymmetry is one aspect of the indeterminacy I investigate here.

In response to the question that the young woman at the beginning of the chapter submitted to the mufti's authority about whether her husband had divorced her, he wrote a fatwa that regulated kinship by deauthorizing an intimate relationship. The fatwa scene indicates the intimacy of the legal advice given in a fatwa. The mufti did not, however, initiate this regulatory scene; he was responding to the woman's request that he diagnose the relationship. This is indicative of the fatwa's temporality, demonstrating how the fatwa responded to and marked an act that had already taken place, as well as how the mufti only encountered the relationship through the lens of the istifta. The fatwa defined the dispute after the fact. At the same time, the questioner's decision to bring her conundrum to the mufti placed it within his purview, acknowledging the mufti's authority to diagnose human actions according to Islamic law. The questioner was the initiating actor, or agent, of the fatwa scene even as she submitted her question, and the status of her marriage, to the mufti's legal (and moral) expertise. Further, the dynamics of this conversation placed the mufti in a position of responsiveness rather than one in which he would have been able to initiate injunctions, even as his status as a legal authority constituted a hierarchical power relation between the two parties.

Only once did I read two separate istiftas about the same situation during my fieldwork. I reproduce these two fatwas here, as they bring the dialogic character of fatwas into relief.

Fatwa 36

Istifta

What do you command, learned mufti, in the following situation: Phul Babu gave his wife Rifat Khatun a divorce while Rifat Khatun was three months pregnant. Now Phul Babu is no longer acting as a husband, and he does not give either allowance or any of the things that Rifat Khatun was given at her wedding. According to the Quran and Hadis what is Rafaat Khatun entitled to?

Al-Jawab

In this situation, the husband said talaq. Therefore, there has been a divorce. 'Iddat will be performed once the child is born. Until that time, the husband must pay for living expenses. The wife is entitled to her *mahr* and to her dowry.

Fatwa 49

Istifta

What do you have to say, learned religious 'ulama, about the following problem? Zayd's relation[,] Phul Babu, divorced his wife Rifat Khatun when he was in a drunken state. Rifat Khatun was even three months pregnant at the time. Now, after having given the divorce, Phul Babu is ashamed of his mistake, and he is ready to build a life with his wife [*sharik-i hayat banane ke liye taiyar hai*]. So please tell us what we can do in the light of the Quran and the Hadis.

Al-Jawab

If talaq was given three times, then without observing halalah, it is not legal to remarry. If talaq was given one or two times, upon reconciling [*ruju kar ke*] he may live with his wife.

Fatwa 36 was dated 1 Jumada al-awwal, 1427 (May 29, 2006), and Fatwa 49 was dated 3/5 Jumada al-awwal, 1427 (May 30, 2006). The istifta in Fatwa 49 appears to have been written by a different person from the earlier one, both because of the way the question is framed and because of the handwriting. Whereas the handwriting in Fatwa 36 is shaky and loose, suggesting that it had been executed by someone who is not used to writing much, the penmanship in Fatwa 49 is even and refined. In terms of their content, Istifta 36 requests information about the wife's responsibility in the case of divorce. It neither challenges the divorce nor asks for reunion. The fatwa given in response affirms the divorce and draws out the consequences. Istifta 49, on the other hand, begs to know how and whether the couple can be reunited. The fatwa in this exchange is notable in part because it picks up the register of uncertainty that the istifta raises through the fact of the husband's drunkenness and transforms it into a conditional statement about felicity conditions. While drunkenness is rendered irrelevant in the fatwa, it implicitly raises the question of how the divorce was carried out, introducing possibility and uncertainty rather than delineating the outcome.

Fatwa 49, further, spells out the consequences of talaq ul-ba'in, in particular the requirement of performing halalah. Halalah is the much-contested provision of Hanafi law that if a husband and wife have been irrevocably divorced, the only way for them to remarry is if the wife marries another man, consummates that marriage, and is then divorced by him. At that point, the original couple can marry one another again. Historian Judith Tucker writes that halalah follows a "hadith narrative that held that the Prophet had said she must 'taste the sweetness of another' before she could be lawful again to her first husband" (1988, 88). Tucker has discussed some fatwas in which the mufti delineates what constitutes penetration for the purposes of consummating the intermediary marriage (2008, 88) as well as the legal debates about who the interim husband should be and whether the wife could marry him with the express intent of remarrying her first husband (2008, 88). This was an issue that was quite present in my own field work, as Mufti Ahmed explained to me that it was a punishment of both husband and wife for the husband's immoral, though legal, act of unilaterally and irrevocably divorcing his wife. Halalah was also a politically charged issue, with Shaista Amber, the founder of the All India Muslim Women's Personal Law Board, vociferously condemning the injunction to perform halalah, claiming that it was against the spirit of Islam. She also contested the efficacy of halalah, for, as she put it, no knowledgeable woman would actually go through with the practice. Together, the two fatwas suggest one way in which fatwas participate in dialogues that exceed them: each of these fatwas responds to a different aspect and consequence of divorce, one focusing on consequences of divorce and the other on the possibility of reunion.

The dialogue captured in Fatwas 36 and 49 has several important qualities: they are belated responses, and they are indeterminate. The fatwas in particular pick up and draw out the consequences of indeterminacy, rather than reach a decision. The following fatwa shares these qualities, again employing on the conditional tense to evoke indeterminacy.

Fatwa 10

Istifta

What do you command, learned mufti, about the following issue about Zayd: Zayd had drunk so much alcohol [*sharab*] that he barely made it home. In this condition, Zayd acted in an extreme way, and said many words to Hind. There were people there who told Hind's family that Zayd gave Hind a talaq. But

Zayd and other people who were there say that Zayd did not say any such things to Hind. Hind wants to know according to the shariʿa, does she have to leave Zayd or no?

Al-Jawab
If he did not give a talaq, then there has been no divorce.

The way in which the question is framed is leading—even in a genre that rarely gives clear information about who is asking the question and what they hope to accomplish with it. "Hind wishes to know" whether she has to leave her husband, suggesting that she does not wish to leave him but is concerned that she may be required to do so legally. The mufti might have responded that in fact she was de facto divorced, because by becoming drunk her husband had apostatized and thereby ended the marriage. Instead, he responded with a conditional ("If he did not give a talaq, then . . .") and ignored the fact of drunkenness. The messiness of the situation that gave rise to this request—the husband's drunkenness, which may or may not be habitual, Zayd's relationship with Hind, their implied wishes for the relationship to continue—is simultaneously beyond the boundaries of the request and central to it. Because there was so much room for the mufti to pronounce on the information implied but not directly articulated by the question, this particular fatwa makes clear how the mufti works in a register of belatedness (because his response must follow from an event that has taken place) and indeterminacy (because the specificities of his response are contingent on the question that initiated the dialogue and have effects beyond his knowledge or reach).

Fatwas share the characteristic of indeterminacy with other legal speech acts, though they differ in being indeterminate by design. Jacques Derrida (1986) gives a particularly useful account of this type of legal temporality in his analysis of the act of founding. Derrida (1986, 10) wrote that the American Declaration of Independence is emblematic of the "fabulous retroactivity" of founding: in signing the Declaration, "we the people" was both brought into being and given the right to sign. "We the people" did not exist before the signature, but instead will have come into being as an entity defined by its authorization to sign. Earlier I touched on this analysis because it shows the cohabitation of the constative and the performative; here, it is the temporality of this cohabitation that becomes relevant.

Marianne Constable (2014) draws on Derrida to argue that legal acts more broadly entail a future perfect tense. One example she gives of this legal temporality is the working of precedent in a common law system. The future perfect of a judgment lies in the fact that it "may become precedent" but only if in fact "an appropriately related case arises, at which point it *will have become* precedent" (2014, 74, emphasis in original). This example does two things. First, it illustrates the workings of retroactivity: a particular judgment is or provides precedent. Second, it clarifies the indeterminacy of legal speech. It can always be otherwise—there may be precedent for something, but if for whatever reason, political or otherwise, that precedent is not taken up, it is simply a judgment, a possibility unrealized beyond the case it decides. By virtue of being diagnostic, fatwas share this temporality: in providing an authoritative interpretation of what has transpired between disputants—for example, whether a couple did or did not divorce—the fatwa inaugurates a future in which they will (or will not) have been divorced. However, this future perfect rests on a conditional—*if* he did not give a talaq, you are not divorced—thereby invoking its own incompleteness and indeterminacy. In other words, this future prefect reveals how the fatwa's authority relies on social conditions to which it responds but extend beyond it. As with a judgment that will only have become precedent if a similar case arises after it is made, and if the social, political, and legal conditions are such that a judge takes it up, a fatwa will only have altered the state of affairs of a couple's relationship if they separate. The productivity of a legal speech act relies on a particular response in the social world.

Fatwas on talaq ul-ba'in are simultaneously authoritative—reflecting the learned opinion of a jurist—and dialogical—deferring to the terms of the question and to an uncertainty regarding how they will be taken up. With this kind of intervention, the indeterminacy of the fatwa's formulation reflects the mufti's fallibility, but also obscures the way in which there can be only one right way to respond in a given situation. Mufti Ahmed told me on numerous occasions that although he or another jurist might make a mistake in answering a certain question, this fallibility did mean that there was no right answer; so, while following any given fatwa is optional, ignoring the correct one is a sin. The fatwa recipients therefore receive, along with the fatwa, the responsibility to heed the solution that correctly applies to the situation in which they find themselves. Practically, in the Indian legal system where mahila panchayats and dar ul-qazas' decisions are not enforced by the state, parties in a dispute also assume the responsibility to follow the judgment they receive. However, in the case of mahila panchayats and dar ul-qazas this is because the state does not authorize these institutions' decisions as legally binding. In the case of fatwas, such dependence on the parties' own decision to follow the advice is inherent in the legal form. Even, that is, in a Muslim state, fatwas differ from other judgments precisely in that fatwas are *nonbinding advice* given by a legal authority, not binding judgments that must be obeyed.

Talaq ul-Ba'in and Fatwas's Secularism

Hussein Agrama has argued that fatwas in the state-run al-Azhar seminary in Cairo are asecular and that the fatwa council is an asecular space (2012, 186–187). His argument is that the practice of fatwa giving "does not partake of the problem-space of secularism, that ensemble of questions and stakes anchored by the question of where to draw the line between religion and politics, and where the limits of religion should be" (2012, 186). The fatwa council, he argues is "indifferent" to the distinction between religion and politics, whereas making that distinction is the definitive work of secularism. Agrama's evidence for this, in large part, comes out of the fatwa exchanges he observed at al-Azhar. He convincingly shows that the muftis are concerned with the pedagogical aspect of their interventions, and he demonstrates that many of the conversations focus on the emotional relationship between a disputing couple. He concludes, therefore, that fatwas are a matter of the care of the self, and of pedagogy, rather than sharing with the law courts questions about public order and reform of the family (186). It appears in Agrama's analysis that the fatwa council is where the family can be really private and really religious—subject only to ethical guidance provided according to good faith interpretations of the Islamic source texts.

I disagree with Agrama's assessment of fatwas as asecular for two primary reasons. First, to examine fatwas on divorce as untouched by secularism and by the secular regulation of the family is to accept the secular premise that divorce and reconciliation are private matters that can be separated from the state's interest in the family. Second, it is to accept that because the fatwa council does not explicitly debate questions of public order and the family, it can be neatly separated from the political work of delineating the relation between religion and law/politics.

In India, fatwas are touched by, and help to make, the secular present. This is, first, because they are a matter of public debate, as we saw in the *Madan* case, discussed in chapter 4—*Madan* insisted that fatwas require their own judgment, and that the Supreme Court must declare that they are benign. Second, the subject about which fatwas in Delhi are most frequently sought—talaq ul-ba'in—is the object of an even more vociferous debate, one that heated up again in 2016 and 2017. While the debate surrounding the *Shayara Bano* case, which I have discussed in chapter 2, focused on the legality of talaq ul-ba'in itself, those understood to enable the practice—qazis and muftis like those with whom I conducted my fieldwork—were explicitly implicated. And the critics are not all wrong: the fatwas I have analyzed here at once obey the boundaries around personal law, responding only to questions that fall within them,[12] and actively animate a jurisdiction that contradicts state courts' judgments, authorizing talaq ul-ba'in when the state courts would not.

Finally, the state, too, cares about talaq ul-ba'in, although its care is expressed in a contradictory fashion, by simultaneously vilifying, disavowing, and maintaining the practice. With several telling exceptions, judgments on talaq ul-ba'in concern themselves with the economic facets of divorce (and of staying married), which they approach by regulating and restricting the felicity conditions of talaq ul-ba'in. Because of this focus, talaq ul-ba'in judgments highlight the political economy of divorce and marriage, asking who will take responsibility for women no longer contained in and by heterosexual marriage. Judgments on talaq ul-ba'in thus formalize women's economic reliance on kin and community, in contrast to a masculinized sphere of remunerated labor. To substantiate the claim that fatwas, as key mechanisms of diagnosing and adjudicating talaq ul-ba'in, participate in practices of secularism rather than occupying a space untouched by them, I turn in the remainder of this chapter to High Court and Supreme Court jurisprudence on talaq ul-ba'in. The genealogy that follows is not exhaustive, but it points to trends in the jurisprudence and focuses on several representative and high profile cases in order to capture the key tenets and changes of talaq ul-ba'in jurisprudence.[13]

From the perspective of the state, talaq ul-ba'in appears to present a problem for precisely the same reasons that it can be useful for lay Muslims involved in amicable divorces: it is extrajudicial and instantaneous. As a mechanism for regulating marriage and divorce, talaq ul-ba'in ought inherently to be of concern to the state (Donzelot 1997; Foucault 1978; Scott

1996; Surkis 2006, 2010). Indeed, moralizing judicial rhetoric disavows the practice, describing it as spiritually bankrupt (*Parveen Akhtar* [2003]), bad for women (*Rahmat Ullah* [1994]; *Parveen Akhtar* [2003]), unjustifiable either "in the eye of religion or the law" (*Yousuf Rawther* [1971]), and a "monstrosity" (*Mohd. Haneefa* [1972]). Yet in 2013, I learned from a Delhi family court judge that when the court's efforts to reconcile a couple fail, she orders Muslim husbands to pronounce talaq ul-ba'in in court. This is not the aberrant act of a renegade judge: through an analysis of Indian High Court and Supreme Court cases on talaq ul-ba'in, I suggest that the judge's inclusion of the practice in the courtroom is in keeping with, rather than contradictory to, the courts' overarching approach of regulating the practice without banning it. Indian judgments, while accepting the legality of talaq ul-ba'in, took considerable space to lay out how abhorrent this practice was; in 2017, the Supreme Court did ban it (see chapter 2 and below). This approach makes the Indian judiciary an outlier: in Egypt, Iraq, Jordan, Kuwait, Lebanon, Morocco, North Yemen, Sudan, and Syria, unintentional talaqs have been outlawed and intentional talaqs have been rendered revocable or valid only with court authorization or registration (T. Mahmood 1995).

In spite of the Indian courts' disapproval of the practice, when talaq-ul-ba'in cases involve the problem of financial support for women they do intervene. I suggest that this is not, as it might seem, evidence that the Indian judiciary has a feminist agenda to address women's disproportionate economic insecurity, its rhetoric of aspiration for women's economic equality notwithstanding. Despite analyses that suggest that personal law is becoming more gender just, legal gains by women are inscribed in a persistent paternalistic logic (Menski 2008; Subramanian 2008, 2014; Vatuk 2001). Such paternalism is reflected in the two different approaches talaq ul-ba'in judgments take. The first ignores talaq ul-ba'in to focus on property rights in divorce, *debating how much women can claim, within what time frame, and from whom.* The second focuses on regulating and restricting talaq ul-ba'in, thereby *enforcing marriage as the site of maintenance distribution.* The approaches nonetheless have convergent effects, as both render women's financial insecurity a private matter while proliferating discourse about this ostensibly private form of divorce. By forcing husbands, families, or the Muslim community to support women who could potentially become destitute, the state keeps in place networks of dependency and paternalistic family structures, reifies a Muslim community as separate, and avoids dealing with broader questions of gender justice and women's economic opportunities. The scholarship on the jurisprudence I consider here notes that, in practice, the precedents set by divorce and alimony cases in High Courts and in the Supreme Court have not been implemented by the lower courts (Menski 2008; Sezgin 2013; Solanki 2011). This observation is key to understanding the limited effect of watershed decisions on the outcomes of maintenance disputes. However, my analysis sets out to do something different: its aim is to interrogate the consequences of the way in which marriage and divorce are related through the question of maintenance in this jurisprudence.

Narendra Subramanian has argued that the reasons for this jurisprudential trend have to do with the courts' respect for cultural autonomy and their skittishness about interpreting Islamic law. In an interview with Subramanian, for example, Judge R. C. Lahoti, who led the two-judge panel in *Shamim Ara* (2002), circumscribing the felicity conditions of talaq ul-ba'in, stated that he did not wish to arouse the ire of conservative 'ulama, which is why he avoided "invalidating all forms of unilateral repudiation even though he believed this would be desirable, because he did not find a basis for such a decree in Islamic traditions" (Subramanian 2014, 250). Another hypothesis for judges' hesitation to ban talaq ul-ba'in is that they doubt their own reasoning abilities when it comes to matters of Muslim personal law. Subramanian shows that high courts rendered talaq ul-ba'in revocable in only ten of the cases reported between 1978 and 2002. By contrast, they have decided in favor of women petitioners seeking permanent maintenance in the majority of cases brought between the 1986 passage of the Muslim Women's (Protection of Rights in Divorce) Act (MWA) and 2001, when the definitive judgment granting divorced Muslim women maintenance, *Danial Latifi*, was issued. Subramanian argues that the courts have more readily ruled in women's favor in maintenance cases because Indian judges were more comfortable reasoning independently about legislation than about "religious traditions" (2014, 249).

While the political fallout from some interventions has certainly provided arguments for treading lightly, I argue here that the failure to ban talaq ul-ba'in was a strategic ambiguity employed by the state. By not banning talaq ul-ba'in, the courts were able to uphold the fiction that the practice was undesirable for the state, thereby perpetuating opportunities for rendering women's economic status a private, family matter of maintenance. At the same time, this interpretive trend is underwritten by the assumption that talaq ul-ba'in is always undesirable for women and, concomitantly, that marriage is always better than male-initiated divorce. This assumption, which has women's best interests in mind, has the effect of limiting women's capacities to forge livelihoods beyond the confines of the heterosexual marital form. In other words, this jurisprudence assumes *both* that Muslim women are oppressed by their husbands *and* that the marital form is descriptively and normatively the only viable option for Muslim women. This appears contradictory. In this way, judgments on talaq ul-ba'in suggest that Muslim marriage is a kind of payment for kinship: Muslim men literally pay by taking on the responsibility for financially supporting their wives, and Muslim women metaphorically pay by living within the confines of marriage.

Making Religion

As the mufti's fatwas and cases like that of Nadia, my ahl-i hadis friend whose divorce I discuss in chapter 1, show talaq ul-ba'in often takes place beyond the purview of the state. Even when talaq ul-ba'in makes its way before state court judges, they have long upheld the view that it is intractable precisely because it is both pervasive and beyond the state's reach. Judgments rhetorically shore up the religious character and specificity of talaq ul-ba'in, making it appear normative to Islam but alien to non-Muslim law and sensibilities. Extensive citations of legal precedents, Quran verses, and exegesis by recognized scholars buttress most judgments. Discussions of talaq ul-ba'in exhaustively discuss the ways in which "talaq" can be pronounced; some further elaborate a general view of divorce in the Quran, the Hadith, and scholarly analyses of them; some note that it is only Hanafi jurists who accept talaq ul-ba'in. These narratives, which are contained in the judgments, are based on legal scholarship and case law. They perform and produce divorce as a complex but also central problem in Islamic scripture, scholarship, and law. Indeed it appears to be *the* intrinsically preoccupying issue of family morality and law for Muslims. It also appears to be a problem for Islamic jurists but not for state courts, even as the state courts present and refract arguments about the Islamic legal basis for moral entailments of Muslim divorce.

Judgments in the Indian judicial system imply that talaq ul-ba'in is peculiar to Islam but pervasive among Muslims. The judgments' rhetoric thereby bolsters the view that marital relationships and their dissolution are religiously significant and that as such they are beyond the reach of secular law. The Supreme Court case *Parveen Akhtar v. Union of India*, for example, states that "talaq-ul-biddat [*sic*] is the most prevalent form of divorce among Muslims in India" (paragraph 7). In *Parveen Akhtar* this claim is part of the larger argument that this form of divorce is "the single most potent cause of [Muslim women's] devastation" both because it is "instantaneous" and because it is so commonly used.[14] In a frequently cited paragraph from the Supreme Court case *Zohara Khatoon v. Mohd. Ibrahim* (1981), the court writes both that unilateral declaration of divorce is the "commonest form" of divorce in "Mohammedan law" and that this is a way of divorcing that is "peculiar to Mohammedan law" (paragraph 19).

In characterizing talaq ul-ba'in as a religious matter at once too pervasive and too distant to be contradicted, state court judgments on the validity of talaq ul-ba'in disavow the state's interest in it. Of course, this disinterest is formal at best. By upholding the legality of talaq ul-ba'in, the state can and has used it as a mechanism for indirectly regulating the family. Its ostensible disinterest in talaq ul-ba'in is even more perplexing given the Court's demonstrable concern with the financial effects of divorce. In what follows, I examine the two dominant approaches the courts have taken to cases involving talaq ul-ba'in, showing that although one ignores talaq ul-ba'in and the other directly addresses it, they converge in their treatment of kin and community as the appropriate sites of financial distribution to women. I suggest, through these analyses, that, contrary to appearances, upholding talaq ul-ba'in is a mechanism for producing Muslim personal law as exceptional and for making women's economic well-being the concern of family and religious communities rather than of the state. In other words, these judgments make explicit the economics of privatizing families and marking them as religious.

Divorce and Destitution

One significant approach to talaq ul-ba'in in the courts has been to focus on the property at stake in divorce. The most famous example of this is *Shah Bano* (1985), which I read here as made up of three parts: the case, the MWA, and the 2001 *Latifi* case. Thus, although *Shah Bano* the case is long over, it continues to impact the way the courts understand the economics of marriage. *Shah Bano* was premised on an understanding of talaq ul-ba'in as a practice beyond the state's reach. Shah Bano was divorced by her husband by talaq ul-ba'in, but from the outset, the court took the talaq ul-ba'in for granted, stating, "Undoubtedly, the Muslim husband enjoys the privilege of being able to discard his wife whenever he chooses to do so, for reasons good, bad, or indifferent. Indeed for no reason at all" (paragraph 3). Instead, the court considered the question of maintenance, concluding that a divorced woman who was unable to maintain herself was entitled to sue for maintenance under the Criminal Procedure Code, article 125. The court upheld Shah Bano's award of maintenance and suggested that she might wish to petition for a higher amount.

In making this judgment, the court articulated links between Muslim divorce and the economies of marriage that continue to shape the parameters of cases of divorced Muslim women's right to maintenance. The court ruled that maintenance was not a personal law issue, to be adjudicated according to Muslim law, but instead a criminal matter. This rendered the failure to provide maintenance an offense not just to wives but to the state. The court thus made maintenance public. At the same time, drawing on Islamic sources, the court relegated the responsibility for destitute Muslim women to the sphere of family and religious community, domesticating the economic fallout of divorce. One potential outcome of this ruling was that destitute Muslim women would require public support.

The MWA of 1986, which has been read as undoing the decision in *Shah Bano*, consolidated the case's findings, specifying that a divorced Muslim woman was entitled to "a reasonable and fair provision and maintenance [to] be made and paid to her within the *iddat* period by her former husband" (MWA 3.1.a). This money was to support her and any children for whom she was responsible. She was also entitled to her mahr and any property she had been given before, during, or after the marriage. The MWA addressed the question of responsibility for divorcées directly: if a divorcée was unable to support herself after the 'iddat period was over, a magistrate could require her relatives, or, failing them, the state waqf board—the body that administers Muslim religious endowments—to support her. That is, the bill clarified that it is first a divorcée's former husband, then her relatives, and then her religious community who bear responsibility for preventing her destitution.

Shah Bano did not end with the MWA. In 2001 the Supreme Court decided for the plaintiff in *Danial Latifi v. Union of India*. *Latifi* was initiated by Shah Bano's lawyer, Danial Latifi, with the express aim of clarifying the MWA and of testing its constitutionality. The Court augmented the award that was due to divorced Muslim women, clarifying that a Muslim husband is required to pay a "reasonable and fair provision for the future" and that the payment must be made within the 'iddat period. If, however, a woman is unable to maintain herself following the 'iddat period, she may sue her relatives and thereafter the state waqf board for maintenance.

Latifi therefore had several effects: it confirmed that divorced Muslim women had a right to maintenance, and it made Muslim husbands and ex-husbands the ideal source of support. While the clarification that Muslim women are entitled to maintenance is important, it comes with the explicit claim that the conjugal couple ought to be the locus of financial support for women. In cases such as Shah Bano's there are good reasons for this—her destitution contrasted sharply with her lawyer husband's sizable income. But whereas the judgment (rightly) bemoans the second-class position of Indian women, noting that they often give up professional aspirations when they marry, it does not adequately take the second-class position of Indian Muslims into consideration (see Sachar Committee Report [Government of India (2006) 2013]). The disproportionate poverty of Muslims in India renders the state's righteous insistence on Muslim men's responsibility to provide alimony an inadequate solution.

The problems of maintenance highlighted by *Shah Bano* and its aftermath are not specific to Muslims. The fact that maintenance is the primary form of property that a divorcée can claim, and that it is usually inadequate to support her, is a thorn in the side of Hindus and Muslims alike. Basu cites a study that found that only 47.4 percent of separated, deserted, or divorced women applied for maintenance and that 42 percent of divorced women had no income to speak of (2015, 143–144). Were it possible, Basu saliently argues, a transfer of property or a larger transfer of funds would be far more advantageous to women. As it is, Muslim and Hindu divorcées alike have to deal with chasing down maintenance payments month after month, often from ex-husbands who themselves lack resources.

In addition to the similarities in practice, the purpose of maintenance in Indian law governing Hindus is the same as in Muslim law cases. With regard to Hindus, the aim of maintenance is to prevent vagrancy and "to compel men to perform the moral obligation that [they] owe to society with respect to his wife and children" (*Bhagwan Datta v. Kamala Devi*, quoted in Agnes 2011, 1:118). As Agnes puts it, the point of maintenance is to require economically better-off members of a family to care for those who are worse off. In so doing it relies on and reinscribes paternalism; successful maintenance claims rest on a woman's ability to prove her sexual morality and her perfor-mance of conjugal duties (Agnes 2011, 1:122; Basu 2015, 143). The talaq cases discussed here, therefore, demonstrate the dual dynamic whereby economic relations in marriage and divorce are governed by state law and courts in such a way as to privatize responsibility for provision. Marriage and its economy are simultaneously privatized and made susceptible to public oversight.

Enforcing Marriage

While *Shah Bano* and *Latifi* confronted the court with questions about main-tenance rather than divorce, subsequent judgments have dealt directly with the legality of talaq ul-ba'in. In spite of their focus on the method of divorce itself, these judgments have been centrally concerned with divorce's outcomes and in particular with financial support for divorcées, a concern that results in reinforcing the distributive function of marriage. The outcomes of such cases have been inconsistent, although the courts have frequently struck down the validity of individual instances of talaq ul-ba'in, thereby asserting sover-eign control over this extrajudicial act by enforcing marriage.

The landmark Supreme Court judgment on talaq ul-ba'in, *Shamim Ara v. State of U.P. and Another* (2002), significantly restricted the practice while retaining its legality under certain circumstances. *Shamim Ara*, like *Shah Bano*, began in 1979 as a suit for maintenance. During the case, the plain-tiff's husband claimed to have divorced his spouse and therefore to be ab-solved of responsibility for providing maintenance. Because the maintenance claim had been contingent throughout on the validity of the divorce, the ques-tion before the Supreme Court on appeal was under what conditions talaq ul-ba'in was legally binding. So although the ruling was issued in 2002, the year after *Danial Latifi* clarified that Muslim divorcées were entitled to main-tenance, the Court ruled that the plaintiff was entitled to maintenance because the husband's 1987 pronunciation of divorce had not been adequately proven. The judgment is considered a landmark on two fronts: while it stops short of banning talaq ul-ba'in, it delineates the conditions that must be met for a given utterance of talaq ul-ba'in to be legally valid; additionally, the judgment was binding on lower courts. Drawing on Gauhati High Court judgments,[15] Judge Lahoti specifies that talaq must be for a reasonable cause and must be preceded by attempts at reconciliation (paragraph 15). Beyond arguing that talaq ul-ba'in must not have been provoked by an ongoing court case, the judgment does not elaborate on "reasonable cause," leaving its definition to judicial discretion.

Shamim Ara restricts talaq ul-ba'in's felicity conditions more extensively than had previous cases, ruling that divorce must be proven and not simply reported to the court. It further rules that "the talaq, to be effective has to be pronounced" (paragraph 18). In other words, it requires that the divorce be given orally rather than in writing. These logocentric regulations make talaq ul-ba'in ever more difficult to prove in court.[16] Proving that a divorce was pronounced is more difficult than producing either a divorce document (*talaq-namah*) or an affidavit attesting to a divorce having been given. Ever more documentation and witness statements are required to demonstrate that a divorce has taken place. More broadly, *Shamim Ara* does not interfere with the legality of a properly pronounced extrajudicial divorce. The judgment goes so far as to suggest that the court *cannot* ban the practice. Instead, it upholds this form of divorce and insists that it and its financial consequences be regulated by the state. In a telling addendum, the decision in *Parveen Akhtar*, which was issued later in 2002, found that although all of the restrictions enumerated in *Shamim Ara*, among other cases, hold specifically that divorce must be preceded by attempts at reconciliation, the section of the Shariat Application Act that upholds talaq ul-ba'in cannot be declared unconstitutional because it is part of personal law. In other words, in spite of the restrictions placed so thoroughly on the institution, banning it remained out of the realm of possibility.

Shamim Ara has been precedent setting in unexpected ways, providing the grounds for women to claim maintenance because they are married. This is because even in cases where the courts could have cited *Latifi* and granted maintenance following divorce, they instead disqualify particular instances of divorce as a route to maintenance. For example, the case *Shabnam Bano v. Mohd. Rafiq* began as a claim for maintenance under CrPC 125 and culminated as a divorce case. Following the maintenance claim, Bano's husband claimed to have divorced her, ostensibly invalidating her right to claim maintenance under CrPC 125. The Supreme Court ultimately reminded the courts of *Shamim Ara* and invalidated the divorce, arguing that "since the petitioner has not been divorced," she may claim maintenance under CrPC 125. In *Iqbal Bano v. State of U.P.* (2007), the Court brought *Shamim Ara* and *Latifi* together to send the case back to the High Court. The case began with a maintenance claim after the couple in question was no longer together. The husband claimed to have divorced his wife, and contested her right to claim maintenance under CrPC 125 because the 'iddat period had passed. The Supreme Court responded with a synopsis of the jurisprudence on talaq ul-ba'in, stating both that the divorce had not been proven according to the standards set by *Shamim Ara* and that as per *Latifi*, Muslim women are entitled to permanent maintenance beyond the 'iddat period.

The Jammu and Kashmir High Court ruling in *Mariyam Akhtar & Anr. v. Wazir Mohammed* (2014) is representative of this jurisprudential trend to uphold marriage in order to grant maintenance. In *Mariyam Akhtar* a Muslim woman was awarded maintenance from her husband on the grounds that he had not divorced her properly. The judgment notes that popular views of Muslim divorce in India have progressed from thinking of it as a mere whim and caprice to thinking of it as a modern legal act, where the distinction between a whim and modern legality is the distinction between the apparently unregulated authority of the husband and regulation by the state courts. The judgment therefore triumphantly articulates a shift from marriage and divorce as matters of private contract to matters of public and state concern. *Mariyam Akhtar* specifies that with the move to modern legality, marriage becomes predictable as a source of financial well-being, stating, "When women have the right to marry, they also have the right to be maintained by their husbands." This public form of marriage carries with it the right to maintenance. The unarticulated corollary of the statement turns out to hold in other such cases: unregulated divorce does not entail a right to maintenance, judicial precedents and legislation to the contrary notwithstanding.

Together, the courts' judgments awarding maintenance on the basis of marriage[17] suggests that the courts' disavowal of talaq ul-ba'in has the unexpected effect of shoring up the privacy of marriage and the male breadwinner ideal.[18] These judgments uphold maintenance claims by enforcing marriage. There is no evidence that the plaintiffs in these cases wished to remain married. But they did wish to receive maintenance. Further, marriage is upheld as the primary institution through which women's financial security is and ought to be distributed—matrimony, it seems, remains the true winner.

In its recognized distributive function, the family is a site of discomfort, even shame, for the Indian judiciary. In *Latifi* the Court suggests that this is in fact a source of dismay. A paragraph buried in the center of the judgment states: "In our society, whether they belong to the majority or the minority group, what is apparent is that there exists a great disparity in the matter of economic resourcefulness between a man and a woman. Our society is male dominated both economically and socially and women are assigned, invariably, a dependent role, irrespective of the class of society to which they belong." The judgment goes on to argue that, in marriage, women of all socioeconomic statuses tend to give up their "avocations," leaving them without resources in the case of divorce. The judges cannot, they state, further address this regrettable social fact, because it is not rightly a matter of religious regulations, which are the subjects at hand. This paragraph articulates at once a critique of the sequestering power of marriage and a desire for a social landscape in which women would be able to support themselves without running from pillar to post seeking charity.

The judgment illustrates the view that because of religious sensitivities, it is necessary to take a circumspect route to the ultimate goal of gender equality. It is therefore perhaps unsurprising that the ways in which the judiciary, among other state and nonstate institutions, makes and reinforces the family as distributive go relatively unremarked; instead, the general idea is that it is legal restraint and realism, recognition of the limits imposed by "culture" on the ground, that keep the judiciary from dismantling the family as relay. Unlike in Donzelot's France (1997), contemporary Indian families' autonomy as an institution of distribution is more strenuously enforced the poorer and more prone to destitution women are. Intensified regulation of talaq ul-ba'in is justified by ostensibly helping women to escape from the brutality of a misogynist divorce mechanism; ironically, the form that this regulation takes reinforces men's accountability for their destitute wives and thereby the privacy of the family. That is, these judgments are a mechanism for perpetuating the distributive quality of the family.[19] This is the irony of *Latifi*'s concern for women: it is embedded in a larger judgment whose effect is to domesticate the potentially disruptive power of divorce by reinscribing the male breadwinner ideal—the view that husbands are responsible for their families—into it.

Constitutional Challenges and Communal Agendas

This chapter has examined the jurisprudence of talaq ul-ba'in in fatwas and in court judgments. Rather than providing a straightforward comparison of the two forums, it has examined the different legal registers in which they address talaq ul-ba'in. Each forum exhibits a different conception of the relationship between divorce and marriage, and their approaches to talaq ul-ba'in are contradictory. Yet, as I suggest here, their collective jurisprudence of talaq ul-ba'in provides insight into the dynamics of secularism as an effect of legal practices.

The jurisprudence of talaq ul-ba'in, as the ensemble of legal registers in which it is addressed, provides a vivid sense of the practices that constitute legal pluralism and its relevance for Delhi Muslims. The mufti's fatwas are simultaneous with court judgments even as the many distinctions—formal, methodological, procedural—between the two forums seem to suggest that they occupy separate, parallel spheres. Fatwas, I have argued, are specific responses to specific questions; they are made partly by the questioners who define their terms. In part because of this, fatwas do not reflect larger judicial agendas, and the responses to particular questions are remarkably consistent. Fatwas, as such belated responses, are not tasked with fact finding but with providing advice conditional on the question.

Court judgments, by contrast, reflect larger judicial and political contexts and agendas, and do not always respond directly to the question at hand. Thus, through examining the cases analyzed here it is apparent that divorce cases are often decided with reference to maintenance, and maintenance complaints end up being decided by means of pronouncements about divorce. These cases, furthermore, often reflect the political contexts in which they are written and judges' attitudes toward the Muslim minority.

The state court judgments fracture divorce as an object, such that it has a kinship component and a distributive, or economic, component. This fracture is an effect both of the judgments issued in court and of the relationship between the courts and the mufti's fatwas. In response to the PIL initiated by *Madan* cited in the previous chapter, the Supreme Court also addressed the matter of fatwas. In much the same way that it advocated tolerance toward dar ul-qazas as merely ADR forums, the Court argued that fatwas are irrelevant to the state because they are merely nonbinding opinions. By ignoring, or even implicitly authorizing, fatwas on talaq ul-ba'in in spite of the fact that the muftis' opinions on what constitutes such a divorce diverge sharply from the prevailing view in the courts, the Supreme Court effectively argues that such divorces are a matter of indifference to it. This indifference, I argue, has two effects. First, it keeps fatwas on talaq ul-ba'in, as well as talaq ul-ba'in itself, available, ensuring further incitements to rule on and regulate the practice. Second, it suggests that inasmuch as divorce is *just* a matter of kin relations, it is a private, religious matter in which the state has no interest.

Constitutional challenges to talaq ul-ba'in help to substantiate this latter point. Two constitutional challenges—the 1994 Tilhari judgment in *Rahmat Ulla and Khatoon Nisa v. State of U.P. and Others*, and the 2017 Supreme Court decision in *Shayara Bano*—share key features. Above all, both cases are efforts to challenge talaq ul-ba'in irrespective of financial facets of divorce in political moments characterized by deep and pervasive communalism. Justice Hari Nath Tilhari's opinion in *Rahmat Ulla and Khatoon Nisa v. State of U.P. and Others* decided against a couple, both of whom told the court they were long divorced. The case concerned whether their land should be treated as a single piece of family-held property, as would be necessary if they were married, or as two separate parcels, as would be correct if they were divorced. Together, the two parcels of land were larger than what one family is allowed to hold under the Land Ceilings Act, so when the court refused to recognize the divorce, the result was state confiscation of a portion of the land. The judgment did not have to be controversial, but the judge, who was Hindu, used a heavy-handed, patronizing tone to condemn much of Muslim personal law, especially Muslim divorce (see also Agnes 2011, 1:160–164). His judgment nullified the divorce and forcefully denounced talaq ul-ba'in more broadly.

Several scholars have noted the communal quality of the judgment, which was issued two years after the destruction of the Babri Masjid in Ayodhya, which Hindus claimed as the birthplace of the lord Ram or *Ram Janambhumi* (Agnes 1999; Kapur and Crossman 1996). The style of the judgment implies that its aim was simply to undermine Muslim law as part of a broader project of undermining Muslims more generally. There seems to be little legal reason for banning talaq ul-ba'in in the context of this case other than the fact that doing so provides an opportunity to berate Muslim law in a way that involves well-off Muslims who could be publically depicted as greedy. The judgment's transparent communalism has in any case undermined its effectiveness, as is evident in the fact that it is rarely cited and was not effective in banning talaq ul-ba'in. It had the opposite effect of pushing extrajudicial divorce off limits.

In 2016, in another moment of intense and increasing communalism, talaq ul-ba'in once again became the judicial and public issue of the moment. In the fall of 2016, the Supreme Court began hearing constitutional challenges to various aspects of Muslim personal law as part of the judicially initiated public interest litigation titled *Muslim Women's Quest for Equality*. The first challenge to talaq ul-ba'in to be heard was *Shayara Bano*. As I have noted in chapter 2, the complexities of current communal politics are emblematized by the confluence of Shayara Bano's and the BJP-led government's views—both were invested in ending talaq ul-ba'in in the interest of justice for Muslim women. Shayara Bano made her petition as a battered former wife who nonetheless did not wish to be divorced, whereas the BJP acted in the interest of winning political points while implying that gender inequality is a Muslim problem. In May 2017 the Court reserved judgment in *Shayara Bano*, striking a deal with the AIMPLB that seemed to renegotiate the place of muftis and qazis in relation to the legal system. The Court and the AIMPLB decided that the latter would instruct qazis to offer wives the choice of refusing to grant their husband the right to talaq ul-ba'in.

This agreement had several effects. First, it elevated the AIMPLB to the status of primary community representative, authorizing it as the voice of "the Muslim community." Second, it sidestepped the question of whether to ban talaq ul-ba'in, an ongoing rather than a pathbreaking approach. Third, it formally acknowledged the place of qazis and muftis in the legal system, not as indifferent to it (as in *Madan*) but as collaborators with it. This agreement thereby distanced the courts from talaq ul-ba'in, once again articulating their disavowal of the practice while leaving it in the hands of religious leaders and couples planning to marry. The agreement also treated divorce as a matter of religion and kinship toward which it was largely indifferent.

The agreement was just an interim step, though. The Supreme Court banned talaq ul-ba'in, and then the MWMB criminalized it in 2017. As the analysis in this chapter shows, such a ban will in certain ways make little difference, at least in terms of the courts. The courts rarely uphold particular cases of talaq ul-ba'in and had restricted it even prior to this judgment to such an extent that in state courts it is nearly impossible to prove. The ban does shift the courts' relationships to qazis and muftis, though, and it is an open question whether Mufti Ahmed and his colleagues will begin to issue different opinions on talaq ul-ba'in. It is also yet to be seen whether this decision will entail any enforcement of the change—for a long time, muftis' fatwas have contravened the courts' narrow parameters and upheld talaq ul-ba'in more extensively than they have. Given the restrictions in place already, and the fact that only Muslim men can still initiate divorce extrajudicially, now by means of pronouncing talaq over a period of three months rather than in one go, the ban is a red herring. Furthermore, as I discussed in chapter 2, by criminalizing Muslim men, the MWMB that followed *Shayara Bano* will likely further undermine the ban.

The questions about gender inequality and differential access to resources that divorce raises have little to do with the distinction between talaq ul-ba'in—which is carried out in one sitting—and talaq-i sunnat—properly carried out over three months. This dimension of divorce is what makes it potentially so disruptive, threatening as it does to undo the sequestering capacity of marriage and to enliven demands on the state, demands that are especially notable when made by members of the large and disenfranchised Muslim minority. The judgments examined here paradoxically militate against such disruption precisely by restricting talaq ul-ba'in and thereby upholding marriage's economy of care as the response to the threat of destitution. It is, thus, time to ban talaq ul-ba'in, as a wide range of very strange bedfellows have said in response to the judgment from the Supreme Court. But it is equally important not to let the ban enable blindness to the reality that the issues of destitution and a failure to imagine lives for women beyond matrimony are at least as urgent as talaq ul-ba'in—although they make for less glamorous newspaper headlines and call for deeper labor on the part of state and nonstate actors.

Conclusion: Talaq ul-Ba'in and the Practice of Secular Governance

The main argument in this book is that religious law is not a domain that emerges by muddling two distinct categories, "religion" and "law," but rather that it constitutes them. This quintessentially secular labor, I have claimed, is not conceptual but practical. The distinction between religion and law is produced in and by everyday religious legal practices in several legal forums and registers. Talaq ul-ba'in is exemplary of this process. To the extent that the state is indifferent to talaq ul-ba'in and to fatwas about it, it is because both are rendered religious rather than legal practices. That is, fatwas are approached as matters of religious practice and belief (and perhaps also ethics) and are dismissed as legal instruments. To the extent that talaq ul-ba'in matters to the courts, it is not a religious matter of kin relations but a legal matter of financial entitlement. This suggests, further, that the "legal"—that which is considered relevant to oversight by state law—is strongly linked to the economics of kinship.

Beyond exposing this key role that divorce plays in the labor of differentiating a private from a public sphere, and with it a religious from a legal one, I am also arguing that this conception of fatwas, in the scholarship as in the courts, is misguided, with important consequences. By emphasizing that fatwas are religious *legal* opinions, in this case on a matter about which the state cares, albeit selectively, I suggest that they represent not a realm outside of secularism but a site of secular labor and secular contradiction. Taking fatwas seriously in this way allows them to challenge prevailing state-centric views of secularism itself, in and beyond India. Fatwa writing is a religious legal practice that is at once read as merely advisory and solely religious and therefore a matter of indifference both to the state and to secularism. Yet it is an ongoing practice of contestation. Binding or not, muftis' opinions continually contest the state jurisprudence on talaq ul-ba'in and raise the question of where authority over divorce really lies.

At the outset of the chapter, I suggested that fatwas and state court judgments exhibited different conceptions of the relation between marriage and divorce. In fatwas, divorce appears to be a problem for kin relations that requires further negotiation—about custody, mahr, maintenance, and residence. Divorce terminates the marriage contract and instantiates new kin, residence, and financial relations. In courts, divorce appears to matter inasmuch as it is a financial problem for the state, which must give and enforce maintenance orders, and, even more worryingly, must deal with destitute women. Marriage solves this problem for the courts. Yet fatwas and judgments regulate talaq ul-ba'in together and in opposition to one another. Fatwas permit divorce when courts rarely do; courts debate maintenance, whereas fatwas have a standard way of addressing it—neither approach grants women sufficient support, and neither imagines a possible life for them beyond matrimony.

One consequence of this relationship is that it demonstrates law's indeterminacy. Fatwas are indeterminate in form because they do not, as constative speech acts, determine the outcome of a question or the dispute of which it is a part. Judgments are indeterminate in content, because they regularly respond to the practice of talaq ul-ba'in but without a final determination on its legality. This particular indeterminacy holds open the place from which fatwas regulate talaq ul-ba'in. In this way, indeterminacy is itself a multifaceted aspect of law, one central to practices of secularism in this legally plural context.

Chapter 6

THE HEALING JURIST

One morning in the summer of 2013, as I sat interviewing Mufti Ahmed in the rooftop room overlooking the Fatehpuri Mosque in Old Delhi that serves as his home office, a family entered. The family—a grandfather, mother, and two children, aged two and five—had first gone to the mufti's room in the mosque, but his son had sent them, unusually, to the mufti's home office. The grandfather told Mufti Ahmed that they had come to see him because the two-year-old had gone to the family's ancestral village and since returning was no longer the same. He would not eat, and he had become very weak. We had been drinking Limca, a lemon soda, and eating biscuits when the family arrived, and Mufti Ahmed offered them some refreshments. The child sipped a bit of soda and nibbled on a biscuit without enthusiasm. When Mufti Ahmed drank from his own glass of Limca, the child's grandfather asked the mufti to pour some of that Limca into the child's glass and tried to get him to drink.

The child's grandfather told Mufti Ahmed that this was a case of *nazar*: that some evil eye had fallen on the child. Mufti Ahmed took a small piece of paper out of his pocket and wrote down the child's name and mother's name on it. He had previously prepared the paper in bulk, writing down a *naqsh*—a number grid whose rows, columns, and diagonals all added up to one of the ninety-nine names of God—on a piece of plain white paper. This particular naqsh is one he gives to remove the effects of the evil eye (*nazar*) from a household and its members. He had recently taken to writing out naqsh and then asking me to cut them apart, stacking them in piles for him to distribute. He folded the paper—the *ta'wiz*—into a small square and gave it to the child's grandfather.

"Wrap this in plastic, tie it with a red string, and have the child wear it around his neck," he advised. "And after you leave, go to the store in the alley outside the mosque and buy a bag of red chilies. Take them to my son, who is sitting in my room in the mosque, and ask him to bless them. When you return home, take a chili and circle it thrice around the boy's head. Repeat this with two more chilies, then burn them in a flame."

The grandfather thanked him, half stood up, and turned back to the mufti, asking him to bless the bottle of water he had carried in with him and the biscuits Mufti Ahmed had given them. Having done so, Mufti Ahmed asked each of the four family members to kneel in front of him so that he could pray for them (*du'a karna*). He placed his hand on their heads, murmured a prayer, and then blew on them three times (*dam karna*). When it was his turn, the grandfather requested that the mufti offer a special prayer to heal his sore foot.

Although this meeting was unusual because it took place in the quiet of the mufti's home office, the request made and remedies offered were variations on the thousands of such exchanges I had observed in the mufti's room at the mosque during my previous fieldwork. The mufti typically met with between fifty and seventy-five people a day during his "public hours," which he held from two p.m. until around five p.m. each afternoon other than Friday. The mufti would often speak with people continuously save for the interruption when he excused himself to perform his ablutions in the small room adjacent to the office and walked to the sanctuary for the late afternoon (*'asr*) or evening (*maghrib*) prayer, depending on the time of year.[1] Each afternoon was dedicated to a particular kind of problem: on Saturdays and Tuesdays the mufti remedied "bad relations" and dislikes or aversions (*nafraten*), while Sundays, Mondays, and Wednesdays he offered cures for love (*muhabbat*), work problems, and physical ailments.

The mufti's office was orderly, and frequent visitors knew and enforced its protocols. Men sat on one side of the mufti and women on the other. When couples came together to consult with him, they often sat at the boundary between the men's side and the women's side, which enabled them to approach the mufti together without undermining the separation between men and women that the mufti gently enforced. There were occasions when people would come to see the mufti and would sit on the wrong side of the room, much as I did on my first visits. When that happened, the mufti would kindly, and with humor, inform the person that he or she ought to move to a seat on the other side. There were also times when the mufti did not bother to enforce gender segregation—sometimes others would do so for him; occasionally the gender division was simply incomplete.

The mufti's disposition of care and patience created the conditions for his therapeutic practice just as it enabled him in his role as a fatwa writer. He attended to most of his petitioners with patience: when regular petitioners approached him, Mufti Ahmed always inquired about their families, often interrupting the petitioners' initial description of their problem with a question about their children or spouse or parents. As in his fatwa practice, in the mufti's therapeutic practice the tone of the interaction was as significant as its content. Although it was extremely rare that the mufti spoke to someone when there was no one else in the room, he created a semiprivate space through his body language. As each person approached him the mufti would turn his head toward him or her. Petitioners would often speak in such low tones that their words were inaudible for all but those sitting just next to them. This attention to privacy meant that it took some time for me to figure out how best to situate myself in the room. Initially, I sat among the petitioners, near the front of the group, and explained to people as they approached the mufti that I was a researcher, and not waiting in line to see him. As time went on, Mufti Ahmed invited me to sit next to him, on the women's side, so that my left side was toward the group of women and my right toward the mufti. In that position, I was better able to hear his conversations with his petitioners and also to speak with them and with him. This new position facilitated conversation with people who had come to see the mufti, many of whom were as curious about my presence at the mosque as I was about theirs. Many women found it amusing that I sat with the mufti day after day, and those who came repeatedly asked more questions with each encounter.

In a formal interview I conducted with Mufti Ahmed during my follow-up research in 2013, he gave an overview of the problems that people brought to him. According to him, among the primary reasons that people approach him were physical ailments, including fainting spells (*be-hosh ho jana*), paroxysms (*daure parne*) caused by jinns (genie) or mental problems (*dimagh men* defect *hota hai*), disturbances caused by jinns (*jinnon ka asr hona*) or by the jinns' aggressiveness (*jadhana hota hai*); and either being anxious (*dil ghabrana*) or unable to sleep (*nind nahin ana*). They also come for their children's health (*sehat*) or because of physical illness (*bimari*). Trouble in human relationships also brings people to the mufti: some people sought better "husband-wife relations" (a phrase Mufti Ahmed gave in English) or because of domestic arguments (*jhagre*), including arguments with neighbors, in-laws, spouses, or children. Finally, people came if their work was not going well (*karobar nahin chal raha*).

The most common remedy that Mufti Ahmed offered was to write a ta'wiz or to personalize one that he had prepared earlier, as in the case of the family I have just described. Mufti Ahmed also used other ritual objects as demanded by the problem at hand, including bones, clothes, and photographs, which I will discuss later. He offered an intercessory prayer (du'a) for each person who came to his office. But the common feature of the remedies Mufti Ahmed offered was that they worked, in speech or in writing, with Quran *ayats* (verses) that he selected to respond to a particular problem: it was the power of these holy words that effected change.

In this chapter, I analyze the work of language through which Mufti Ahmed's healing practice is carried out. I argue that it addresses difficult relationships, physical illness, and everyday troubles with work, joblessness, and "tension" by means of material and embodied speech acts. These speech acts—which take the form of metaphors—produce the relations (*ta'alluqat*) through which God's power travels. Holy words work through the body of the mufti, his enunciations and his breath, and on the bodies of people experiencing trouble as they are ingested through breath, food, drink, or bodily contact.

Unlike the other approaches to adjudication analyzed in this book, including Mufti Ahmed's fatwas, this practice does not provoke debate in legal circles because it appears to be irrelevant from the perspective of law and law-like adjudication. Indeed, from the perspective of the courts, to be concerned with the mufti's healing practice would be to make a category mistake, to meddle with religious (or magical) rather than secular matters. The mufti likewise differentiates between his legal work of fatwa writing and this "charity" work of spiritual healing. One of my arguments here is that the conception—shared by the mufti, his supporters, and his critics—that the connections between bodies, holy words, and divine beings on which healing relies are *religious* in character is itself a secular conceit. The debate about the practice, which many Muslims argue is not religious but superstitious, captures the secular work of co-constituting religion and secularism.

My fieldwork with Mufti Ahmed shows that his healing practice is a way of adjudicating relationship related and other problems through a set of speech acts that differ from those in the other institutions in part because they address not only humans but also jinns, the evil eye, and other nonhuman beings. What this practice, which relies on views of language and its power anathema to secularism, shows is that the process of differentiating religious from legal domains requires defining both. This process of definition produces an excess. In the sphere of marital strife, that excess takes the form of spiritual healing's powerful speech.

There are structural similarities between the mufti's two activities of fatwa writing and healing, the latter of which is also an act of writing in ta'wiz as well as the other remedies the mufti offers. In both situations, the mufti is in a responsive position: he does not initiate or frame the requests or problems but is instead asked to respond. He is called on as authoritative, but his is a belated or responsive authority. Relatedly, in his healing practice, as in his fatwa writing, the mufti offers immediate answers made possible because he draws on an established repertoire both of questions and of responses. In both of these roles, furthermore, the mufti is caught between God and the petitioners, inhabiting two different asymmetrical relationships from and in which he speaks. He is involved in an asymmetrical relationship with the petitioners who approach him in his authoritative capacity as a jurist or as a healer; his ability to respond to these requests is predicated on his involvement in another asymmetrical relationship, with God. As a healer, the mufti is able to transmit the power of the Quran because he inhabits its language. Both as a fatwa writer and as a healer, the mufti participates in circulating knowledge and words whose aim and capacity is to provide guidance and to impact people's everyday lives and problems.

Yet in spite of the structural similarities between the fatwa practice and the healing practice, these are critically distinct. One significant difference between the two practices concerns reception—fatwas are much more broadly accepted as a Muslim form of intervention than healing, which is considered by many to be superstitious. But the more profound difference in the practices is apparent in the ways that language works in each. In fatwas, as we have seen, language is composed of circulating speech acts, both performative and constative. These speech acts and their circulation demonstrate both the importance of speech acts and the limits of the linguistic aspect of the performative. There are excesses—of the body and gender in particular—that cannot be incorporated into the linguistic speech act. In the context of the healing practice, the mufti is not a producer of performatives but of metaphors, and the orderly circulations that constitute the healing practice—of people, problems, words, power, business cards that double as prescriptions—together constitute an object metaphor for the order people seek in their lives.

Addressing Kinship

All individuals who approached Mufti Ahmed while I was conducting fieldwork were unified in their recognition that they needed assistance addressing or ameliorating specific situations—of health, relationships, or work. The kinds of problems that people brought to the mufti correlated with age and gender, reflecting the roles that men and women play in the daily lives from which these problems arose. The patterns of complaints imply that in infancy and youth, the primary dangers to human beings are health-related. Most of the ailments manifested in adolescents, on the other hand, were psychic, not physical, and all were ailments that had the effect of keeping the individual from behaving in a normatively acceptable way. Concerned mothers often complained that their teenagers had taken to wandering (*ghumna*), implying a worrisome restlessness and lack of direction. Unlike with young children, in problems involving youth, the mufti talked about the problem with the subject of the complaint in addition to giving out a remedy. Through these discussions, he encouraged his petitioners to pursue healthy paths, as in the case of one young man whom he advised to stay out of trouble with the police.

For adult petitioners, relationships are the primary reason for approaching the mufti, with work a close second for men and physical illness for women. Both women and men come to the mufti to ask for help with stressed marriages, indicating that the work of maintaining a marital relationship is accepted and taken up by both men and women. On the other hand, men come with work-related injuries and in distress when they cannot find work, while women's troubles manifest themselves physically. The masculinity that is expressed at the mufti's office is closely tied to the ideal of the male bread-winner (Osella and Osella 2006). Women express their roles and their distress differently. For women, marital trouble, the death of a spouse, the illness of a child, or quarrels with the neighbors often manifest themselves in physical symptoms that can be remedied only by addressing the troubled relationships that are their source. For example, when one woman came to the mufti complaining of pain that needed to be "cut" out by his knife, the mufti told me that the source of the pain was the recent death of her husband. Physical and psychic ailments are often entangled in this way, and the mufti treats them together.

Central to this array of problems are marital difficulties, which range from resistance to marriage to domestic conflict. Most of the ta'wiz that the mufti writes and distributes in response to such problems seek to reestab-lish conditions within which family members can live together peacefully or to otherwise put them on the path to resolution. Unlike in dar ul-qazas and in fatwas, people do not seek divorce in the healing office. Notably, these changes can be sought at the mufti's office because the powerful words that he writes on his ta'wiz work through bodies to change physical, psychic, and relational life. Thus, when a woman came to the mosque because her daughter ada-mantly insisted that she did not want to marry, she requested a ta'wiz that would convince her daughter to agree to marry, and the mufti obliged. On a different day, a woman came to ask for help for her twenty-year-old daughter who was acting "crazy" (*pagal*). The mother attributed this behavior to love, explaining to the mufti that her daughter was out of her mind (*dimag kharab hai*) and that she was constantly angry. The woman's suggestion was that in-appropriate love can cause psychic unrest that must be healed;[2] as with the petition from the woman whose daughter did not want to marry, this one suggests that a normative disposition to love, that which may be part of a mari-tal relationship, is crucial to well-being. Forms of disordered love require work and amendment.

More frequently than requests to change the mind of a potential bride were requests to bring a husband back. In one case, a woman came accompanied by two male family members to ask the mufti for help because her husband had left her several months earlier and had refused to give her any maintenance money. Another woman came because she and her husband had been living separately for six months, and she wished to return to him. Another woman came to complain that she and her husband were experiencing difficulties getting along was told by the mufti to read a particular ayat 101 times morning and night. Yet another woman complained to the mufti that although she had been wearing a ta'wiz he had given her around her arm, the husband who had left her had not returned. In each of these cases, women sought to have their marriages restored, and the mufti wrote ta'wiz and prescribed recitations designed to bring this about.

Women's visits to the mufti mark their perseverance in their marriages. They also mark the mufti's office as a site in which the labor of kinship is carried out: taking the time to travel to the mufti and request ta'wiz after ta'wiz is among other acts that people perform in order to reconstitute and maintain kin relations. Furthermore, the ta'wiz itself works on kinship by addressing the relationships between spouses and family members, showing that kinship is maintained by both physical and emotional labor. Ta'alluqat are both the object and the medium of this adjudication method.

Women are not the only ones who undertake such labors of kinship. One man approached the mufti because his wife had left him. The couple had lived in a house that he had built for 25,000 rupees, but after a while his wife had kicked him out of the house. The husband had gone to the police and filed a First Information Report, or FIR, but to no avail. The mufti's office was another potential avenue to reunion to which the husband subsequently turned. The mufti wrote a ta'wiz whose aim was to let him return. More than many of the other narratives I heard in the mufti's office, this one marks the particular form of adjudication that the mufti offers in his healing practice. He cannot and does not claim to offer judgments or resolutions; his ta'wiz are meant to influence particular people and relations. We do not know (and the mufti did not know) under what conditions the wife threw her husband out or the content of the FIR. The mufti did not resolve this dispute or fully address the issues involved. Instead, his ta'wiz intervened by affecting the individuals involved and the spaces they inhabited.

As the following petition shows, though, the ta'wiz does not always seek to affect people in ways that would change the circumstances of their disputes. In this petition, one of the people upset by the dispute became its object of intervention. On an afternoon in June 2013 a young woman approached the mufti looking distraught. She told him that she had come seeking a ta'wiz for her husband because although he had back trouble, he insisted on playing cricket, and she wanted him to stop. As she and the mufti talked, it became clear that she was also worried because while her husband was playing cricket with his injured back, his older brother was busy taking over the family business; she was beside herself with anger because instead of helping her to reason with her husband and convince him to put more of his energies into the business, her mother-in-law was encouraging his pursuit of cricket. Because of this situation, the woman was often bitterly angry, and life with her in-laws had become increasingly frustrating. The ta'wiz that the mufti wrote did not address the woman's husband or her in-laws. Instead, he wrote a ta'wiz to give the petitioner patience (*sabr*) and to diminish her anger (*ghussah*). The mufti had known her family for some time, and he therefore knew that it was true that the mother-in-law did not want her younger son to take over the family business. However, although this meant that the petitioner's anger was justified, he argued that there was nothing she could do to change the convictions of her husband, mother-in-law, or brother-in-law, and that what she should therefore work toward was calming the righteous anger that she suffered on her husband's behalf. When he explained the situation to me, Mufti Ahmed made it clear that the source of this woman's anger was her intense love of her husband, a love that he implied should be tempered to allow her to cultivate a livable role within the family. The mufti did not argue that his ta'wiz would bring a just resolution to the unjust situation, but instead that it would affect the petitioner's disposition, enabling her to live in peace with her in-laws, leading her away from discord.

Although the mufti usually gave ta'wiz designed to effect smooth reconciliation and a return to normal kin relations, as in the preceding petitions, there were several occasions during my fieldwork where he took a different approach. Once, rather than simply giving her the ta'wiz she requested, the mufti joked with a woman who came to him to talk about her deteriorating relationship with her husband. The couple fought frequently, the woman told the mufti, and her husband was constantly telling her what to do. Before giving her a ta'wiz, Mufti Ahmed winked at her and the other women waiting to speak with him and told her that if her husband talks too much and is too difficult, she should simply send him away. The mufti's tone was light, and he did write the requested ta'wiz, but this advice reflected an acknowl-edgment, which I often encountered in dar ul-qazas, that not all problems can be solved and that sometimes exit is the best strategy.

Each of these examples illustrates the structural similarity between fatwas and healing. In each, the mufti was in a notably responsive posi-tion. People not only approached him with their problems at their own ini-tiative, but also provided the terms according to which he decided on a rele-vant remedy. Unlike the fatwa, however, the ta'wiz he offers are not legal opinions that instruct petitioners on how they ought to act or what they ought to do; instead, ta'wiz bear the power to effect such change.

Circulation

The mufti's healing practice is best characterized through the figure of cir-culation. Not only do people and their problems circulate through the mufti's office; so do records, remedies, and powerful words. In an inversion of the bureaucratic practice in both state courts and in the dar ul-qaza, those who visit the mufti for healing keep track of their own records. Mufti Ahmed gives each new petitioner a card that is stamped on one side with the mufti's name, address, office and mobile phone numbers, and e-mail address. On the other side of the card he keeps a log of individual petitioners' histories with him: the dates they visited, the problems they suffered, and the reme-dies he gave them. Before beginning a consultation, the mufti asked each re-turning petitioner for his or her card. When petitioners did not have the card with them, the mufti sternly impressed its importance upon them and then took out a new card to start another record. Mufti Ahmed used this record to follow up with his petitioners about whether they had used the rem-edies he had given them, and if they had, whether they had followed the whole course or had failed to complete the prescription. Thus, although the mufti keeps no records relating to his healing practice, petitioners carried an account, and record, of their trajectory through various stages of healing. Rather than a localized repository, the records, like the remedies, circulate along with petitioners and their problems.

The most common form of remedy offered by Mufti Ahmed—the ta'wiz—is also the one that circulated most literally and in the greatest variety of ways. Ta'wiz are small rectangular pieces of paper that have been inscribed

with holy words. The mufti, whose work of writing I discuss later, emphasizes the uses of ta'wiz, as the key to allowing the ta'wiz's words and their
power to circulate. The uses of the ta'wiz are, by design, much more transparent and accessible than the writing on the ta'wiz themselves. Mufti
Ahmed never let anyone leave his side until he was sure that they had understood what to do with the ta'wiz they had been given.

Ta'wiz can be taken up in an array of ways. Most commonly, Mufti Ahmed
folded the amulet into a small square and gave it to the petitioner, whom he
instructed to wrap it in plastic and to tie it with a red string. He instructed
the petitioner to tie the string either around his or her neck like a necklace
or around the upper arm. When children were sick—usually, the mufti told
me, with diarrhea, fever, or vomiting—Mufti Ahmed wrote amulets that
they were to hang around their necks. The amulets' powerful words could
also be effective in other ways: sometimes, especially when petitioners came
with problems in love, the mufti gave them amulets to hang in the doorframe
of the affected house. This way the words could permeate the household,
rather than keeping the evil eye away from only one individual child or
adult. Mufti Ahmed also instructed several petitioners to place amulets in
strategic parts of the house to target particular troubles. A woman who was
having trouble with her husband was told to place an amulet under his side
of the mattress. Another was asked whether she would be able to slip an
amulet into her husband's pocket without him knowing. These were both
ways to harness and target the power of the words even without the knowledge or consent of the person to whom they were directed.

The amulets' words were often distributed among several people, as many
of the problems that petitioners brought to the mufti were not personal health
issues, but rather relationship troubles. Mufti Ahmed frequently prescribed
ingesting the words on the amulet when petitioners approached him with
ailments affecting a whole family or several neighbors. He told his petitioners, for instance, to steep the ta'wiz in a pot of tea or in a bottle of water. The
holy words, which were written in saffron ink, dissolved into the liquid, so
everyone involved in the problem could consume them. Once I asked the
mufti why he had told a woman who came to see him about a difficult marital situation to dissolve an amulet's words in a bottle of water. He had told
her that she and her husband should drink the water. Mufti Ahmed replied
that through the amulet, love would enter the husband and wife, and "if there
is love between them, and good behavior, then everything will be fine." Some-

times people involved in a quarrel would be told to drink from different bottles in which two different amulets had been dissolved. Thus, each of them would be impacted by the words addressing his or her particular condition.

Trees were another way to distribute the ta'wiz's words. When I first came to the Old Delhi mosque where the mufti lived and worked, I noticed that the tree in the part of the courtyard closest to his office seemed to shimmer. As I approached it, I saw that what gave the tree this appearance were many small pieces of paper folded into squares, quite a few of them wrapped in plastic. Each square of paper hung from a branch or leaf of the tree by a thread, many of which were red.

Ta'wiz were by far the most common but not the only vehicles by means of which the mufti transmitted "holy words" into troubled contexts, changing the people, relationships, and even the space they inhabited. In dire cases, for example, animal bones are used as powerful remedies. In one such case, a middle-aged woman who came to see the mufti on a daily basis while I was conducting my research presented him with entrenched trouble in the house. Usually the problems this woman presented to the mufti blended in with other people's requests for general relief. "Main pareshan hunh" (I have troubles), she would say, her troubles mixing with those of others in the mosque—aches, pains, a disobedient child. But one day she came to the mosque with a plastic bag full of goat bones. The mufti had asked her to bring these after she had recounted a family feud that had recently escalated. Everyone, she told him, was angry with everyone else, and the atmosphere in the household was deteriorating. On this particular afternoon, the mufti peered inside the plastic bag holding the bones and quickly returned it to her, telling her that these were not properly prepared. When she asked him, perplexed, what the problem was, he told her that they were not thoroughly dried. She was to return another day with eight properly dried goat bones. When she returned several days later, the bones she carried were thoroughly dried. Mufti Ahmed wrote the names of her children and the other people involved in the dispute on a piece of paper, which he carefully added to the bones in the plastic bag. He told the woman that he would transfer the names from the paper onto the bones, keep them over night, and return them to her. She was to bring eight more bones the following day.

Mufti Ahmed asked for bones in cases of severely "bad relations." In these cases, he told me, there was a strong possibility that some black magic (*jadu*) was involved;[3] numerous Quran ayats had the potential to cure this magic.

To address this jadu, the mufti worked with God's words (*Allah ka kalam*). He took the bones, recited the relevant ayats, and wrote them on the bones along with the names of everyone involved in the dispute. He then asked the person who had brought the bones to wrap them in plastic and to keep them for a period of time.

Reading, Writing, and Arithmetic

Circulation, as I have suggested, is the mode through which the mufti heals: he puts certain objects and words into circulation so that they intersect with people and their problems. But the power to heal is carried into such circulation in the form of specific words and numbers, along with acts of recitation or reading.

On ta'wiz, holy words take the form of a grid, called a naqsh, each of whose fields contains a number, and whose rows and columns add up to one of the ninety-nine names of God or to a Quran verse. Others carry a verse, or ayat, from the Quran. Some ta'wiz are inscribed both with a naqsh and with an ayat. Mufti Ahmed has two different methods of writing ta'wiz. Sometimes he writes out a Quran ayat or a naqsh, or both, as he converses with someone about their particular problem. Usually, however, he uses one of the six ta'wiz he prepared in advance. These ta'wiz are piled in six stacks on the desk in front of him. Each of these six ta'wiz serves a different purpose: one is to heal children; another to mend relationships and to increase love; a third is for men who suffer from depression or whose work is not going well; a fourth is for improving marital relationships; a fifth removes the effects of the evil eye from a household; and the last is for success.

The mufti does not give these ta'wiz haphazardly, for each condition must be addressed by the ayat or name or attribute of God relevant to it. "Just like medicine that the doctor gives," each ta'wiz has a different purpose and remedies a specific condition, the mufti told me. In another discussion about the ta'wiz, the mufti gave the analogy of going to the pharmacy. "When we go to the pharmacy [chemist], we take a specific [*khas*, literally, special] medicine that will cure our illness [*jo humari bimari ke liye fa'ideh-mand ho*]. We don't need to take all of the medications in the pharmacy."

However, in spite of this insistence on particularity, there are several genres of problems that can and should be addressed similarly.[4] For example, problems of love (*muhabbat*) require Sura al-Ikhlas (Quran 112). Al-Ikhlas[5] is one of the shortest chapters of the Quran, and it is important because it affirms the oneness (*tauhid*) of God as well as His eternal nature and His transcendence. Al-Ikhlas opens with the injunction "Say" (*qul*). The sura commands believers to recite some of the central tenets of the faith—the unity, eternity, and uniqueness of God. But what is it about these words, in a sura that Droge (2013) translates as "Devotion," and that others refer to as "the Unity," that is particularly suitable for problems of love? I asked Mufti Ahmed this question many times in different ways, and he told me in response that these words were especially powerful. He also referred me to a book titled *Ai' nah-i 'Amaliyat*, a long analysis of and manual about healing with amulets. Reading it, he told me, would provide insight into his practice. The book, which is full of sample ta'wiz and ta'wiz to be given in response to a vast array of problems, states that the naqsh representing Sura al-Ikhlas is "an elixir of love and loyalty/sincerity/attachment (*ikhlas*)." In a different context, John Bowen's Isak informants told him that the al-Ikhlas invests those who recite it with power because it contains "powerful meanings" (1993). Each of these references suggests that al-Ikhlas is not a powerful means of healing because of its referential value—it does not explicitly discuss healing or love. Instead, the ta'wiz is a recitation of the power that resides in devotion to Allah alone.

The other mode of writing that the mufti uses—the seemingly precise science of rendering ayats or verses into number grids, or naqsh—further emphasizes that the power of God's words lies not in their referential quality but in their transformative capacity as vehicles of God's power. While the mufti and *Ai'nah-i 'Amaliyat* describe the writing of naqsh as a precise series of calculations, in practice it is a process by means of which power is conveyed. *Ai'nah-i 'Amaliyat* outlines a complex system through which Quran verses and the names of God are transposed into numbers and arranged on a grid. Each letter of the Arabic alphabet has a value, beginning with *alif*, whose value is 1, and ending with *ghain*, whose value is 1,000. Thus, any word written in Arabic also has a numeric value.[6] Each naqsh, the mufti told me, has a different sum because each represents its own holy word.[7] *Ai'nah-i 'Amaliyat* lays out a mathematical formula for creating ta'wiz. First, the healer has to calculate the numerical value of the relevant Quran verse. Then the healer has to subtract twelve from this value and divide the result by three. If there is a remainder, this can be added in one of the columns. This system does not quite match the one the mufti explained to me, in which the sum of an ayat determines the numbers that will go into the grid, and the act of writing must follow a certain pattern: the pen jumps from square to square, not sequentially from left to write or top to bottom, but following a pattern that was difficult to discern just through observation.

In spite of the seeming precision of this formula and Mufti Ahmed's insistence that his ta'wiz are written according to this method, of his six standard ta'wiz only one of them matches any of the hundreds reproduced in *Ai' nah*. Likewise, I was unable to find verses that correspond with the values to which his ta'wiz add up. This discovery was surprising, given Mufti Ahmed's insistence on the clarity and systematic nature of the healing he offers and in particular of the ta'wiz he prescribes. But as with Amma, the healer whose work Joyce Flueckiger (2006) documents, mathematical precision seems to be less important than the ability to diagnose a situation and to respond with holy words.

This brief analysis reiterates what many others have said: God is the basis and origin of healing in Islamic practices like this one (Bowen 1993; Flueckiger 2006; Messick 1993). Another Urdu text to which the mufti referred me puts it most clearly: ta'wiz, its author writes, are religiously permissible only on the condition that the user does not believe that the words have any effect in themselves but acknowledges that they are empowered by Allah. Joyce Flueckiger's study of a Muslim woman healer in Hyderabad, India, also makes the point that amulets carry power that is recognized as originating with God. She writes, "The efficacy of the amulets [that the healer writes] does not depend primarily upon the semantic content of their words but upon the spiritual authority they represent and embody and the authority with which they are dispensed" (2006, 68). This authority, Flueckiger elaborates, resides in the Arabic letters themselves, which are "powerful, filled with *barkat* [auspicious blessings]. As the channel through which the revelation was transmitted, they are experienced as the very word of God" (2006, 68).

The power of Quranic Arabic to hold and transmit the word of God reflects, as Brinkley Messick (1993) has argued, a logocentrism similar to that identified by Jacques Derrida (1976) in the Western philosophical tradition. For example, Messick (1993, 212), writing about Islamic legal training and practice in Yemen, notes that in the traditions of the Hadith, the justness and authenticity of words can be affirmed only if they can be linked to the Prophet through a chain of recitation. Messick therefore argues that the primary power and guarantee of authenticity in the Islamic tradition is not writing but speech, highlighting a focus on correct and attributed recitation that he calls "recitational logocentrism" (1993, 25). Textual authority is established through ancestry, authorship, dissemination, and reputation (1993, 16). The practice of recitation therefore transmits the perfection and power of God's word as revealed in the Quran. Notably, this recitation may be spoken or written, as in the case of the mufti's inscriptions on the ta'wiz he distributes.

Mufti Ahmed offered a similar argument about the power of recitation in our conversations about healing. He told me, "It [my healing] is Allah's word [*Allah ka kalam*] and the words and prayer [*du'a*] of the prophet, Hazrat Muhammad, peace by upon him," suggesting that the power of his healing practice lies in God's "holy words," as he refers to them in English. On another occasion, Mufti Ahmed told me, "Reciting[8] the verses of the Quran Sharif while I bless someone is very beneficial [*fa'ideh-mand*] for sending illness away [*bimari ko dur karna*], for burning the evil eye [*nazar jelana*], and for putting an end to magic [*jadu ko khatm karna*]." Notably, in the mufti's analysis the recitation or reiteration of the Quran is powerful.

In his analysis of sermon giving in Egypt, Charles Hirschkind argues that the perfection of Quranic Arabic has yet another implication: its efficacy resides in the recipient's ability to take that language in. Classically, rhetorical embellishments in sermon-giving were minimal, as the words uttered were "a perfect unification of beauty and truth" (Hirschkind 2006, 34). The agency of the words was "located in God" and in the "disciplined ears and hearts of listeners" (Hirschkind 2006, 39). This disciplined ear has been revived with the circulation of sermon tapes in contemporary Egypt, now with the goal of morally transforming the listener (2006, 55). Despite the differences between these contexts—in Hirschkind's, learning to listen was a practice of self-cultivation in which Muslims participated while the mufti's healing practice addressed Hindus alongside literate and illiterate Muslims—receiving powerful words is, in both, a carefully crafted practice. In both contexts, people aspired to have the power that resides in the words of God to transform them. The process by which this happens in the healing practice did not, however, require expertise on the part of the recipient, nor is it best understood as a practice of self-cultivation, as Hirschkind shows to be the case in sermon audition. Instead, in the healing practice, communicating the power of "holy words," as the mufti often called them, required their recipient to use them, and to embody them, by painstakingly following the mufti's directions.

The Responsive Mufti

Each of the examples I have given above emphasizes the mufti's act of recitation. But in order to offer the appropriate recitation, the mufti must settle on an understanding of the problem and an approach to ameliorating it. One way he does this is by listening to objects. Once, a woman came to request the mufti's help for her son, who had recently been distracted and who had begun to wander around the neighborhood (ghumna). She could not convince her son to come with her to see the mufti, so instead she brought a photograph of him with her. This also happened when the petitioner was too ill to come in person to see the mufti. Instead of consulting with the person in this situation, the mufti would study the photograph. He told me that as he studied the image he prayed over it, which allowed him to more accurately assess the condition of the sick person and to provide a remedy for the problem. He focused on the photograph and therefore on the person, as he contemplated the person's ailment.

Clothing could serve a similar purpose. One afternoon, a young woman came to the mufti's office with her cousin and her aunt and a number of other female relatives. Each of them ultimately spoke to Mufti Ahmed about a problem they were having, but the primary reason they had come to the mosque was because the young woman was soon to be married. She told the mufti that her mother had died several years earlier, and she and the rest of the family were concerned that there could still be spirits lingering from the death. They wanted to ensure that these spirits would not interfere with the wedding. The mufti told the woman that she should bring him a *qamiz* (top) and a *dupatta* (scarf) that he could read (pardhna) and figure out what, if anything, she ought to worry about. The next day, the girl brought the mufti a plastic bag with a quamiz and a dupatta inside. The mufti asked for the girl's name and for her mother's name.[9] He wrote this information on a piece of paper and told her to return the following day for his response.

I asked Mufti Ahmed why he requested that this woman bring him her clothing. He told me that by looking at clothing that she had worn and that had not been washed subsequently, "I can sometimes see something obvious in the clothing. Sometimes I look at the clothing while I recite verses. That way I can tell whether some nazar is there, or jadu, or what it is . . . While I am reading over it, I think about it, and then an idea comes about what I should do about it and then I perform the healing [*ham 'ilaj karte hain*], and return the clothing." When the woman returned for her qamiz and dupatta the next day, the mufti told her that everything was fine, and she could proceed with her wedding without worry. In each of these diagnostic acts, the objects made the troubled people present to the mufti. In this process, the intimate connection between apt observation or listening and apt recitation becomes clear: as the mufti listens, the idea of what he should do, which ayats he should recite, comes to him, producing a unity of diagnosis and cure by means of a connection between the mufti and the petitioner.

The unifying feature of the mufti's healing practices we have seen in the cases examined so far is that, in each one, the mufti relied on and produced ta'alluqat, relations, through which God's powerful words traveled. As the ethnographic analysis above suggests, these relations were forged through language, which was not always a medium of communication or even referential but which acted as a material conductor. As others have also noted (Spadola 2014; Flueckiger 2006; Keane 2013), once words of the Quran have been transposed into writing on the ta'wiz, they are not intended to be read or even seen. When they are given as amulets to be worn, hung up in a tree or on a doorframe, or hidden under a pillow, the mufti himself folds them carefully, words facing inward, so that all that he hands to the person requesting help is a small white square (though I did on a few rare occasions see people open them up and peek inside as though confirming that the words were really there). When the words are to be ingested, they are often not hidden in the same way—the mufti hands taviz written in saffron water out flat and open, or sometimes inserts them into a small envelope made of recycled paper. These ta'wiz are not intended for reading but for transduction (Keane 2013), a process that obliterates them as legible signs. This suggests that the capacity for healing rests in the materiality of writing, in the "potency that derives from the very capacity to transform the word from one semiotic modality to another" (Keane 2013, 9).

However, the mufti's healing practice and his interpretation of it suggest that rather than resting only on the *form* language takes (its materiality in writing), healing also relies on the embodied quality of language. In other words, the materiality of language is crucial to the transmission of power, but this transmission is complete only because of another transformation, from writing to incorporation in the body of the petitioner. It is important to Mufti Ahmed's healing practice that hearing or reciting the words of the Quran and drinking or touching them are equally beneficial.[10] Mufti Ahmed made this explicit: "If reading [parhna] the Quran has an effect [*tasir*] so too does wearing it [*pahinna*]." Both are methods of bringing divine pronouncements that are transmitted in speech (by the Angel Jibra'il and through the Prophet) and recorded in scripture into physical contact with the bodies of those who need spiritual, physical, or social healing.

The Quran's holy words are beneficial because they act, or in Mufti Ahmed's words, they have an "impact" [*words ka impact*], when he mobilizes them appropriately. If so mobilized, these words affect the body or mind of the afflicted person. Mufti Ahmed explained this to me as follows: "Small words have an impact. When we say something good, we are happy. When we say something in anger, we see red. A person's whole body is angered. We read the mystery of Allah's word (the Quran) and people can benefit greatly from it." Speech, embodied language, affects the bodies of speaker and recipient. When we speak or hear angry words both our physical and our emotional lives are affected. Likewise, God's words, appropriately brought into a relation with bodies, alter them in beneficial ways. The mufti continued: "Writing verses of the Quran Sharif and du'as from the Hadith of the Prophet Muhammad and tying them [the ta'wiz on which they are written] around the neck is very beneficial. And it is very beneficial to write verses of the Quran Sharif in saffron [*kesar se*], or with a pen and then to dip it in water [*pani men dalke*] and give it to someone to drink [*pilaya ja'e*]." The particular qualities of language, illustrated through the widespread experience of being angered by words, make the rituals effective, as they enable God's power to enter and transform human bodies, relationships, and lives: Quran ayats enter ears and mouths; they touch necks and upper arms. When these powerful words are mobilized in these ways, anyone can hypothetically benefit from them: the illiterate, the person lacking knowledge of the Quran, the Hindu, the child, the recalcitrant. This is something that even the mufti's most scathing critics sometimes come close to conceding. A group of strict ahl-i hadis[11] women with whom I studied the Quran spent long hours trying to convince me that the mufti's work was a form of black magic. But first they speculated that his healing practice might be one way for illiterate Muslims ignorant of the Quran's words to benefit from their power nonetheless.[12]

Mufti Ahmed's interpretation of holy words highlights the significance of writing's materiality, which enables ingestion or incorporation. Because of this relationship between words, writing, and ingestion, Mufti Ahmed's spiritual healing cannot be sufficiently analyzed without grappling with the confounding question of how language is bodily. Indeed, the question that his practice raises is, How does language heal (and not only physical ailments) through the body? Put otherwise, What is language here that it heals through the body? My suggestion is that Mufti Ahmed's way of working with words mines one of their capacities that has been overlooked by analysts of ritual and of law alike: the capacity to bring together spirit and matter, mind and body. This is a characteristic of language to which some feminist scholars attend in a way that enables us to take seriously the account the mufti gives of transmitting God's powerful words.

The two lines of intervention I turn to here posit language as producer of and produced by a link between cognition and physicality. The first of these interventions, Veena Das's (2007) work on violence and pain, ethnographically approaches the skeptical suspicion that "my soul and my body, while necessarily distinct, are not merely contingently connected" (Stanley Cavell, quoted in Das 2007, 41). Das works with Wittgenstein and Cavell to examine what she calls "language as the bodying forth of words" (2007, 40). Her ethnographic and philosophical question is, How can one ethically approach and represent the pain of another, given that pain is usually understood as that which is incommunicable? Through her reading of Wittgenstein's account of feeling one's pain in another's body, Das argues that pain does not destroy communication but instead "makes a claim on the other—asking for acknowledgment that may be given or denied" (2007, 40). Through a reading of the story "Khol Do" by Saadat Hasan Manto, Das argues that language can also make a claim on the body in pain, that it can beckon and provide the promise of a future by affirming someone's life. In Manto's story, the title of which literally means open it, in Hindi/Urdu, a father searches for his daughter, who was lost to him during the Partition violence. When he finds her, the daughter appears to be a corpse who has been wheeled into the clinic. The doctor who brings her into the room orders someone to open the window—*khol do*. When he gives the order, she moves to untie the strings that hold up her pants. Her father, seeing the movement, says, "My daughter is alive!" In Das's analysis, the significance of this story is that through it we can see how speech makes a claim on another, and how this claim can also be a hailing of the body. The father's speech not only addresses his daughter (inadvertently). Her response is both an effect of other scenes of address (which are also scenes of power) and makes her a subject.

The hail is this kind of address: one that works within a relation of power in such a way that the subject both recognizes herself in the address and that it is brought into being as a particular kind of subject by it.[13] Also significant, though, is the fact that the daughter's gesture, the speech of her body, which is induced by her own misunderstanding of the verbal command, produces meanings distant from her intentions. This speaking body does not communicate violation but life, even if violation is what the daughter expects.

It is precisely this excess of the speaking body's language that Shoshana Felman (2002) examines in her reading of J. L. Austin and Don Juan. Writing in the register of playful literary criticism, Felman (2002) responds to Derrida's argument that speech acts can be performative because they are structured as writing, which we know to be citable and therefore to exceed the intentions of its author. Felman's reply to this is not a refutation but a reminder that speech can only come into being as a physical act, in her example through the organ of the mouth, and that speech nonetheless exceeds the conscious intentions of its utterer. That is, speech is embodied, but the body is not a guarantor of authenticity, not, as Derrida would have it, because it shares the structure of writing, but because the relationship between the speaker and speech is not fully intentional. Felman's analysis of Austinian speech act theory focuses on the act of promising, and specifically on the promise to marry that Don Juan so compulsively makes and breaks. Felman shows that the promise to marry is a privileged site from which to identify the relationship between language and the body because the promise to marry is the promise of a sexual relationship, which is a particular relationship between bodies. In her afterword to Felman's book, Judith Butler illuminates this point, arguing that "the speaking body functions as a chiasmatic relay between the promise and the disposition of the sexual body that the promise is meant to bind" (Felman 2002, 118). The speech act "I do" in the context of a wedding ceremony is a promise that two bodies will relate over the course of time in a particular way and in this sense hail one another. But as Don Juan shows over and over again, this promise to dispose one's body in a particular way over time can be and often is undone by the actions of the one who has made the promise.

Both Felman and Das show how language hails the body. This hail, we see in their texts, is both semantic and talismanic. Its power resides both in meaning and in misfire. Thinking of language in this way helps to think through the mufti's healing practice. The words he wrote on ta'wiz, and the du'as he uttered over people and chilies, have important semantic content— they are the words of the Prophet, and they hail bodies of jinns, neighbors, husbands—not as an effect of the mufti's intentions but as an effect of God's utterances. In other words, the mufti's language exceeds him as his speaking body becomes the conduit for words that he has been inspired to recite, in writing and in speech. The language itself produces effects on the bodies of those it addresses by coming into contact with them through ingestion, inhalation, audition, and proximity. So while it is true, as others have argued, that ta'wiz are not meant to be read by their recipients, the writing they contain hails both by virtue of what it says and by virtue of who and what it touches.

Unlike in Felman's account, the body is not scandalous here: this language must move through bodies and must hail bodies. Furthermore, this language can move as it does because it is recitational and iterative: correct recitation of God's language affects bodies directly and by impacting their physical environments. Thus, what Felman and Das enable us to see is how this form of healing is linguistic, not in the sense that it is a matter of statements and meanings but in the sense that it is constituted by the workings of embodied language. However, unlike these conceptions of language, the mufti's healing practice relies at each juncture on the presence of the metaphysical in the language—both spoken and written—itself. These words ultimately act because the mufti's writing and speech recite, reiterate, and reinstantiate the power at the origin of the Prophet's own recitational act.

Conclusion: Law and Religion in the Healing Practice

Healing practices like Mufti Ahmed's exist throughout South Asia, North Africa, and the Middle East. In South Asia, these practices are approached through a vocabulary that evokes legal adjudication. For example, in her book on the Sufi shrine (*dargah*) Husain Tekri in northern India, Carla Bellamy notes that individuals who come to the shrine seeking relief from their problems often refer to its activities using a legal vocabulary. Not only does she remind us that a "dargah" refers both to a royal court and to a court of law; she tells us that pilgrims at the shrine say they are there to register a petition (*'arz*) and at the end of their ordeals they wait for a decision or judgment (*faisalah*) (Bellamy 2011, 9). Anand Taneja (2013) has also noticed that legal language and practice pervade pilgrims' approaches to Firoz Shah Kotla, a Sufi shrine in Delhi. Taneja found that pilgrims file petitions with jinns at the shrine, miming the actions required to approach bureaucratic government offices or courts of law: these petitions are photocopied and submitted at various locations in the shrine, accompanied by the petitioner's photograph and address.

These accounts suggest that dargahs do not respect a strict boundary between "law" and "religion," where law is a secular process of adjudicating disputes in reference to uniform and universal rules and procedures, and religion is a private matter of belief. At the same time, these accounts do not imply that dargahs are spaces of religious law of the sort I have examined in the rest of the book. Instead, the configuration of law and religion, as well as the outcomes of cases in dargahs is transformative in a different way than judgments in courts or opinions in fatwas. Like court judgments and fatwas, the spiritual healing practice offers directives to be followed. However, unlike court judgments and fatwas, correctly following these directives addresses problems by transforming both people and the broader cosmological relationships that afflict them and produce their problems.

Significantly, this cosmological transformation, which calls on and to jinns, the evil eye, and other afflicting spirits, marks this form of adjudication both as nonlegal and nonreligious in the secular sense. Long-standing consensus among inheritors of nineteenth-century Muslim reformers in South Asia is that healing practices like the mufti's are superstitious, not religious. In Pakistan (N. Khan 2006; Ewing 1997) and in India (Bellamy 2011) alike, many Muslims dismiss such practices as ill-advised at best and as *shaitani* (evil) at worst. Unlike in Morocco, practices in India have not been remade into a matter of pride, national or otherwise, for the middle classes (Spadola 2014). Instead it alternately incites curiosity and provokes disapproval. Spiritual healing is, nonetheless, the most democratic form of adjudication I have addressed here. Illegible as law or even adjudication is from the perspective of the state courts, it is nonetheless an important resource for managing— psychically and spiritually—domestic arguments and the kinds of troubles that bring litigants to all of the other forums I have discussed in this book.

CONCLUSION

Divorcing Traditions

Divorcing traditions—of Hanafi jurists, sufi healers, ordinary Muslim women, and state courts; in dar ul-qazas, dar ul-iftas, and mahila panchayats; by ta'wiz, fatwas, and cases—are the object of this ethnography. These legal forums constitute divorcing traditions in the sense that each forum draws on a number of sources to address specific and personal, if widespread, problems of how to live in the present. More specifically, each forum in its own way guides ordinary Muslims as they grapple with how to respond, as Muslims, to marital disputes, domestic violence, and abandonment. Talal Asad's conception of tradition as he elaborated it in his 1986 essay, "The Idea of an Anthropology of Islam," captures the character of the legal traditions I study. Asad writes, "A tradition consists essentially of discourses that seek to instruct practitioners regarding the correct form and purpose of a given practice that, precisely because it is established, has a history" (1986, 14).[1] In this formulation, a tradition is animated by active engagement with its past, which shapes practices in the present and the future. An *Islamic* discursive tradition, he further argues, is "simply a tradition of Muslim discourse that addresses itself to conceptions of the Islamic past and future, with reference to a particular Islamic practice in the present" (1986, 14). Muslims are inducted into particular practices in this tradition "*as* Muslims" (1986, 15, emphasis in original). This conception of the Islamic tradition emphasizes its sources, which are from the past, and its continuity. But this continuity is not stasis; it is a practice or a number of practices that are learned and are implemented as a way of moving into the present and the future. In other words, a tradition in Asad's sense is dynamic and mobile.

Each of the forums I have discussed in this book draws on the Quran and the Hadith, although each forum approaches these sources by means of different interpretive approaches and informed by different kinds of knowledge. The qazis and the mufti not only rely on the Quran and the Hadith but on Islamic legal sources and traditions of jurisprudence in which they are experts. Mahila panchayat members, on the other hand, work with their knowledge, from parents, from Quran study groups, and some of them from girls' madrasas, in order to ground their advice to fellow Muslim women. In his healing work, the mufti draws on a different form of expertise, this one grounded in Sufi mystical traditions that some Muslims consider to be superstition. All of these forums, nonetheless, participate in what Asad calls an Islamic discursive tradition, highlighting Asad's own point that a discursive tradition is not only a tradition of experts but includes the interpretive work undertaken by ordinary Muslims.

In arguing that these forums all participate in an Islamic discursive tradition I am also suggesting that such a tradition, in which Muslims are advised how to live their marital relations and their divorces *as* Muslims is far from hermetic. These are spaces the state has neither co-opted nor abandoned but with which the state intersects. Asad's concept of tradition is helpful here as it draws attention to the complex and power-laden relations within and between the various divorcing, and legal, traditions I examine here. As Saba Mahmood noted, a key element of Asad's analysis of tradition is that he "places an emphasis on relations of power that are necessary both for the propagation of a tradition in relation to other discursive traditions and to the processes by which certain practices and arguments become hegemonic within a tradition" (2005, 115n56). If, as I argue, the different traditions of Muslim divorce in India, in state and nonstate forums both, do not work independently of each other but instead intersect, these intersections reflect and instantiate relations of power both within and between forums.

Thus, the history of Muslim clerical involvement in making Indian law is evident in the Dissolution of Muslim Marriages Act, and the harmony between the dar ul-qazas' reliance on the sources of this legislation and the state courts' reliance on the legislation itself brings these histories and practices together. In another way, the reconciliation imperative apparent in the mahila panchayat binds practices of Muslim interpretations of marriage to state and global discourses about the importance of reconciliation as a priority and the virtues of pragmatism in the face of scarcity. The story is not all about convergence, however. Fatwas and court cases on talaq ul-ba'in provide perhaps the best example of contestation. In his fatwas, the mufti implicitly rejects the state's interpretation of talaq ul-ba'in and upholds the practice as external to the state. This contestation, too, is part of a tradition of Indian politics and part of a history of Muslim participation in the creation of India as an independent state and of Indian practices of law. These intersections not only make Indian secularism, which is the main argument of *Divorcing Traditions*, they also shape the discursive tradition.

My larger argument in this book is that the very plurality of forums, each with its own traditions of divorce adjudication, together makes Indian secularism. Secualrism, I have maintained, is a practical and not a conceptual project. There are three ways in which the forums I study make secularism. First, the legal experts with whom I did my research have implicitly accepted the secular division between religion and law as the basis for their authority to adjudicate these cases. In other words, qazis and muftis do not set out to practice secular law let alone to uphold the state's secular character. Nonetheless, their work of adjudication fits within the parameters the state sets for religious authority, as it concerns matters that fall within the jurisdiction of personal law. Litigants, too, play a role in upholding this division of labor, as their choice of adjudication venue likewise follows the parameters defined by the state's legal system.

Second, in addition to the division of labor that they uphold, adjudication proceedings themselves also participate in a practical (as opposed to discursive) dialogue with state courts over jurisdiction. This is especially clear in the case of fatwas on talaq ul-ba'in, where although the mufti does not respond to questions about matters other than those that fall under the jurisdiction of personal law, his advice frequently runs directly counter to the state courts' rulings on this type of divorce. In this sense, making Indian secularism is not just about obeying a set division between secular and religious domains; it is also about engaging, often implicitly, in practical debates over jurisdiction. This is how Indian secularism is animated by legal pluralism. Third, this dialogue, with all its asymmetries, orbits around Muslim divorce. Indian FLE at once works by positing family as religious and private (which is true for all religious communities in India but which is especially politically loaded for Muslims) and by adjudicating marriage and divorce through the question of property.

The political implications of this argument seem to become more rather than less pronounced as the months pass. This book will come to press at a time when secularism is again (as always, but more strenuously) on the tip of everyone's tongue. The question of secularism is so alive now largely because statements and acts asserting who belongs to the Indian nation are pervasive. In 2014 the Hindu Right once again achieved political and electoral ascendancy in India. News media and some emerging scholarship suggest that this has come with a tremendous increase in cases of violence against those considered "other" to the Hindu majority.[2] Notably, outsider status has been applied not only to Muslims but also to other "beef-eaters," in particular Dalits. Acts of violence against these groups, following patterns we have seen before, appear to be ignored if not sanctioned by the government at various levels—police, local politicians, the prime minister.[3] In this political climate, it may be that the most important lesson of this research is that Muslim law and Muslim politics are not other to the secular Indian state after all, either historically or in practice.

In a 2015 meditation on Indian secularism, the renowned historian Romila Thapar has argued that the history of religion in pre-colonial India is the history of sects rather than of monolithic religious groups, or religious groups that claimed to be monolithic. This, she argues, was true even with the arrival of Islam, an arrival that she argues was marked by an expanded exploration of religious ideas and an increase in the number and variety of sects. Her point is that if India is to secularize in keeping with its history, Indians ought to continue to practice an array of religions composed of a broad range of practices. Yet even as these various practices persist, the "religious identity of the Indian, whatever it may be, has to give way to the primary secular identity of an Indian citizen" (2015). Her specific call is to secularize education and to secularize civil laws, the latter by "resolving differences" between civil laws and laws of religions and castes. In other words, Thapar calls for producing a single, unified, civil law that would no longer be subject to discrepancies.

Thapar's argument about the necessity of recognizing that Indian religious history is a history of plurality is critical, in particular with regard to the place of Islam in that plurality. But her conclusion that what India needs is a unified civil law is both out of step with her own emphasis on plurality and also unconvincing from the perspective of the research that forms the core of this book. Specifically, might it not be equally important to come to terms with the plurality, including the legal plurality, of the Indian present—not to celebrate multiplicity or to indulge in the fiction that pluralism is a solution to communal violence, to religious nationalisms, or to inequalities produced in and by such plural orders, but in order to begin in a different place?

That this legal pluralism is so apparent in a study of Muslim divorce does not make it a panacea. But attending to the way that this legal pluralism produces the effect of a system of secularism enables a recognition, which is currently absent from debates about Islam, personal law, and secularism, that practices of secularism and practices of the two current forms of religious law relevant to Indian Muslims—personal law and Islamic law—are both in significant ways *Indian laws*. These two forms of religious law demonstrate the plurality of sources and interpretations and tensions and intersections of which the Indian present is forged. Recognizing this practical plurality, with all of its contradictions and its drawbacks, as well as its resources, may enable us to turn our attention to the question of what practices of law and politics—"religious" and "secular"—entrench the inequalities about which Thapar is concerned and to leave behind the red herring that Muslim personal law currently provides.

In contemporary India, secularism demands that personal law stand for religious norms. To insist that secularism requires eliminating such personal laws is therefore ironic. What we see when we look closely is that in considering Indian law, and in asking about the sources of structural inequality (gender, class, caste), we need to consider these legal practices as part of the Indian legal sphere, not as aberrations at its heart—not as the mark of incomplete secularism but as one of its major sites. The argument that practices of secularism both rely on and reinforce religious difference and inequalities between majority and minority religions seems to contest Irfan Ahmad's insight that for members of the Indian Muslim minority, secularism is nothing if not an antimajoritarian project (2009). It is, instead, a promise of interreligious equality that at least provides the grounds to protect minority religions. For this reason the Islamist organization Jamaat-e-Islami, which Ahmad studied, embraced secular democracy following Indian independence.

Yet, while this is the promise of secularism, the structure of the legal system has entrenched Muslim difference and thereby Hindu majoritarianism and linked both to the Woman Question. This means that minority religions, in particular Islam, are widely reduced to a matter of gender inequality, which is deduced from women's comportment and from divorce laws. The mahila panchayat shows both that the challenges facing poor women across communities are more similar than they are different from one another and that Muslims are understood to have qualitatively different circumstances that do not permit them to fully participate in alliances with Hindu women in similar situations. This is one effect of Indian secularism, which rests on a view of Muslims as a consolidated community. *Divorcing Traditions* shows that the centrality of divorce to Muslim legal forums is not about a core of the Hanafi legal tradition. Instead, divorce is at the core of what these forums attend to because the secular state has defined the family as religious and because divorce is a problem that the state courts grapple with only in select and often contradictory ways. Kinship must, therefore, be part of any serious account of the workings of secularism. This book's most important conclusion may be that grappling with secularism's violence in order to pursue its promise of equality requires addressing the ideology and the legal regimes that uphold FLE and thereby perpetuate gender inequality in marriage and divorce as centerpieces of secular practice.

Notes

Chapter 1

1. I am drawing here on Talal Asad's notion of the Islamic discursive tradition, which he analyzes as: "a tradition of Muslim discourse that addresses itself to conceptions of the Islamic past and future, with reference to a particular Islamic practice in the present" (1986, 14). Later in this essay, he writes that an Islamic practice is one "into which Muslims are inducted *as* Muslims" (1986, 15). In the case of the mahila panchayat, participating in the Islamic discursive tradition is, ironically, predicated on certain secular precepts. In particular, the mahila panchayat leaders address these disputes to women as Muslims in marital disputes because the personal law system has made the Muslim family into a religious institution. Matters of criminal law, for example, do not come before any of the forums I study even though there are nuanced Islamic jurisprudential traditions of criminal law.

2. For comparative examination of religious personal laws in postcolonial states, see, for example, Sezgin 2013 and An-Naim 2010.

3. As Karuna Mantena shows, Henry Maine, legal theorist and Law Member in the Viceroy's Council in post-1857 India, was an early critic of the way that the British changed native customary law by integrating it into the colonial court system (2010, 107–113). An extensive scholarship demonstrates the many ways in which preexisting

legal practices and norms were altered in this process. See especially Cohn 1996; Derrett 1999; Galanter and Dhavan 1989; and Kugle 2001.

4. The smaller minorities have developed their own personal laws, each through unique engagements with British and Indian law. On Parsi law, see Sharafi 2014. On Christian personal law, see N. Chatterjee 2010a, 2010b. On Jewish personal law, see Derrett 1964; Roland 1998.

5. The British did not formally assume administrative control of India until 1857, yet they began introducing legal changes and impacting the authority granted to different legal adjudicators much earlier, as the Hastings Declaration indicates.

6. There is one major caveat to this, which I discuss at length in the next chapter: Article 44 of the Constitution of India contains a Uniform Civil Code as a Directive Principle. This means that the constitution articulates an aspiration to homogenize personal laws such that all Indians, regardless of confession, would be governed by the same laws of marriage, divorce, inheritance, adoption, and succession.

7. Some of this literature insists on the equality of these normative systems, arguing that they ought to be treated equally as laws, regardless of the differences in their origins and the enforcement mechanisms relevant to them (Griffiths 1986). Others (Moore 1993) demand that we recognize the distinctions between state-enforced law and norms enforced by other mechanisms.

8. I discussed the immediate influences on Hastings's plan above, but it is important to note here that Sir William Blackstone's influential *Commentaries on the Laws of England*, originally published between 1765 and 1769, included separate sections on master and slave, husband and wife, parents and children, guardians and wards, and corporations (1962, bk. 1, chaps. 14–18). Wolfram Müller-Freienfels has argued that Blackstone's *Commentaries* is one of the first British legal texts to have separated out laws relating to the family (2003, 39–40).

9. In Veena Talwar Oldenburg's words: "I am tempted to conclude that it is not dowry that endangers women's lives, but marriage itself. Much has always been said about the 'dangers' of marriage, and the position of potential bride and wife, but the institution itself remains robust—the ineluctable and unquestioned destination toward which all young women travel. It is this compulsive unitary vision that severely limits the choices of bridegivers" (2002, 213).

10. The success of these codification projects made India a "peculiar anomaly" vis-à-vis the persistent failure of codification projects in Britain (Mantena 2010, 91). Mantena suggests that many theoretical and practical factors enabled codification to succeed in India where it failed in Britain; among these factors was the idea that codification would introduce certainty into law (95). For Henry Maine, advanced forms of codification were instruments for enacting legal change without falling into the disarray of "judge's law" (Mantena 2010, 102). The broad project of codification in late colonial India therefore shares a set of characteristics with Savigny's theory of contract law. This was in spite of the fact that, as Mantena shows, Savigny viewed codification as a sign of immaturity or decline, as relevant only when sources of law and legal authority were weak (101–102).

11. Agarwal notes that in the postcolonial period the act's effect has varied by state either because it has been amended to include agricultural land or because customary

laws of inheritance were not strong before 1937, and there was therefore no ground not to comply (1994, 232–233).

12. See also S. Mahmood (2016, 111–148) on Egyptian personal status law.

13. On the relationship between households and markets in industrialized contexts, see Harris 1984; Oakley 1974; Barrett and MacIntosh 1982; and Simpson 1998.

14. This is Fernando's term, which she uses to refer to "women and men committed to practicing Islam as French citizens and to practicing French citizenship as pious Muslims" (2014b,13).

15. The word "secularism" was not inserted into the Preamble of the Indian Constitution until 1976, yet the Constituent Assembly debates included discussions about secularism and Muslim personal law (see Bajpai 2002).

16. See Irfan Ahmad (2009) for an analysis of secularism as the political promise to treat minority citizens as equals of members of the majority.

17. There are four schools (*madhab*) of legal interpretation within Sunni Islam (Makdisi 1979) and two major schools within Shi'a Islam. The vast majority of Indian Muslims are Sunni and follow the Hanafi school of Sunni law. For a detailed history and analysis of Sunni jurisprudence, see Hallaq 1999.

Chapter 2

1. Because talaq ul-ba'in is instant, sometimes a husband has not thought through the consequences of divorce and later, with his wife, wishes to resume the marriage. As I discuss in chapter 5, the process required for the couple to remarry one another is called *halala*. To perform halala, a divorcée must marry another man and consummate the marriage. If her second husband divorces her, she can then remarry the first husband.

2. The case was *Prakash & Ors. v. Phulavati & Ors.* See Masoodi 2017.

3. As Anuj Bhuwania has argued, the PIL is hailed in India and internationally as a democratizing instrument because it opens every facet of political life to judicial scrutiny initiated by any member of the public (2017). What comes along with this, Bhuwania argues, is both a valorization of anti-proceduralism, and sloppy, openly politicized jurisprudence. In the case of the *Muslim Women's Quest for Equality*, the political valence of the PIL is evident.

4. The MWMB has yet to be passed by the Rajya Sabha, or upper house of parliament. It will only become law if and when it is approved both by the Rajya Sabha and the president of India.

5. This is ironic, given that a similar approach to domestic violence characterized Criminal Procedure Code 498A, which criminalizes dowry demands; 498A has been criticized for its chilling effect on women who do not think they will benefit from their husbands' being jailed. In 2006 feminist lawyers and advocates succeeded in pushing the Protection of Women from Domestic Violence Act through the legislature. This act puts into place civil procedures of redress for domestic violence, partly in order to encourage women to come forward without fear that their relatives will face immediate arrest.

6. As Partha Chatterjee has noted, the early postcolonial period was especially rife with reforms of Hindu religious practices, including rights to temple entry for dalits and

the criminalization of temple dedications of girls. For Chatterjee, this marks one of the contradictions of Indian secularism. I suggest here that this is in fact one of the several ways that Indian secularism brings into relief a facet of most, if not all, secular states: a tension between disestablishment and the regulation of religion. See Chatterjee 2004, chapter 6.

7. Religious personal law coexists in the Constitution with a Directive Principle pushing the state to enact a UCC. Supporters of the UCC frame the code as promising to complete Indian secularism. See, for example, Agnes 1999; Sunder Rajan 2003.

8. In 2001 the Supreme Court decided another landmark case, *Danial Latifi v. Union of India*, which I discuss in chapter 5, that clarified that such generous provisions were in fact the correct interpretation of the MWA.

9. In Nathaniel Roberts' words: "dalits refers to members of Indian castes outside Hindu society's traditional fourfold social structure known as the varna system. Dalits were once known by a variety of English terms, like *untouchables*, *Pariahs*, and *outcastes*, as well as by native terms such as *avarna, chandala,* and *panchama*" (2016, xiii). Dalits, like Muslims, are known to eat beef, which some caste Hindus do not, or ought not. One major issue that tracks this identification of otherness, therefore, is the spate of violence against people accused of killing cattle or eating beef, as well as bans on killing or eating beef—in this way, otherness is not only a matter of religion but also of caste. See, for a very small sample of a much larger body of reports, Wire Staff 2016a, c; Bhatia 2016; Pisharoty 2016.

10. I rely on Gayer and Jaffrelot's (2012) figures in the paragraphs that follow.

11. Caste panchayats are often run by the dominant caste group in a village (Cohn 1987, 554–574). On caste panchayats in several different communities, see Hayden 1999; Holden 2003; Solanki 2011; and Moore 1993.

12. On the complex and varied formations of caste panchayats, see, e.g., Bharadwaj 2012; Chowdhry 2007.

13. "In the village context, for example, biradari refers to the entire village, overriding difference of caste, class, and creed. In the context of a caste group, a biradari is a social group made up of males who believe they are descended from a common male ancestor, which makes them equal and brothers" (Chowdhry 2007, 95–96; see also Solanki 2011).

14. For a good overview of this literature, see Holden 2003.

15. Scholars agree that for panchayats to work in women's interests, they must include women members. Prem Chowdhry argues that all-male caste panchayats perpetuate patriarchal power (2007, 100–101); additionally, Solanki (2011) demonstrates that when women participate in them, panchayats can be more sympathetic to their claims. For further analysis of gender and panchayats, see Kapadia 2002, pt. 3.

16. In another example of this approach, Aradhana Sharma (2008) studies how a network of women's organizations designed as a GONGO—a government-organized NGO—benefits from government status while still keeping a critical distance from the government.

17. It stipulated that all hearings should be set within three days of an initial complaint, and maintained that within sixty days some kind of legal relief should be in place.

18. The original formulation, "I will not do the wrong thing," refers to the possibility that his relatives might try to steal Rehana's property.

19. While Hindu families are also understood to be religious in everyday conversation, Muslim religiosity is more frequently depicted as a problem for women's rights, in spite of much evidence to the contrary.

20. For ethnographic accounts of kinwork in India, see Pinto 2011; Ramberg 2014, 2015; and Trawick 1990.

Chapter 3

1. There is a third dar ul-qaza in the trans-Yumuna area of Delhi in which I was able to do a limited amount of research. However, because the qazi in that dar ul-qaza was less convinced that he wanted to allow an observer, I never attended hearings there.

2. Faskh has often been translated as an "annulment" of marriage, but as it does not eliminate the marital history, instead divorcing the couple, the term "annulment" is misleading.

3. There is one inheritance case included in the overview above, which is why I say I have looked at thirty-three cases.

4. Parveez Mody (2008) shows that simply getting in to talk to a judge in the Delhi district courts can be a daunting task. The corridors of the district court brim with touts who are both necessary because they know how to navigate the court system and an impediment because they demand payment for their services.

5. For a detailed history and analysis of Deoband, see Metcalf 1982.

6. To illustrate his point, the qazi recounted a tale about Hazrat Ali (son-in-law of the Prophet Muhammad) and a Jew. Hazrat Ali lost his armor and saw a Jew wearing it. He accused the Jew of having stolen the armor and brought him before the qazi. The qazi heard the case and asked Ali to produce two witnesses. When Ali was only able to produce one admissible witness, the qazi decided in the Jew's favor because of lack of evidence. Overcome by the qazi's equity, the Jew later became a Muslim. This story is about the qazi's unwavering fairness when adjudicating between a Jew and a Muslim but also illustrates his dedication to procedure.

7. Although dowry is sometimes assumed to be relevant only to Hindu, and not to Muslim, marriages, in fact it is widely practiced in all of India's religious traditions. Sylvia Vatuk has found that dowries among Muslims marrying within their extended families (*khandan*) are relatively low, whereas families whose daughters marry beyond the family (where the groom is from a *ghair khandan*) must be prepared to pay significant dowries and to face further dowry demands (2014, 40).

8. A lakh is a unit in the number system used in India. It is equivalent to 100,000 USD.

9. A tola is a measure of weight equivalent to 11.6 grams. The amount in question here is about 150 grams.

10. Unani medicine is a "system of Greek medicine that has evolved within the Muslim world" (Flueckiger 2006, 99).

11. Most Indians give dowry, whereas mahr is a specifically Muslim practice.

Chapter 4

1. For an analysis of the *Madan* case as indicative of an institutional turn in legal pluralism in India, see Redding 2010.

2. Among those concerned about the prevalence of divorce by apostasy are the Begum of Bhopal, Begum Sharifa Hamid Ali, president of the All India Woman's Council, and Thanawi (De 2009; Zaman 2008, 29).

3. Qazi Kamal, of the AIMPLB dar ul-qaza, was also trained in the seminary at Deoband. As Zaman notes, Deoband was founded to reorient Islamic learning both toward the study of the *hadith* (reported teachings of the Prophet) and toward a "strong emphasis on Islamic law" (2008, 3). The Deobandis were also dedicated to spreading their text-based approach to Islam to ordinary Muslims (Zaman 2008, 3).

4. Some scholars (F. Khan 2008; Masud 1996; and Jones 2010) refer to this as a fatwa, while others (Zaman 2008) refer to it as a treatise. I pick up the latter terminology, as it is a compilation of responses to fatwas intended to make a doctrinal intervention.

5. This is Zaman's translation.

6. The DMMA states that a Muslim woman is entitled to divorce if (1) her husband has been missing for four years; (2) her husband has neglected or failed to provide maintenance for two years; or he has taken an additional wife unlawfully; (3) her husband has been sentenced to prison for seven years or longer; (4) the husband has failed to perform his marital obligations for three years; (5) the husband was impotent at the time of marriage and remains impotent; (6) the husband has been insane for two years or is suffering from leprosy or a "virulent venereal disease"; (7) she was given in marriage before age eighteen, the marriage has not been consummated, and she renounces it by age nineteen; (8) her husband treats her cruelly: (a) physically assaults her or makes her life miserable even if the cruelty is nonphysical; (b) associates with women of ill repute; (c) attempts to get her to lead an immoral life; (d) disposes of her property or prevents her from exercising her legal rights over it; (e) obstructs her observance of religious practice; (f) if he has more wives than one he does not treat them equitably according to the Quran (DMMA 1939 2:i–viii).

7. In her work in the Imarat-i Shari'a in Bihar, Sabiha Hussain (2007) found the same requirements for faskh.

8. See chapter two for a detailed discussion of the case.

9. The IPC "lays down categories of offenses and stipulates punishment," while the CrPC "lays down procedural rules for investigation and trial" (Agnes 1992, 25).

10. CrPC 498A states: "Whoever, being husband or the relative of the husband of a woman, subject[s] women to cruelty shall be punished with imprisonment for a term which may extend to three years and shall also be liable to fine. Explanation—for the purposes of this section, 'Cruelty' means a) any willful conduct which is of such a nature as is likely to drive the woman to commit suicide or to cause grave injury or danger to life, limb or death whether mental or physical of the woman; or b) harassment of the woman where such harassment is with a view to coercing her or any person related to her [to] meet any unlawful demand for any property or valuable security or is on account of failure by her or any person related to her to meet such a demand."

11. I mention Egypt in particular here because it is in this context that scholars have explicitly begun to consider the question of secularism. However, because they are non-state forums, dar ul-qazas should also be differentiated from "shari'a courts" in Iran (Osanloo 2009), Kenya (Hirsch 1998), Zanzibar (Stiles 2009), and numerous other national contexts.

Chapter 5

1. Bombay High Court Judge J. Batchelor used this phrase in his judgment in the 1905 case *Sarabai v. Rabiabai*. In this case, a widow was denied maintenance by the court because her husband had reportedly issued a talaq ul-ba'in when he was still healthy and died during the subsequent 'iddat period. Although she was never informed of the talaq, the court held that it was nonetheless "good in law, though bad in theology."

2. This range of questions is similar to those asked of the mufti with whom Gregory Kozlowski (1995) conducted ethnographic research in Hyderabad.

3. In India this has long been cited as a major difference between Hindu and Muslim marriage, although, as Uberoi (1995) pointed out, the ostensible gulf in marital practice between members of these communities is overstated.

4. On the particularities of the marriage contract, see Pateman 1988; Mir-Hosseini 2000. I have argued that in the context of Muslim Indian marriages the contract is ambivalent but is, under the right circumstances, a potential tool for democratizing marriage (Lemons 2013).

5. I am not suggesting that the "gate of ijtihad" had closed (Hallaq 1984)—that independent interpretation is no longer possible. Instead, Mufti Ahmed's recourse to ijma' is a reflection of the kinds of questions he has asked, questions for which there are clear responses in the tradition.

6. In Austin's text, the performative "I divorce you" sneaks in just before Don Quixote, as an example of the misfire that occurs when a speech act is not accepted. "Consider 'I divorce you,' said to a wife by her husband in a Christian country, and both being Christians rather than Mohammedans. In this case it might be said, 'nevertheless he has not (successfully) divorced her: we admit only some other verbal or non-verbal procedure'; or even possibly 'we (*we*) do not admit any procedure at all for effecting divorce—marriage is indissoluble.' This may be carried so far that we reject what may be called a *whole code* of procedure, e.g. the code of honor involving dueling: for example, a challenge may be issued by 'my seconds will call on you,' which is equivalent to 'I challenge you,' and we may merely shrug it off. The general position is exploited in the unhappy story of Don Quixote" (Austin 1975, 27).

7. In her study of fatwas from seventeenth- and eighteenth-century Syria and Palestine, Judith Tucker has made a similar argument, suggesting that the triple talaq may in fact be one way that a resourceful woman could secure an escape from marriage *and* maintain her entitlement to mahr and maintenance payments since talaq (like faskh) does not require her to give these up (1998, 91–92).

8. Mahr, as discussed in the previous chapter, refers to money or property due to a woman from her husband. While ideally mahr is given at the time of marriage, often

the husband's family withholds at least half of the property to be granted to the wife in case there is a divorce. In practice, divorcées rarely receive this money (Vatuk 2001).

9. Chambers-Letson writes: "As a result of the simultaneous *making* of law and instantaneous force of the law as established fact . . . the legal production of subjects . . . occurs not as purely constative or purely performative, but as both" (2013, 21).

10. Brinkley Messick (1993) thinks through this quality of the performative by drawing on Bakhtin's notion of "authoritative discourse." Bakhtin writes: "The authoritative word demands that we acknowledge it, that we make it our own; it binds us, quite independent of any power it might have to persuade us internally; we encounter it with its authority already fused to it. The authoritative word is located in a distanced zone, organically connected with a past that is felt to be hierarchically higher. It is, so to speak, the word of the fathers" (1981 quoted in Messick 1993, 342n). In a later article, Messick writes that "it is only in the theory of the unilateral act that this authoritative intentionality can, for some, approach being 'fused' with the spoken word. Otherwise, the 'authoritative word' exists only in the deeper, or prior 'language' of human intentions" (2001, 178).

11. Because indeterminacy is a key term in Agrama's analysis of secularism, it is worth noting that it does something quite different here. The indeterminacy of Agrama's analysis is the constant conundrum that he argues secularism produces: the impossibility of knowing what is properly religious and what secular, and the consequent compulsion to separate the two (2012, chap. 2). Here, as will become clear, I am concerned with a legal speech act that does not determine its own effect but that instead remains indeterminate until the parties involved respond to it through their actions and decisions.

12. There have, in recent years, been several highly publicized cases of fatwas that breach this boundary of personal law. Most notably, a woman named Imrana was allegedly raped by her father-in-law, and in the wake of the event, someone (later revealed to be a journalist) solicited a fatwa on the matter from Darul Uloom Deoband. The fatwa declared that Imrana could no longer be married to her husband. The fatwa sparked tremendous controversy globally. For a thoughtful discussion, see Metcalf 2006.

13. For a more exhaustive list of cases, see Agnes 2011, 1:60–64.

14. Here the court is citing Sayeda Hamid's *Voice of the Voiceless: Status of Muslim Women in India* (2000).

15. These cases are *Jiauddin Ahmed v. Mrs. Anwara Begum* (1978) and *Must. Rukia Khatun v. Abdul Khalique Laskar* (1981). Judge Baharul Islam wrote both judgments.

16. Notably, with few exceptions (including *Dagdu S/o Chotu Pathan, Latur v. Rahimbi Dagdu Pathan, Ashabi Minor D/o Dagdu Pathan and Naimatbi Minor D/o Dagdu Pathan* [2002], *Mariyam Akhtar & Another v. Wazir Mohammed* [2014], and *Fazlur Rahman v. Masummat Ayasha and Another* [1929]), debates over the kind of evidence required to establish talaq ul-ba'in in the courts do not refer to the Indian Evidence Act. Instead, judgments refer to the Quran and commentaries, and to textbooks on Muslim law (see *Shamim Ara*, paragraph 7). Indeed, most of the argumentation in the cases focuses on the felicity conditions of divorce, stating that a divorce needs to be proven without substantiating what kind of documentation or witness statements would constitute such proof.

17. In addition to the cases discussed above, the following exemplify this trend: *Begum Bee* (2011), *Karunissa Begum W/o Aslamkhan v. Aslamkhan S/o Akbar Ali Khan* (2008), and *Masrat Begum v. Abdul Rashid Khan & Another* (2014). In the latter case, the court left the matter undecided, pending a ruling on whether the couple had been divorced, stating that the maintenance claim hung on this decision; *Reshma v. Rashid & Another* (2008), and *Syed Maqsood v. State of A.P. and Another* (2002). One notable exception to this pattern is *Mohammed Ali Jinnah v. Balgees Beevi* (2014), in which the divorce was simply accepted by the court, and the ex-wife was granted maintenance.

18. Two notable exceptions to this are *Yousuf Rawther v. Sowramma* (1971) and *Masroor Ahmed v. State (NCT of Delhi) & Another* (2007).

19. Werner Menski has argued that this approach to personal law is a specifically Indian method for harmonizing law without imposing a uniform civil code. He at the same time argues that by insisting that husbands are responsible for their wives and families, the Indian judiciary avoids "full gender equality in copied western garb," instead insisting on a "culture-specific re-appraisal of moral responsibility." This stance unfortunately reifies the family and "culture-specific moral responsibility," suggesting that the male breadwinner ideal is somehow indigenous to India rather than itself a relatively recent innovation (2008).

Chapter 6

1. Because prayer times are based on the position of the sun, during the summer months *'Asr* prayer falls at about five P.M. and *maghrib* at about eight-thirty P.M. In mid-December *Al-asr* falls at about three P. M. and the *maghrib* at about five-thirty P. M.

2. The dangers of psychic unrest that come with nonnormative or excessive love are not the subject of this chapter. For an excellent analysis of the problem, see Pinto 2014.

3. This kind of magic, jadu, entails the evil spells that jinns and Satan cast using techniques including mesmerism or particular spells. Spells, both good and bad, can have an impact on the soul. The kind of magic that causes relationships to deteriorate is referred to as *haqiqi*. It is mentioned in Quran 2:102 in reference to those who did not follow the Quran but instead "what the satans used to recite," books of magic spells. The one use of magic that is mentioned in the verse is in reference to the separation of a husband from a wife. This is clearly black magic, the use of which disqualifies someone from heaven.

4. In this way the healing practice bears a strong resemblance to the fatwa-writing practice. In both cases, the mufti hears a specific case and responds to its details, giving an answer that is simultaneously individually tailored and generic.

5. "In the Name of God, the Merciful, the Compassionate / Say: 'He is God, One, / God, the / Everlasting Refuge, / Who has not begotten, and has not been begotten / And equal to Him is not any one.'"

6. Annemarie Schimmel's *The Mystery of Numbers* (1994) discusses various mystical number systems, including the Kabala and Islamic number systems.

7. Some naqsh are written so that each row and each column add up to one of the ninety-nine names of God, while others add up to a number that refers to a Quran ayat.

A frequently used naqsh adds up to 11,843, the number that represents Sura Ya-Sin, which Mufti Ahmed and many others refer to as the "heart of the Quran." Another powerful verse is Ayat al-Kursi (the verse of the throne), which many understand to be a particularly powerful ayat. Naksh were important, Mufti Ahmed told me, because it is impossible to write out long Quran verses on ta'wiz because there is not enough space, and doing so would take too long. The power of the Quran's words can be transported instead by means of these numbers.

8. The mufti uses the verb *parhna*, literally "to read," when he describes this part of the healing ritual. However, for the reasons elaborated by Flueckiger (2006), I translate this as a recitation. The mufti never read from the Quran while engaged in healing; instead, he recited the verses that came to mind, verses that he knows by heart.

9. Amma, the healer with whom Joyce Flueckiger studied healing in Hyderabad, used the numerical value of the names of the mother and the afflicted person to attain a diagnosis of the source of the problem. Although when Mufti Ahmed explained the system of numbers to me he also asked for my name and my mother's name and added together "Katherine" and "Mary" to arrive at a value of 910, he never mentioned using this value in a process of diagnosis. He did often ask petitioners for their names and the names of their mothers and of anyone else involved in the matter at hand. He would write these names on the ta'wiz or *falitah* [wicks to be burned], but did not to my knowledge incorporate them into the naksh.

10. This marks a distinction with some other studies of similar healing rituals. For example, El-Tom (1985) argued that the Berti of Sudan understand that recitation of the Quran is superior to its ingestion, as recitation is ingestion by the superior organ of the body, the mind.

11. The ahl-i-hadiis, which means "people of the Hadith," is a group of Muslims who place great emphasis on the Hadith, the sayings and actions of the Prophet as recorded by his followers, than other groups. This leads to several practical differences—for example, in Delhi ahl-i-hadiis women have a section of the mosque in which they pray on Fridays. In Delhi there is notable tension between the ahl-i-hadiis and the Barelwis and other Muslim groups living in the city. I never heard vitriolic comments, but was well aware that the family with whom I lived thought it strange and somewhat suspect that I went on Fridays and other days to visit with ahl-i-hadiis women. Katherine Ewing (1997) notes that in Pakistan, the ahl-i-hadiis are among the Muslim groups who have been strictest about eliminating "local practices" like visiting *pirs* [Sufi saints] and seeking ta'wiz in their pursuit of reform.

12. Naveeda Khan (2006, 2012) discusses various Sunni approaches to knowing the Prophet, and demonstrates that in contemporary Lahore, jinns are simultaneously dismissed and relied on. Her nuanced analysis of a jinn living in the household of a Sunni Urdu and Islamiyat teacher in Lahore shows the role and place of jinns even in households one might expect to refuse them.

13. This language relies on Althusser's concept of interpellation. In the essay "Ideology and the Ideological State Apparatuses," Alhusser depicts a street scene in which a pedestrian, hearing someone call "you there!," turns around. Althusser writes that with this turn, "he becomes a *subject*. Why? Because he recognized that the hail was really directed at him" (1971, 174). The subject recognizes herself because she is already em-

bedded in the ideology that makes it evident to her that she is the addressee. At the same time, it is her own response by means of which she becomes a subject, by heeding the call. In what follows, I think through what it might mean if the hailing of the subject is also hailing of the body.

Conclusion

1. Asad draws here on the philosopher Alisdair MacIntyre's analysis (1984).
2. See, for example, S. Gupta 2016 and Burke 2015.
3. This is reminiscent of what many have shown about communal riots, whether in the 1990s (Hansen 1999, 2001; R. Chatterji and Mehta 2007), or more recently in Gujarat (in 2002), or Muzaffarnagar (in 2013) (Ramakumar 2016; Fazal 2013; Larouche 2017).

BIBLIOGRAPHY

Abu-Lughod, Lila. 2002. "Do Muslim Women Really Need Saving? Anthropological Reflections on Cultural Relativism and Its Others." *American Anthropologist* 104(3): 783–790.

Action India. 2001. *Collective Journeys: Celebrating 25 Years of Action India*. N.p.: Action India. In the author's possession.

Adcock, C. S. 2014. *The Limits of Tolerance: Indian Secularism and the Politics of Religious Freedom*. Oxford: Oxford University Press.

Agarwal, Bina. 1994. *A Field of One's Own: Gender and Land Rights in South Asia*. Cambridge: Cambridge University Press.

Agmon, Iris. 2006. *Family and Court: Legal Culture and Modernity in Late Ottoman Palestine*. Syracuse, NY: Syracuse University Press.

Agnes, Flavia. 1992. "Protecting Women against Violence? A Review of a Decade of Legislation, 1980–1989." *Economic and Political Weekly* 27(17): WS19–W21, WS24–WS33.

——. 1999. *Law and Gender Inequality*. Oxford: Oxford University Press.

——. 2008. "Hindu Conjugality: Transition from Sacrament to Contractual Obligations." In *Redefining Family Law in India*, edited by Archana Parashar and Amita Dhanda, 236–257. Delhi: Oxford University Press.

——. 2011. *Family Law*. Vol. 1 and 2. Oxford: Oxford University Press.

——. 2012. "From Shah Bano to Kausar Bano: Contextualizing the 'Muslim Woman' with a Communalized Polity." In *South Asian Feminisms*, edited by Anya Loomba and Ritty Lukose, 33–53. Durham, NC: Duke University Press.

——. 2016. "Muslim Women's Rights and Media Coverage." *Economic and Political Weekly* 51(20). http://www.epw.in/journal/2016/20/web-exclusives/muslim-womens-rights-and-media-coverage.html.

Agrama, Hussein Ali. 2005. "Law Courts and *Fatwa* Councils in Modern Egypt: An Ethnography of Islamic Legal Practice." diss., Johns Hopkins University.

——. 2010. "Ethics, Tradition, Authority: Toward an Anthropology of the Fatwa." *American Ethnologist* 37(1): 2–18.

——. 2012. *Questioning Secularism: Islam, Sovereignty, and the Rule of Law in Modern Egypt*. Chicago: University of Chicago Press.

Ahmad, Irfan. 2009. *Islamism and Democracy in India: The Transformation of Jamaat-e-Islami*. Princeton, NJ: Princeton University Press.

All India Muslim Personal Board. 2001. *Compendium of Islamic Laws / Majmu'ah-i Qawanin-i Islami*. New Delhi: All India Muslim Personal Board.

Al-Sharmani, Mulki. 2013. "Qiwama in Egyptian Family Laws: 'Wifely Obedience' between Legal Texts, Courtroom Practices and Realities of Marriages." In *Gender and Equality in Muslim Family Law: Justice and Ethics in the Islamic Legal Tradition*, edited by Ziba Mir-Hosseini, Kari Vogt, Lena Larsen, and Christian Moe, 37–56. New York: I. B. Tauris.

Althusser, Louis. 1971. *Lenin and Philosophy, and Other Essays*. New York: Monthly Review Press.

Anand, Kunal. 2016. "The Fight against Triple Talaq Has an Unexpected Friend, the Muslim Women of the RSS!" *India Times*, May 31.

Anderson, Michael R. 1993. "Islamic Law and the Colonial Encounter in British India." In *Institutions and Ideologies: A SOAS South Asia Reader*, edited by David Arnold and Peter Robb, 165–185. Routledge, NY: Psychology Press.

An-Naim, Abdullahi Ahmed. 2010. *Islam and the Secular State*. Cambridge, MA: Harvard University Press.

Asad, Talal. 1986. "The Idea of an Anthropology of Islam." Occasional Papers Series. Washington, DC: Georgetown University Center for Contemporary Arab Studies.

——. 1993. *Genealogies of Religion*. Baltimore, MD: Johns Hopkins University Press.

——. 2003. *Formations of the Secular*. Stanford, CA: Stanford University Press.

——. 2006. "Trying to Understand French Secularism." In *Political Theologies: Public Religions in a Post-Secular World*, edited by Hent DeVries and Laurence E. Sullivan, 494–526. New York: Fordham University Press.

Austin, John Langshaw. 1975. *How to Do Things with Words*. Oxford: Oxford University Press.

Bajpai, Namita. 2016. "Allahabad High Court Terms 'Triple Talaq' as Unconstitutional." *Indian Express*, December 8. http://www.newindianexpress.com/nation/2016/dec/08/triple-talaq-unconstitutional-rules-allahabad-high-court-1546965.

Bajpai, Rochana. 2002. "The Conceptual Vocabularies of Secularism and Minority Rights in India." *Journal of Political Ideologies* 7(2): 179–198.

Bakhtin, Mikhail. 1981. *The Dialogic Imagination: Four Essays*. Translated by C. Emerson and M. Holquist. Austin: University of Texas Press.

Bano, Sabeeha. 2003. "Cunning, Deceit, and Vindictiveness: Case Studies of Divorced Muslim Women and Men in North India." In *Divorce and Remarriage among Muslims in India*, edited by Imtiaz Ahmed, 207–230. New Delhi: Manohar.

Barrett, Michèle, and Mary McIntosh. 1982. *The Antisocial Family*. New York: Verso.

Basu, Srimati. 1999. *She Comes to Take Her Rights: Indian Women, Property, and Propriety*. Albany: State University of New York Press.

———. 2005. *Dowry and Inheritance*. Delhi: Women Unlimited.

———. 2008. "Separate but Unequal: Muslim Women and Un-uniform Family Law in India." *International Feminist Journal of Politics* 10(4): 495–517.

———. 2015. *The Trouble with Marriage: Feminists Confront Law and Violence in India*. Oakland: University of California Press.

Baxi, Upendra. 1992. "'The State's Emissary': The Place of Law in Subaltern Studies." In *Subaltern Studies VII: Writings on South Asian History and Society*, edited by Chatterjee Partha and Gyanendra Pandey, 247–264. Delhi: Oxford University Press.

———. 2007. "Siting Secularism in the Uniform Civil Code: A 'Riddle Wrapped inside an Enigma?'" In *The Crisis of Secularism in India*, edited by Anuradha Dingwaney Needham and Rajeswari Sunder Rajan, 267–293. Durham, NC: Duke University Press.

Bellamy, Carla. 2011. *The Powerful Ephemeral: Everyday Healing in an Ambiguously Islamic Place*. Berkeley: University of California Press.

Benda-Beckman, Keebet von. 1981. "Forum Shopping and Shopping Forms: Dispute Processing in Minankabao Village." *Journal of Legal Pluralism* 13(19): 117–159.

Bhan, Gautam. 2009. "'This Is No Longer the City I Once Knew': Evictions, the Urban Poor and the Right to the City in Millennial Delhi." *Environment and Urbanization* 21(1): 127–142.

Bharadwaj, Suraj Bhan. 2012. "Myth and Reality of the Khap Panchayats: A Historical Analysis of the Panchayat and Khap Panchayat." *Studies in History* 28(1): 43–67.

Bhargava, Rajeev. 1998. *Secularism and Its Critics*. Oxford: Oxford University Press.

———. 2010. *The Promise of India's Secular Democracy*. Oxford: Oxford University Press.

Bhatia, Sidarth. 2016. "From Beef Vigilantism to Flag Nationalism, Indian Politics Hits a New Low." *The Wire*, October 8. https://thewire.in/71799/beef-vigilantism-flag -nationalism-indian-politics-hits-new-low.

Bhuwania, Anuj. 2017. *Courting the People: Public Interest Litigation in Post-Emergency India*. Cambridge: Cambridge University Press.

Bilgrami, Akeel. 2014. *Secularism, Identity, and Enchantment*. Cambridge, MA: Harvard University Press.

Blackstone, William. 1962. *Commentaries on the Laws of England*. Boston: Beacon Press.

Bowen, John. 1993. *Muslims through Discourse: Ritual and Religion in Gayo Society*. Princeton, NJ: Princeton University Press.

Brown, Wendy. 2006. *Regulating Aversion: Tolerance in the Age of Identity and Empire*. Princeton, NJ: Princeton University Press.

Burke, Jason. 2015. "Inside the Indian Village Where a Mob Killed a Man for Eating Beef." *The Guardian*, October 3. https://www.theguardian.com/world/2015/oct/03 /inside-bishari-indian-village-where-mob-killed-man-for-eating-beef.

Butler, Judith. 1991. "Imitation and Gender Insubordination." In *Inside/Out: Lesbian Theories, Gay Theories*, edited by Diana Fuss, 13–31. New York: Routledge.

———. 2002. *Antigone's Claim: Kinship between Life and Death*. New York: Columbia University Press.

———. 2004. *Undoing Gender*. New York: Routledge.

Caeiro, Alexandre. 2011. "The Making of the Fatwa." *Archives de Sciences Sociales des Religions* 155: 81–100.

Carroll, Lucy. 1982. "Talaq-i-Tafwid and Stipulations in a Muslim Marriage Contract: Important Means of Protecting the Position of the South Asian Wife." *Modern Asian Studies* 16(2): 277–309.

———. 1989. "Law, Custom and Statutory Social Reform." In *Women in Colonial India*, edited by J. Krishamurthy, 1–26. Delhi: Oxford University Press.

Chambers-Letson, Joshua Takano. 2013. *A Race So Different: Performance and Law in Asian America*. New York: New York University Press.

Chatterjee, Moyukh. 2017. "The Impunity Effect: Majoritarian Rule, Everyday Legality, and State Formation in India." *American Ethnologist* 44(1): 118–130.

Chatterjee, Nandini. 2010a. "English Law, Brahmo Marriage, and the Problem of Religious Difference: Civil Marriage Laws in Britain and India." *Comparative Studies in Society and History* 52(3): 524–552.

———. 2010b. "Religious Change, Social Conflict and Legal Competition: The Emergence of Christian Personal Law in Colonial India." *Modern Asian Studies* 44(6): 1147–1195.

Chatterjee, Partha. 1998. "Secularism and Tolerance." In *Secularism and Its Critics*, edited by Rajeev Bhargava. Oxford, Delhi: Oxford University Press.

———. 2004. *The Politics of the Governed: Reflections on Popular Politics in Most of the World*. New York: Columbia University Press.

Chatterji, Roma, and Deepak Mehta. 2007. *Living with Violence: An Anthropology of Events and Everyday Life*. New York: Routledge.

Chopra, Radhika, Filippo Osella, and Caroline Osella. 2004. *South Asian Masculinities: Context of Change, Sites of Continuity*. New Delhi: Women Unlimited.

Chowdhry, Prem. 2007. *Contentious Marriages, Eloping Couples: Gender, Caste, and Patriarchy in Northern India*. New Delhi: Oxford University Press.

Cohn, Bernard S. 1987. *An Anthropologist among the Historians and Other Essays*. Oxford: Oxford University Press.

———. 1996. *Colonialism and Its Forms of Knowledge*. Princeton, NJ: Princeton University Press.

Constable, Marianne. 2010. "Speaking the Language of Law: A Juris-dictional Primer." *English Language Notes* 48(2): 9–15.

———. 2014. *Our Word Is Our Bond: How Legal Speech Acts*. Stanford, CA: Stanford University Press.

Cormack, Bradin. 2007. *A Power to Do Justice: Jurisdiction, English Literature, and the Rise of Common Law, 1509–1625*. Chicago: University of Chicago Press.

Coulson, Noel. J. 1964. *A History of Islamic Law*. Edinburgh: Edinburgh University Press.

Dalmia, Vasudha. 1997. *The Nationalization of Hindu Traditions: Bharatendu Harischandra and Nineteenth Century Banaras*. Delhi: Oxford University Press.

Dalmia, Vasudha, and Heinrich von Stietencron. 1995. *Representing Hinduism: The Construction of Religious Traditions and National Identity*. New Delhi: Sage Publications.

Das, Veena. 2007. *Life and Words: Violence and the Descent into the Ordinary*. Berkeley: University of California Press.

De, Rohit. 2009. "Mumtaz Bibi's Broken Heart: The Many Lives of the Dissolution of Muslim Marriages Act." *Indian Economic and Social History Review* 46(1): 105–130.

Deeb, Lara. 2006. *An Enchanted Modern: Gender and Public Piety in Shi'i Lebanon*. Princeton, NJ: Princeton University Press.

Derrett, Duncan. 1964. "Jewish Law in Southern Asia." *International and Comparative Law Quarterly* 13(1): 288–301.

——. 1999. *Religion, Law and the State in India*. Delhi: Oxford University Press.

Derrida, Jacques. 1976. *Of Grammatology*. Baltimore: Johns Hopkins University Press.

——. 1982. *Margins of Philosophy*. Chicago: University of Chicago Press.

——. 1986. "Declarations of Independence." *New Political Science* 7(1): 7–15.

Donzelot, Jacques. 1997. *The Policing of Families*. Baltimore: Johns Hopkins University Press.

Droge, Arthur. 2013. *The Quran: A New Annotated Edition*. Sheffield, UK: Equinox.

Eaton, Richard M. 1993. *The Rise of Islam and the Bengal Frontier, 1204–1760*. Vol. 17. Berkeley: University of California Press.

Eisenstadt, S. N. 2000. "Multiple Modernities." *Daedalus* 129(1): 1–29.

El Hajjami, Aïcha. 2013. "The Religious Arguments in the Debate on the Reform of the Moroccan Family Code." In *Gender and Equality in Muslim Family Law: Justice and Ethics in the Islamic Legal Tradition*, edited by Ziba Mir-Hosseini, Kari Vogt, Lena Larson, and Christian Moe. London: I. B. Tauris.

El-Tom, Abdullahi Osman. 1985. "Drinking the Koran: The Meaning of Koranic Verses in Berti Erasure." In *Popular Islam South of the Sahara*, edited by John D. Peel and C. C. Stewart, 414–431. Manchester, UK: Manchester University Press.

Engels, Friedrich. (1884) 2010. *The Origin of the Family, Private Property and the State*. New York: Penguin Classics.

Ewing, Katherine. 1997. *Arguing Sainthood*. Durham, NC: Duke University Press.

Fazal, Tanweer. 2013. "Lineages of a Riot: Muzaffarnagar Foretold." Hindu Centre for Politics and Public Policy, October 3. http://www.thehinducentre.com/the-arena/article5186233.ece.

Federici, Silvia. 1975. "Wages against Housework." In *The Politics of Housework*, edited by Ellen Malos, 187–194. New York: New Clarion Press.

Felman, Shoshana. 2002. *The Scandal of the Speaking Body: Don Juan with J. L. Austin, or Seduction in Two Languages*. 2nd ed. Stanford, CA: Stanford University Press.

Fernando, Mayanthi L. 2014a. "Intimacy Surveilled: Religion, Sex, and Secular Cunning." *Signs* 39(3): 685–708.

——. 2014b. *The Republic Unsettled: Muslim French and the Contradictions of Secularism*. Durham, NC: Duke University Press.

Fisch, Jörg. 1983. *Cheap Lives and Dear Limbs: The British Transformation of the Bengal Criminal Law, 1769–1817*. N.p.: F. Steiner.

Flueckiger, Joyce Burkhalter. 2006. *In Amma's Healing Room: Gender and Vernacular Islam in South Asia*. Bloomington: Indiana University Press.

Foucault, Michel. 1978. *The History of Sexuality*. Vol. 1. New York: Vintage.

Fyzee, Asaf Ali Ashgar. 1974. *Outlines of Muhammadan Law*. Delhi: Oxford University Press.

Galanter, Marc. 1981. "Justice in Many Rooms: Courts, Private Ordering, and Indigenous Law." *Journal of Legal Pluralism and Unofficial Law* 13(19): 1–47.

——. 1998. "Hinduism, Secularism, and the Indian Judiciary." In *Secularism and Its Critics*, edited by Rajeev Bhargava. Oxford: Oxford University Press.

Galanter, Marc, and Upendra Baxi. 1979. "Panchayat Justice: An Indian Experiment in Legal Access." In *Access to Justice*, Vol. 3, *Emerging Issues and Perspectives*, edited by Mauro Cappelletti and Bryant Garth, 341–86. Milan: Sijthoff and Noordhoff-Alphenaandenrijn.

Galanter, Marc, and R. Dhavan. 1989. *Law and Society in Modern India*. Delhi: Oxford University Press.

Gayer, Laurent. 2012. "Safe and Sound: Searching for a 'Good Environment' in Abul Fazl Enclave, Delhi." In *Muslims in Indian Cities: Trajectories of Marginalisation*, edited by Laurent Gayer and Christophe Jaffrelot, 213–236. London: HarperCollins.

Gayer, Laurent, and Christophe Jaffrelot, eds. 2012. *Muslims in Indian Cities: Trajectories of Marginalisation*. London: HarperCollins.

Geertz, Clifford. 1983. *Local Knowledge: Further Essays in Interpretive Anthropology*. New York: Basic Books.

Ghosh, Durba. 2006. *Sex and the Family in Colonial India: The Making of Empire*. Cambridge: Cambridge University Press.

Ghosh, Papiya. 1997. "Muttahida Quamiyat in Aqalliat Bihar: The Imarat i Sharia, 1921–1947." *Indian Economic and Social History Review* 34(1): 1–20.

Gilmartin, David. 1981. "Kinship, Women and Politics in Twentieth Century Punjab." In *Extended Family: Women and Political Participation in India and Pakistan*, edited by Gail Minault. Delhi: Chanakiya Publications.

Government of India. 2008. Baseline Survey of North-East District, NCT Delhi. Minority Concentrated Districts Project. Ministry of Minority Affairs. Delhi: Jamia Millia Islamia.

——. (2006) 2013. *Sachar Committee Report and Status of Follow Up Action (as on 31.01.2013)*. New Delhi: Ministry of Minority Affairs.

Griffiths, John. 1986. "What Is Legal Pluralism?" *Journal of Legal Pluralism and Unofficial Law* 18(24): 1–55.

Grover, Shalini. 2011. *Marriage, Love, Caste and Kinship Support*. New Delhi: Social Science Press.

——. 2016. "Jural Relations of Middle Class Marriage and Women as Legal Subjects in the Imaginary of 'New India.'" *Australian Journal of Anthropology*. doi: 101111/taja 12188.

Guenther, Alan M. 2003. "Hanafi Fiqh in Mughal India: The Fatāwá-i ʿĀlamgīrī." In *India's Islamic Traditions: 711–1750*, edited by Richard Eaton, 209–233. New Delhi: Oxford University Press.

Gupta, Akhil. 1998. *Postcolonial Developments: Agriculture and the Making of Modern India*. Durham, NC: Duke University Press.

——. 2012. *Red Tape: Bureaucracy, Structural Violence, and Poverty in India.* Durham, NC: Duke University Press.

Gupta, Smita. 2016. "Politics of Meat Ban Creating Polarisation." *The Hindu*, March 28. http://www.thehindu.com/news/national/politics-of-meat-ban-creating-polarisation /article7708079.ece.

Hallaq, Wael. 1984. "Was the Gate of Ijtihad Closed?" *International Journal of Middle East Studies* 16(1): 3–41.

——. 1999. *A History of Islamic Legal Theories: An Introduction to Sunni Usul-al-Fiqh.* Cambridge: Cambridge University Press.

Halley, Janet. 2011. "What Is Family Law?" Part 1. *Yale Journal of Law and the Humanities* 23(1): 1–109.

Halley, Janet, and Kerry Rittich. 2010. "Critical Directions in Comparative Family Law: Genealogies and Contemporary Studies of Family Law Exceptionalism." *American Journal of Comparative Law* 58(4): 753–951.

Hamid, Sayeda. 2000. *Voice of the Voiceless: Status of Muslim Women in India.* New Delhi: Report for the National Commission for Women.

Hansen, Thomas Blom. 1999. *The Saffron Wave: Democracy and Hindu Nationalism in Modern India.* Princeton, NJ: Princeton University Press.

——. 2001. *Wages of Violence: Naming and Identity in Postcolonial Bombay.* Princeton, NJ: Princeton University Press.

——. 2011. "Secular Speech and Popular Passions: The Antinomies of Indian Secularism." In *After Secular Law*, edited by Winnifred Sullivan and Mateo Taussig-Rubbo, 261–281. Stanford, CA: Stanford University Press.

——. 2013. "Secularism, Popular Passion, and Public Order in India." In *Contesting Secularism: Comparative Perspectives*, edited by Anders Berg-Sørensen, 207–232. London: Routledge.

Harris, Olivia. 1984. "Households as Natural Units." In *Of Marriage and the Market*, edited by, Kate Young, Carole Wolkowitz, and Roslyn McCullagh. London: Routledge and Kegan Paul.

Hasan, Zoya, and Ritu Menon. 2004. *Unequal Citizens: A Study of Muslim Women in India.* New Delhi: Oxford University Press.

Hayden, Robert. 1999. *Disputes and Arguments among Nomads: A Caste Council in India.* New Delhi: Oxford University Press.

Hidayatullah, M., and Arshad Hidayatullah. 2001. *Mulla Principles of Mohamedan Law.* Lexis Nexis Butterworths.

Hirsch, Susan. 1998. *Pronouncing and Preserving: Gender and the Discourse of Disputing in an African Islamic Court.* Chicago: University of Chicago Press.

Hirschkind, Charles. 2006. *Ethical Soundscapes: Cassette Sermons and Islamic Counterpublics.* New York: Columbia University Press.

Holden, Livia. 2003. "Custom and Law Practices in Central India: Some Case Studies." *South Asia Research* 23(2): 115–134.

——. 2008. *Hindu Divorce: A Legal Anthropology.* Aldershot, England: Ashgate Publishers.

Hong Tschalär, Mengia. 2017. *Muslim Women's Quest for Justice.* Cambridge: Cambridge University Press.

Hull, Matthew. 2012. *Government of Paper*. Berkeley: University of California Press.

Hussain, Sabiha. 2007. "Shariat Courts and Women's Rights in India." Occasional Papers Series. Delhi: Center for Women's Development Studies.

Jackson, Michael. 2011. *Life within Limits: Well-Being in a World of Want*. Durham, NC: Duke University Press.

Jackson, Sherman. 2001. "Kramer versus Kramer in a Tenth/Sixteenth Century Egyptian Court: Post-Formative Jurisprudence between Exigency and Law." *Islamic Law and Society* 18(1): 27–51.

Jaising, Indira. 2009. "Bringing Rights Home: Review of the Campaign for a Law on Domestic Violence." *Economic and Political Weekly* 44(44): 50–57.

——. 2017. "Besides Gender Justice, Triple Talaq Case Was Also about Separating Religion and State in Family Law." *The Wire*, August 23. https://thewire.in/170195/triple-talaq-gender-justice-separation-of-state-from-religion/.

Jakobsen, Janet R., and Ann Pelligrini. 2008. *Secularisms*. Durham, NC: Duke University Press.

Jalal, Ayesha. 2000. *Self and Sovereignty: Individual and Community in South Asian Islam since 1850*. London: Routledge.

Jeffery, Patricia. 1979. *Frogs in a Well: Indian Women in Purdah*. London: Zed Press.

Jones, Justin. 2010. "'Signs of Churning': Muslim Personal Law and Signs of Contestation in Twenty-First Century India." *Modern Asian Studies* 44(1): 175–200.

Kapadia, Kirin, ed. 2002. *The Violence of Development*. London: Zed Books.

Kapur, Ratna, and Brenda Crossman. 1996. *Subversive Sites: Feminist Engagement with Law in India*. New Delhi: Sage Publications.

——.1996. "Secularism: Bench-Marked by the Hindu Right." *Economic and Political Weekly* 31(38): 2613–2617, 2619–2627, 2629–2630.

Keane, Webb. 2013. "On Spirit Writing: Materialities of Language and the Religious Work of Transduction." *Journal of the Royal Anthropological Institute* 19(1): 1–17.

Kennedy, Duncan. 2010. "Savigny's Family/Patrimony Distinction and Its Place in the Global Genealogy of Classical Legal Thought." *American Journal of Comparative Law* 58(4): 811–841.

Khan, Fareeha. 2008. "Traditionalist Approaches to Shari'a Reform: Maulana Ashraf 'Ali Thanawi's *Fatwa* on Women's Right to Divorce." PhD diss., Department of History, University of Michigan.

Khan, Naveeda. 2006. "Of Children and Jinn: An Inquiry into an Unexpected Friendship during Uncertain Times." *Cultural Anthropology* 21(2): 234–264.

——. 2012. *Muslim Becoming: Aspiration and Skepticism in Pakistan*. Durham, NC: Duke University Press.

Kholoussy, Hanan. 2010. *For Better, For Worse: The Marriage Crisis that Made Modern Egypt*. Stanford, CA: Stanford University Press.

Kozlowski, Gregory C. 1995. "Loyalty, Locality, and Authority in Several Opinions (Fatawa) Delivered by the *Mufti* of the Jami'at Nizamiyyah Madrasah, Hyderabad, India." *Modern Asian Studies* 29(4): 893–927.

Kugle, Scott Alan. 2001. "Framed, Blamed and Renamed: The Recasting of Islamic Jurisprudence in Colonial South Asia." *Modern Asian Studies* 35(2): 257–313.

Larouche, Catherine. 2017. "'Developing' Muslims? Islamic Charity, Minority Politics and Violence in Uttar Pradesh." PhD diss., Department of Anthropology, McGill University.

Lasch, Christopher. 1979. *Haven in a Heartless World: The Family Besieged*. New York: Basic Books.

Lazarus-Black, Mindie. 2007. *Everyday Harm: Domestic Violence, Court Rites, and Cultures of Reconciliation*. Urbana-Champaign: University of Illinois Press.

Lemons, Katherine. 2013. "When Marriage Breaks Down, How Do Contracts Matter? Marriage Contracts and Divorce in Contemporary North India." In *Marriage in Globalizing Contexts: Exploring Change and Continuity in South Asia*, edited by Shalini Grover, Ravinder Kaur, and Rajni Palriwala, 371–388. Delhi: Orient Blackswan.

———. 2016. "The Politics of 'Livability': Tutoring Kinship in a New Delhi Women's Arbitration Center." *Political and Legal Anthropology Review* 39(2): 244–260.

Live Law News Network. 2016. "Centre Urges SC to Abolish Triple Talaq, Polygamy [Read Affidavit]." *Live Law*, October 8. http://www.livelaw.in/centre-urges-sc-abolish-triple-talaq-polygamy/.

Lodhia, Sharmila. 2009. "Legal Frankensteins and Monstrous Women: Juridical Narratives of the 'Family in Crisis.'" *Meridians: Feminism, Race, Transnationalism* 9(2): 102–129.

Madan, T. N. 1987. "Secularism in Its Place." *Journal of Asian Studies* 46(4): 747–759.

———. 1998. "Secularism in Its Place." In *Secularism and Its Critics*, edited by Rajeev Bhargava, 297–320. Oxford: Oxford University Press.

Mahmood, Saba. 2005. *The Politics of Piety*. Princeton, NJ: Princeton University Press.

———. 2013. "Sexuality and Secularism." In *Religion, the Secular, and the Politics of Sexual Difference*, edited by Linell Cady and Tracy Fessenden, 47–58. New York: Columbia University Press.

———. 2016. *Religious Difference in a Secular Age: A Minority Report*. Princeton, NJ: Princeton University Press.

Mahmood, Tahir. 1995. *Statutes of Personal Law in Islamic Countries*. Delhi: India and Islam Research Council.

———. 2002. *The Muslim Law of India*. Delhi: LexisNexis Butterworths.

Majumdar, Rochona. 2009. *Marriage and Modernity: Family Values in Colonial Bengal*. Durham, NC: Duke University Press.

Makdisi, George. 1979. "The Significance of the Sunni Schools of Law in Islamic Religious History." *International Journal of Middle East Studies* 10(1): 1–8.

Mani, Lata. 1998. *Contentious Traditions: The Debate on Sati in Colonial India*. Berkeley: University of California Press.

Manoukian, Setrag. 1996. "Fatwas as Asymmetrical Dialogues: Muhammad Karmin Khan Kirmani and his Questions." In *Islamic Legal Interpretation: Muftis and Their Fatwas*, edited by Muhammad Khalid Masud, Brinkley Messick, and David S. Powers, 162–172. Oxford: Oxford University Press.

Mantena, Karuna. 2010. *Alibis of Empire: Henry Maine and the Ends of Liberal Imperialism*. Princeton, NJ: Princeton University Press.

Masoodi, Ashwaq. 2017. "The Thorny Issue of Triple Talaq: While Women Rights Activists See Banning Triple Talaq as a Means of Ensuring Gender Equality, Opponents of the Ban See It as the First Step towards a Uniform Civil Code." *LiveMint*, January 13. http://www.livemint.com/Politics/Ial1al8yQxmyuAjDDNKhGJ/The-thorny-issue-of-triple-talaq.html.

Masud, Muhammad Khalid. 1996. "Apostasy and Judicial Separation in British India." In *Islamic Legal Interpretation: Muftis and Their Fatwas*, edited by Muhammad Khalid Masud, Brinkley Messick, and David S. Powers, 193–203. Oxford: Oxford University Press.

Masud, Muhammad Khalid, Brinkley Messick, and David S. Powers. 1996. *Islamic Legal Interpretation: Muftis and Their Fatwas*. Oxford: Oxford University Press.

Maurer, Bill. 2013. "Jurisdictions in Dialect: Sovereignty Games in the British Virgin Islands." In *European Integration and Postcolonial Sovereignty Games: The EU Overseas Countries and Territories*, edited by Rebecca Adler-Nissen and Ulrik Pram Gad, 130–144. London: Routledge.

McClure, Kirstie M. 1990. "Difference, Diversity, and the Limits of Toleration." *Political Theory* 18(3): 361–391.

Menon, Nivedita. 2007. "Living with Secularism." In *The Crisis of Secularism in India*, edited by Anuradha Dingwaney Needham and Rajeswari Sunder Rajan, 118–140. Durham, NC: Duke University Press.

Menski, Werner. 2008. "The Uniform Civil Code Debate in Indian Law: New Developments and Changing Agenda." *German Law Journal* 9(3): 211–250.

Merry, Sally Engle. 1990. *Getting Justice and Getting Even: Legal Consciousness among Working-Class Americans*. Chicago: University of Chicago Press.

——. 2001. "Rights, Religion, and Community: Approaches to Violence against Women in the Context of Globalization." *Law and Society Review* 35(1): 39–88.

——. 2006. "Transnational Human Rights and Local Activism: Mapping the Middle." *American Anthropologist* 108(1): 38–51.

Mertz, Elizabeth. 1994. "Legal Language: Pragmatics, Poetics, and Social Power." *Annual Review of Anthropology* 23: 435–455.

Messick, Brinkley. 1993. *The Calligraphic State: Textual Domination and History in a Muslim Society*. Berkeley: University of California Press.

——. 2001. "Indexing the Self: Intent and Expression in Islamic Legal Acts." *Islamic Law and Society* 8(2): 151–178.

Metcalf, Barbara Daly. 1982. *Islamic Revival in British India: Deoband, 1860–1900*. Delhi: Oxford University Press.

——. 2006. "Rape, Islam, and Law in India." *Islamic Studies* 45(3): 389–412.

Mir-Hosseini, Ziba. 2000. *Marriage on Trial: A Study of Islamic Family Law; Iran and Morocco Compared*. London: I. B. Tauris.

Modern, John Lardas. 2013. "Confused Parchments, Infinite Socialities: The Immanent Frame." Accessed December 20, 2016. http://blogs.ssrc.org/tif/2013/03/04/confused-parchments-infinite-socialities/.

Mody, Parveez. 2008. *The Intimate State*. New York: Routledge.

Moore, Erin. 1993. "Gender, Power, and Legal Pluralism: Rajasthan, India." *American Ethnologist* 20(3): 522–542.

———. 1998. *Gender, Law and Resistance in India*. Tucson: University of Arizona.

Mufti, Aamir. 1995. "Secularism and Minority: Elements of a Critique." *Social Text* 45: 75–96.

Mukhopadhyay, Maithrayee. 1998. *Legally Dispossessed: Gender Identity and the Process of Law*. Calcutta: Stree.

Müller-Freienfels, Wolfram. 2003. "The Emergence of Droit de Famille and Familien-recht in Continental Europe and the Introduction of Family Law in England." *Journal of Family History* 28(1): 31–51.

Nader, Laura. 1990. *"Harmony Ideology": Justice and Control in a Zapotec Mountain Village*. Stanford, CA: Stanford University Press.

———. 1993. "Controlling Processes in the Practice of Law: Hierarchy and Pacification in the Movement to Reform Dispute Ideology." *Ohio State Journal on Dispute Resolution* 9(1): 1–25.

———. 2002. *The Life of the Law*. Berkeley: University of California Press.

Nair, Harish V. 2016. "Centre Files Affidavit in SC Opposing Triple Talaq, Calls Practice Discriminatory." *India Today*, October 8. http://indiatoday.intoday.in/story/triple-talaq-uniform-civil-code-womens-rights-centre-secularism/1/783051.html.

Nair, Janaki. 1996. *Women and Law in Colonial History*. New Delhi: Kali for Women Press.

Nair, Shalini. 2016. "Govt., Law Board: Framing the Triple Talaq Argument." *Indian Express*, October 14. http://indianexpress.com/article/explained/shayara-bano-law-board-triple-talaq-supreme-court-3077695/.

Nandy, Ashis. 1998. "The Politics of Secularism and the Recovery of Religious Toleration." In *Secularism and Its Critics*, edited by Rajeev Bhargava. Oxford: Oxford University Press.

———. 2007. "Closing the Debate on Secularism: A Personal Statement." In *The Crisis of Secularism in India*, edited by Anuradha Dingwaney Needham and Rajeswari Sunder Rajan, 107–117. Durham, NC: Duke University Press.

Navaro-Yashin, Yael. 2002. *Faces of the State: Secularism and Public Life in Turkey*. Princeton, NJ: Princeton University Press.

Needham, Anuradha Dingwaney, and Rajeswari Sunder Rajan, eds. 2007. *The Crisis of Secularism in India*. Durham, NC: Duke University Press.

Oakley, Ann. 1976. *Women's Work: Housewives Past and Present*. New York: Random House.

Okin, Susan M. 1989. *Justice, Gender, and the Family*. New York: Basic Books.

Oldenburg, Veena Talwar. 2002. *Dowry Murder: The Imperial Origins of a Cultural Crime*. Oxford: Oxford University Press.

Osanloo, Arzoo. 2009. *The Politics of Women's Rights in Iran*. Princeton, NJ: Princeton University Press.

Osella, Caroline, and Filippo Osella. 2006. *Men and Masculinities in South India*. London: Anthem Press.

Pandey, Gyanendra. 2007. "The Secular State and the Limits of Dialogue." In *The Crisis of Secularism in India*, edited by Anuradha Dingwaney Needham and Rajeswari Sunder Rajan, 157–176. Durham, NC: Duke University Press.

Parashar, Archana. 1992. *Women and Family Law Reform in India: Uniform Civil Code and Gender Equality*. Delhi: Sage Publications.

Parashar, Archana, and Amita Dhanda, eds. 2008. *Redefining Family Law in India*. Delhi: Oxford University Press.

Pateman, Carole. 1988. *The Sexual Contract*. Stanford, CA: Stanford University Press.

Peletz, Michael G. 2002. *Islamic Modern: Religious Courts and Cultural Politics in Malaysia*. Princeton, NJ: Princeton University Press.

Pinto, Sarah. 2011. "Rational Love, Relational Medicine: Psychiatry and the Accumulation of Precarious Kinship." *Culture, Medicine, and Psychiatry* 36(3): 376–395.

——. 2014. *Daughters of Parvati: Women and Madness in Contemporary India*. Philadelphia: University of Pennsylvania Press.

Pisharoty, Sangeeta Barooah. 2016. "Muslim Residents Fearful after Gurgaon Police Make First 'Beef' Arrests." *The Wire*, February 4. https://thewire.in/20833/muslim-residents-fearful-after-gurgaon-police-make-first-beef-arrests.

Povinelli, Elizabeth. 2002. *The Cunning of Recognition*. Princeton, NJ: Princeton University Press.

——. 2011. *Economies of Abandonment*. Durham, NC: Duke University Press.

Rafat, Zakiya. 2003. "Muslim Women's Divorce and Remarriage in a Town of Western Uttar Pradesh." In *Divorce and Remarriage among Muslims in India*, edited by Imtiaz Ahmed, 75–100. New Delhi: Manohar.

Ramakumar, R. 2016. "Jats, Khaps and Riots: Communal Politics and the Bharatiya Kisan Union in Northern India." *Journal of Agrarian Change* 17(1): 22–42.

Ramberg, Lucinda. 2013. "Troubling Kinship: Sacred Marriage and Gender Configuration in South India." *American Ethnologist* 40(4): 661–675.

——. 2014. *Given to the Goddess: South Indian Devadasis and the Sexuality of Religion*. Durham, NC: Duke University Press.

——. 2015. *Conjugality Unbound: Sexual Economies, State Regulation and the Marital Form in India*, edited by Srimati Basu and Lucinda Ramberg. New Delhi: Women Unlimited.

Randeria, Shalini. 2006. "Entangled Histories: Civil Society, Caste Solidarities, and Legal Pluralism in Post-Colonial India." In *Civil Society: Berlin Perspectives*, edited by John Keane, 213–242. New York: Berghahn Books.

Rasheed, Mohammad Arif. 2003. "Muslim Women and the Dowry Prohibition Act, 1961: A Study of Selected Divorce Cases." In *Divorce and Remarriage among Muslims in India*, edited by Imtiaz Ahmed, 343–366. New Delhi: Manohar.

Redding, Jeffrey. 2010. "Institutional v. Liberal Contexts for Contemporary Non-state, Muslim Civil Dispute Resolution Systems." *Journal of Islamic State Practices in International Law* 6(1).

——. 2013. "Secularism, the Rule of Law, and Shari'a Courts: An Ethnographic Examination of a Constitutional Controversy." *Saint Louis University Law Journal* 57: 339.

Richland, Justin. 2011. "Hopi Tradition as Jurisdiction: On the Potentializing Limits of Hopi Sovereignty." *Law and Social Inquiry* 36(1): 201–234.

——. 2013. "Jurisdiction: Grounding Law in Language." *Annual Review of Anthropology* 42: 209–226.

Roland, Joan G. 1998. *The Jewish Communities of India: Identity in a Colonial Era.* Piscataway, NJ: Transaction.

Rosen, Lawrence. 2000. *The Justice of Islam.* Oxford: Oxford University Press.

Rudolph, Lloyd I., and Susanne Hoeber Rudolph. 1987. *In Pursuit of Lakshmi: The Political Economy of the Indian State.* Chicago: University of Chicago Press.

Sangari, Kumkum, and Sudesh Vaid. 1989. *Recasting Women: Essays in Colonial History.* New Delhi: Kali for Women.

Sarin, Jitendra. 2016. "Triple Talaq Misunderstood but Can't Trump Constitutional Rights: Allahabad HC." *Hindustan Times,* December 8. http://www.hindustantimes .com/india-news/triple-talaq-unconstitutional-violates-rights-of-women-allahabad -hc/story-DK2jCqoEtEMwXpvVaLja2H.html.

Sarkar, Sumit, and Tanika Sarkar. 2008. *Women and Social Reform in Modern India: A Reader.* Bloomington: Indiana University Press.

Schacht, Joseph. 1950. *The Origins of Muhammadan Jurisprudence.* Oxford: Clarendon Press.

———. 1964. *An Introduction to Islamic Law.* New York: Clarendon Press.

Schimmel, Annemarie. 1994. *The Mystery of Numbers.* New York: Oxford University Press.

Scott, Joan Wallach. 1996. *Only Paradoxes to Offer.* Cambridge, MA: Harvard University Press.

———. 2007. *The Politics of the Veil.* Princeton, NJ: Princeton University Press.

———. 2011. *The Fantasy of Feminist History.* Durham, NC: Duke University Press.

Sekhon, Joti. 1999. "Grassroots Social Organization and Empowerment in India: The Case of Action India Women's Program." In *Democratization and Women's Grassroots Movements,* edited by Jill M. Bystydzienski and Joti Sekhon, 25–48. Bloomington: Indiana University Press.

Sethi, Aman. 2006. "Uneasy Reprieve." *Frontline* 23(20).

Sezgin, Yüksel. 2013. *Human Rights under State-Enforced Religious Family Laws in Israel, Egypt, and India.* Cambridge: Cambridge University Press.

Sharafi, Mitra. 2014. *Law and Identity in Colonial South Asia: Parsi Legal Culture, 1772– 1947.* New York: Cambridge University Press.

Sharda, Shailvee. 2016. "Triple Talaq Unconstitutional, It Violates Rights of Muslim Women: Allahabad. High Court." *Times of India,* December 8. http://timesofindia .indiatimes.com/india/Triple-talaq-unconstitutional-it-violates-rights-of-Muslim -women-Allahabad-high-court/articleshow/55869880.cms.

Sharma, Aradhana. 2008. *Logics of Empowerment: Development, Gender, and Governance in Neoliberal India.* Minneapolis: University of Minnesota Press.

Simpson, Bob. 1998. *Changing Families: An Ethnographic Approach to Divorce and Separation.* New York: Berg.

Singha, Radhika. 1998. *A Despotism of Law: Crime and Justice in Early Colonial India.* Delhi: Oxford University Press.

Skovgaard-Petersen, Jakob. 1997. *Defining Islam for the Egyptian State: Muftis and Fatwas of the Dār al-Iftā.* Leiden: Brill.

Smith, Donald Eugene. 1963. *India as a Secular State.* Princeton, NJ: Princeton University Press.

Solanki, Gopika. 2011. *Adjudication in Religious Family Laws: Cultural Accommodation, Legal Pluralism, and Gender Equality in India*. New York: Cambridge University Press.

Soneji, Davesh. 2012. *Unfinished Gestures: Devadāsīs, Memory, and Modernity in South India*. Chicago: University of Chicago Press.

Sonneveld, Nadia. 2012. *Khul' Divorce in Egypt: Public Debates, Judicial Practices, and Everyday Life*. Cairo, Egypt, and New York: American University in Cairo Press.

Sousa Santos, Bonavoantura de. 1987. "Law: A Map of Misreading. Toward a Postmodern Conception of the Law." *Journal of Law and Society* 14(3): 279–302.

Spadola, Emilio. 2014. *The Calls of Islam: Sufis, Islamists, and Mass Mediation in Urban Morocco*. Indianapolis: Indiana University Press.

Sreenivas, Mytheli. 2004. "Conjugality and Capital: Gender, Families, and Property under Colonial Law in India." *Journal of Asian Studies* 63(4): 937–960.

Srinivas, M.N. 1984. "Some Reflections on Dowry." Delhi: Oxford University Press.

Stepan, Alfred. 2011. "The Multiple Secularisms of Modern Democratic and Non-democratic Regimes." In *Rethinking Secularism*, edited by Craig Calhoun, Mark Jurgensmeyer, and Jonathan VanAntwerpen, 114–144. New York: Oxford University Press.

Stiles, Erin. 2009. *An Islamic Court in Context*. New York: Palgrave MacMillan.

Stolcke, Verena. 1984. "Women's Labors: The Naturalization of Social Inequality and Women's Subordination." In *Of Marriage and the Market: Women's Subordination Internationally and Its Lessons*, edited by Kate Young, Carol Woklowitz, and Roslyn McCullagh, 159–177. London: Routledge and Kegan Paul.

Sturman, Rachel. 2012. *The Government of Social Life in Colonial India: Liberalism, Religious Law, and Women's Rights*. Cambridge: Cambridge University Press.

———. 2014. "Indian Indentured Labor and the History of International Rights Regimes." *American Historical Review* 119(5): 1439–1465.

Subramanian, Narendra. 2008. "Legal Changes and Gender Inequality: Changes in Muslim Family Law in India." *Law and Social Inquiry* 33(631): 631–672.

———. 2014. *Nation and Family: Personal Law, Cultural Pluralism, and Gendered Citizenship in India*. Stanford, CA: Stanford University Press.

Sullivan, Winnifred Fallers. 2005. *The Impossibility of Religious Freedom*. Princeton, NJ: Princeton University Press.

Sunder Rajan, Rajeswari. 2003. *The Scandal of the State: Women, Law, and Citizenship in Postcolonial India*. Durham, NC: Duke University Press.

Sunder Rajan, Rajeswari, and Zakiya Pathak. 1992. "Shahbano." In *Feminists Theorize the Political*, edited by Judith Butler and Joan Scott, 257–279. New York: Routledge.

Surkis, Judith. 2006. *Sexing the Citizen*. Ithaca, NY: Cornell University Press.

———. 2010. "Hymenal Politics: Marriage, Secularism, and French Sovereignty." *Public Culture* 22(3): 531–556.

Tambar, Kabir. 2014. *The Reckoning of Pluralism: Political Belonging and the Demands of History in Turkey*. Stanford, CA: Stanford University Press.

Taneja, Anand. 2013. "Jinnealogy: Everyday Life and Islamic Theology in Post-Partition Delhi." *HAU: Journal of Ethnographic Theory* 3(3): 139–167.

Tarlo, Emma. 2003. *Unsettling Memories*. Berkeley: University of California Press.

Taylor, Charles. 2007. *A Secular Age*. Cambridge, MA: Harvard University Press.

Tejani, Shabnam. 2007. "Reflections on the Category of Secularism in India: Gandhi, Ambedkar, and the Ethics of Communal Representation, c. 1931." In *The Crisis of Secularism in India*, edited by Needham Anuradha Dingwaney and Rajeswari Sunder Rajan, 45–65. Durham, NC: Duke University Press.

——. 2008. *Indian Secularism: A Social and Intellectual History, 1890–1950*. Bloomington: Indiana University Press.

Thapar, Romila. 2015. "What Secularism Is and Where It Needs to Be Headed." *The Wire*, October 18. http://thewire.in/12539/what-secularism-is-and-where-it-needs-to-be -headed/.

Travers, Robert. 2007. *Ideology and Empire in Eighteenth-Century India: The British in Bengal*. Cambridge: Cambridge University Press.

Trawick, Margaret. 1990. *Notes on Love in a Tamil Family*. Berkeley: University of California Press.

Tucker, Judith. 1998. *In the House of the Law: Gender and Islamic Law in Ottoman Syria and Palestine*. Berkeley: University of California Press.

——. 2008. *Women, Family and Gender in Islamic Law*. Cambridge U.K.: Cambridge University Press.

Uberoi, Patricia. 1995. "When Is Marriage Not a Marriage? Sex, Sacrament, and Contract in Hindu Marriage." *Contributions to Indian Sociology* 29(1–2): 319–345.

Van der Veer, Peter. 1994. *Religious Nationalism: Hindus and Muslims in India*. Berkeley: University of California Press.

Vatuk, Sylvia. 2001. "'Where Will She Go? What Will She Do?' Paternalism toward Women in the Administration of Muslim Personal Law in Contemporary India." In *Religion and Personal Law in Secular India*, edited by Gerald James Larson, 226–250. Bloomington: Indiana University Press.

——. 2008. "Divorce at the Wife's Initiative in Muslim Personal Law: What Are the Options and What Are Their Implications for Women's Welfare?" In *Redefining Family Law in India*, edited by Archana Parashar and Amita Dhanda, 200–235. London: Routledge.

——. 2013. "The 'Women's Court' in India: An Alternative Dispute Resolution Body for Women in Distress." *Journal of Legal Pluralism and Unofficial Law* 45(1): 76–103.

——. 2014. "Change and Continuity in Marital Alliance Patterns: Muslims in South India, 1800–2012." In *Marrying in South Asia: Shifting Concepts, Changing Practices in a Globalising World*, edited by Ravinder Kaur and Rajni Palriwala, 28–48. Hyderabad: Orient BlackSwan.

——. 2017. *Marriage and Its Discontents: Women, Islam, and the Law in India*. New Delhi: Women Unlimited.

Vogel, Lise. 1995. *Woman Questions: Essays for a Materialist Feminism*. New York: Routledge.

Warner, Michael. 2012. "Was Antebellum America Secular?" *The Immanent Frame* (blog). Accessed December 20, 2016. http://blogs.ssrc.org/tif/2012/10/02/was -antebellum-america-secular/.

Weitzman, Lenore J. 1985. *The Divorce Revolution: The Unexpected Social and Economic Consequences for Women and Children in America*. New York: Free Press.

Welchmann, Lynn. 2011. "A Husband's Authority: Emerging Formulations in Muslim Family Law." *International Journal of Law, Policy and the Family* 25(1): 1–23.

Whitehead, Anne. 1984. "'I'm Hungry Mum': The Politics of Domestic Budgeting." In *Of Marriage and the Market: Women's Subordination Internationally and Its Lessons*, edited by Kate Young, Carol Woklowitz, and Roslyn McCullagh, 93–116. London: Routledge and Kegan Paul.

Williams, Rina Verma. 2006. *Postcolonial Politics and Personal Laws*. Delhi: Oxford University Press.

Wire Staff. 2016a. "Man Arrested for WhatsApp Message on Beef Dies in Police Custody." *The Wire*, October 12. https://thewire.in/72556/beef-whatsapp-custodial-death.

———. 2016b. "Triple Talaq Unconstitutional, Says Allahabad High Court." *The Wire*, December 8. http://thewire.in/85399/triple-talaq-allahabad-high-court.

———. 2016c. "Two Muslim Women Attacked over Beef Rumours; Police Watch." *The Wire*, July 27. https://thewire.in/54224/muslim-women-beaten-beef-rumour.

Yngvesson, Barbara. 1988. "Making Law at the Doorway: The Clerk, the Court, and the Construction of Community in a New England Town." *Law and Society Review* 22(3): 409–448.

Yusuf, K. M. 1965. "The Judiciary in India under the Sultans of Delhi and the Mughal Emperors." *Indo-iranica* 18(4): 1–12.

Zaman, Muhammad Qasim. 2002. *The Ulama in Contemporary Islam: Custodians of Change*. Princeton, NJ: Princeton University Press.

———. 2008. *Ashraf Ali Thanawi: Islam in Modern South Asia*. Oxford: Oneworld Publications.

Zantout, Mida. 2008. "Khul': Between Past and Present; Islamic Law and Law of the Muslim World." New York Law School Research Paper Series 08–14.

Legal Cases

Bai Tahira v. Ali Hussein Fidaali Clothia and Anr. AIR 1979 SC 362

Begum Bee and Moulan Bee v. Shaikh Hussain and Anr. (2011) LAWS(APH), Criminal Petition 2286 of 2008

Dagdu S/o Chotu Pathan, Latur v. Rahimbi Dagdu Pathan, Ashabi Minor D/o Dagdu Pathan and Naimatbi Minor D/o Dagdu Pathan. (2002) 2003(1) BomCR Cri

Danial Latifi v. Union of India. 2001 (7) SCC 740

Fazlur Rahman v. Musammat Ayasha and Anr. AIR 1929 Pat 81

Fuzlunbi v. K. Khader Vali and Anr. AIR 1980 SC 1730

Harvinder Kaur v. Harminder Singh. AIR 1984 Del 66

Iqbal Bano v. State of U.P. (2007) INDLAW SC 618

Jiauddin Ahmed v. Mrs. Anwara Begum. (1978) 1 GLR 375

Kharunissa Begum W/o Aslamkhan v. Aslamkhan S/o Akbar Ali Khan. (2008) BomCR Criminal Application 829 of 1997

Mariyam Akhtar & Anr. v. Wazir Mohammed. (2014) Jammu and Kashmir Cr.Rev.50/2005

Masrat Begum v. Abdul Rashid Khan & Anr. (March 3, 2014). Accessed September 29, 2016. https://indiankanoon.org/doc/29284431/

Masroor Ahmed v. State (NCT of Delhi) and Anr. (2007) ILR 2 Delhi 329

Mohammed Ali Jinnah v. M. Balgees Beevi. (2014). Accessed September 29, 2016. https://indiankanoon.org/doc/82381651/

Mohd. Ahmed Khan v. Shah Bano Begum. AIR 1985 SC 945

Mohd. Haneefa v. Pathummal Beevi. 1972 KerLT 512

Must. Rukia Khatun v. Abdul Khalique Laskar. (1981)1 GLR 375

Parveen Akhtar v. Union of India. (2002) 1 LW370

Pathayi v. Mideen. 1968 KLT 763

Prakash and Others v. Phulawati and Ors. Civil Appeal No. 7217 of 2013

Rahmat Ullah and Khatoon Nisa v. State of U.P. and Ors. II (1994) DMC64

Reshma v. Rashid & Anr. (2008) High Court of Uttarakhand. First Appeal 18 of 2007

Sarabai v. Rabiabai. (1905) ILR 30 Bombay 537

Saroj Rani v. Sudharshan Kumar Chadha. 1984 AIR 1562

Shabnam Bano v. Mohd. Rafiq & Ors. RLW 2009 (4) Raj 3158

Shamim Ara v. State of U.P. and Anr. 2002(3) ACR 3013 (SC)

Shayara Bano v. Union of India and Others. Supreme Court Writ Petition No. 118 of 2016

Srimati Hina and Another v. State of UP and 2 Others. WRIT-C No. 51421 of 2016

Syed Maqsood v. State of A.P. and Anr. (2002) AIR 2003 AP 123

T. Sareetha v. Venkatasubbiah. AIR 1983 AP 356

Vishwa Lochan Madan v. Union of India. (July 7, 2014) Writ Petition 386 of 2005, SC

Yousuf Rawther v. Sowramma. AIR 1971 Ker 261

Zohara Khatoon v. Mohd. Ibrahim. AIR 1981 1243

Legislation

Constitution of India

Criminal Procedure Code (CrPC) 125

Criminal Procedure Code (CrPC) 498A

Dissolution of Muslim Marriages Act, 1939

Family Courts Act 2e, 1984

Indian Evidence Act, 1872

Indian Penal Code 406

Muslim Women's (Protection of Rights on Divorce) Act, 1986

Protection of Women from Domestic Violence Act, 2005

Restitution of Conjugal Rights (RCR)

Shariat Application Act, 1937

Urban Land (Ceiling and Regulation) Act, 1976

INDEX

Note: Page numbers with a *t* indicate tables.

Lightning Source UK Ltd.
Milton Keynes UK
UKHW040618120219
336958UK00001B/61/P